Hothouse Management:
Acquisitions, Takeovers, and LBOs

HOTHOUSE MANAGEMENT:
Acquisitions, Takeovers, and LBOs

A Harvard Business Review Paperback

Harvard Business Review paperback No. 90043

ISBN 0-87584-296-8

The *Harvard Business Review* articles in this collection are available as individual reprints, with the exception of "Takeovers: Last Chance for Self-Restraint," "Hostile Takeovers: What Should Be Done?" and "How to Acquire a Company." Discounts apply to quantity purchases. For information and ordering contact Operations Department, Harvard Business School Publishing Division, Boston, MA 02163. Telephone: (617) 495-6192, 9 a.m. to 5 p.m. Eastern Time, Monday through Friday. Fax: (617) 495-6985, 24 hours a day.

Editor's Note: Some articles in this book may have been written before authors and editors began to take into consideration the role of women in management. We hope the archaic usage representing all managers as male does not detract from the usefulness of the collection.

Printed in the United States of America by Harvard University, Office of the University Publisher.
93 92 91   5 4 3 2 1

Contents

Acquisitions and Corporate Diversification

Raiders and LBOs:
If You Can't Stand
the Heat . . .

Takeovers: folklore and science

Public criticism of the takeover market is largely unfounded and unproductive

Michael C. Jensen

Criticism of the increasing number and complex collection of mergers, tender offers, leveraged buy outs, and proxy offerings has come from consumers, government, and business. The general negative reaction focuses on the amount of money involved and the complex managerial maneuvering among industrial giants.

In the view of some financial economists, however, corporate takeovers are the logical outgrowth of competitive struggles in the free market. If you accept the assumption that shareholders are the most important constituency of the modern corporation, then these mergers and acquisitions make sense because they increase the value of the shares held in the target company.

Michael Jensen, one of the foremost proponents of this argument, has examined the various criticisms of corporate takeover activity and found many to be based on faulty logic. His conclusions are as controversial as the subject: takeovers are good for shareholders, golden parachutes are not unreason-

able, mergers do not create monopoly power, takeovers serve a unique economic function. Whether you accept the underlying basis of his assertions, you will find them fascinating, for they bring the discussion out of the realm of prejudice. At the very least, they serve as a logical basis for realistic further investigation.

Mr. Jensen is LaClare Professor of Finance and Business Administration at the Graduate School of Management, University of Rochester, founder and director of the Managerial Economics Research Center, and founding editor of the Journal of Financial Economics. *During the academic year 1984-1985, he is visiting professor at the Harvard Business School. He is the author of numerous articles and editor of several books, including (with Clifford W. Smith, Jr.)* The Modern Theory of Corporate Finance *(McGraw-Hill, 1984).*

Illustration by Karen Watson.

From 1981 to 1983, the number of large U.S. corporate acquisitions grew at a rate roughly double that of the 1970s and even exceeded the one realized during the famous merger wave of the 1960s. The drama of 2,100 annual takeovers valued at more than $1 million—much of it played out in heated, public battles—has generated an enormous amount of criticism, not only from politicians and the media but also from high-level corporate executives.

Commenting in the *Wall Street Journal* on the Bendix and Martin Marietta takeover battle, for example, Lee Iacocca, chairman of Chrysler, argued:

"It's not a merger. It's a three-ring circus. If they're really concerned about America, they'd stop it right now. It's no good for the economy. It wrecks it. If I were in the banking system I'd say no more [money] for conglomerates for one year."

A former director at Bendix added:

"I think...it's the kind of thing corporate America ought not to do, because the poor stockholder is the one whose interest is being ignored in favor of the egos of directors and executives. And who the hell is running the show—the business of making brakes and aerospace equipment—while all of this is going on?"

In a 1984 *New York Times* piece on the "surge of corporate mergers," Felix Rohatyn noted:

"All this frenzy may be good for investment bankers now, but it's not good for the country or investment bankers in the long run. We seem to be living in a 1920s, jazz age atmosphere."

Just as the public outcry over excesses on Wall Street in the early 1930s led to the Glass-

Author's note: I am indebted to Armen Alchian, Karl Brunner, Harry DeAngelo, Leo Herzel, Charles Plosser, Richard Rosett, Richard Ruback, Clifford Smith, Jr., Robert Sproull, Alan Underberg, and Ned Wass for comments and assistance.

Editor's note: All references are listed at the end of the article.

Steagall Act regulating banking, so the latest criticisms of mergers have brought enormous political pressure to bear on Congress to restrict takeovers. The July 1983 report of the SEC Advisory Committee on Tender Offers contained 50 recommendations for new regulations. Democratic Representative Peter Rodino has cosponsored a bill that would require advance notice of proposed acquisitions resulting in assets of $5 billion and 25,000 employees and a judgment by the Antitrust Division of the Justice Department or the FTC whether such acquisitions "serve the public interest."

The popular view underlying these proposals is wrong, however, because it ignores the fundamental economic function that takeover activities serve. In the corporate takeover market, management teams compete for the right to control – that is, to manage – corporate resources. Viewed in this way, the market for control is an important part of the managerial labor market, which is very different from, and has higher stakes than, the normal labor market. After all, potential chief executive officers do not simply leave their applications with personnel officers. Their on-the-job performance is subject not only to the normal internal control mechanisms of their organizations but also to the scrutiny of the external market for control.

Imagine that you are the president of a large billion-dollar corporation. Suddenly, another management team threatens your job and prestige by trying to buy your company's stock. The whole world watches your performance. Putting yourself in this situation leads to a better understanding of the reasons behind the rhetoric, maneuverings, and even lobbying in the political and regulatory sectors by managers for protection from unfriendly offers.

The Bendix attempt to take control of Martin Marietta in 1982 gained considerable attention because of Marietta's unusual countertakeover offer for Bendix, called the "Pac-Man defense," whose principle is: "My company will eat yours before yours eats mine."[1] Some describe this kind of contest as disgraceful. I find it fascinating because it makes clear that the crucial issue is not whether the two companies will merge but which managers will be in control.

At the end of the contest, Bendix held 67% of Martin Marietta while Martin Marietta held 50% of Bendix. United Technologies then entered as Martin Marietta's friend and offered to buy Bendix. But it was Allied, coming in late, that finally won the battle with its purchase of all of Bendix's stock, 39% of Martin Marietta's, and a promise not to buy more. When the dust had cleared, shareholders of Bendix and Martin had both won; their respective shares gained roughly 38% in value (after adjusting for marketwide stock price change). Allied's shareholders, on the other hand, lost approximately 8.6%.[2]

Given the success and history of the modern corporation, it is surprising how little the media, the legal and political communities, and even business executives understand the reasons behind the complexities and subtleties of takeover battles. Prior to the last decade, the academic community made little progress in redressing this lack of understanding. But research efforts in business schools across the country have recently begun to overcome it.

In this article I summarize the most important scientific evidence refuting the myths that swirl around the controversy. The research shows that:

☐   Takeovers of companies by outsiders do not harm shareholders of the target company; in fact, they gain substantial wealth.

☐   Corporate takeovers do not waste resources; they use assets productively.

☐   Takeovers do not siphon commercial credit from its uses in funding new plant and equipment.

☐   Takeovers do not create gains for shareholders through creation of monopoly power.

☐   Prohibition of plant closings, layoffs, and dismissals following takeovers would reduce market efficiency and lower aggregate living standards.

☐   Although managers are self-interested, the environment in which they operate gives them relatively little leeway to feather their nests at shareholders' expense. Corporate control-related actions of managers do not generally harm shareholders, but actions that eliminate actual or potential takeover bids are most suspect as exceptions to this rule.

☐   Golden parachutes for top-level executives are, in principle, in the interest of shareholders. Although the practice can be abused, the evidence indicates that shareholders gain when golden parachutes are adopted.

☐   In general, the activities of takeover specialists benefit shareholders.

Before exploring the evidence, I consider why shareholders are the most important constituency of the modern corporation and why their interests must be held paramount when discussing the current wave of acquisitions and mergers.

The nature of the corporation

Stockholders are commonly portrayed as one group in a set of equal constituencies, or "stakeholders," of the company. In fact, stockholders are *not* equal with these other groups because they are the ultimate holders of the rights to organization control and therefore must be the focal point for any discussion concerning it.

The public corporation is the nexus for a complex set of voluntary contracts among customers, workers, managers, and the suppliers of materials, capital, and risk bearing. The rights of the interacting parties are determined by law, the corporation's charter, and the implicit and explicit contracts with each individual.

Corporations, like all organizations, vest control rights in the constituency bearing the residual risk.[3] (Residual risk is the risk associated with the difference between the random cash inflows and outflows of the organization.) In partnerships and privately held companies, for example, these residual claims and the organizational control rights are restricted to major decision agents (directors and managers); in mutuals and consumer cooperatives, to customers; and in supplier cooperatives, to suppliers.

Corporations are unique organizations because they make no restrictions on who can own their residual claims and this makes it possible for customers, managers, labor, and suppliers to avoid bearing any of the corporate residual risk. Because stockholders guarantee the contracts of all constituents, they bear the corporation's residual risk. The absence of restrictions on who can own corporate residual claims allows specialization in risk bearing by those investors who are most adept at the function. As a result, the corporation realizes great efficiencies in risk bearing that reduce costs substantially and allow it to meet market demand more efficiently than other organizations.

Although the identities of the bearers of residual risk may differ, all business organizations vest organizational control rights in them. For control to rest in any other group would be equivalent to allowing that group to "play poker" with someone else's money and would create inefficiencies that lead to the possibility of failure. Stockholders as the bearers of residual risk hold the right to control of the corporation, although they delegate much of this control to a board of directors who normally hire, fire, and set the compensation of at least the CEO.

Proof of the efficiency of the corporate organizational form shows dramatically in market performance. In principle, any marketer can supply goods and services. In reality, all organizational forms compete for consumers, managers, labor, and supplies of capital and other goods. Those that supply the goods demanded by customers at the lowest price win out. The dominance of the corporate form of organization in large-scale nonfinancial activities indicates that it is winning much of this competition.

Acquisition folklore

Takeovers can be carried out through mergers, tender offers, and proxy fights, or sometimes through elements of all three. A tender offer made directly to the stockholders to buy some or all of their shares for a specified price during a specified time period does not require the approval of the target company's management or board of directors. A merger, however, is negotiated with the company's management and, when approved by its board of directors, is submitted to the shareholders for approval. In a proxy contest the votes of the stockholders are solicited, generally for the election of a new slate of directors.

Takeovers frequently begin with what is called a "friendly" merger offer from the bidder to the target management and board. If management turns down the offer, the bidder can, and often does, take the offer directly to the shareholders in the form of a tender offer. At this point, target company managers usually oppose the offer by issuing press releases condemning it as outside the shareholders' best interest, by initiating court action, by requesting antitrust action against the bidder, by starting a countertakeover move for the bidder, and by other actions designed to make the target company a less desirable acquisition.

Target company management often casts about for a "white knight"—a friendly merger partner who will protect the "maiden" from the advances of the feared raider and, more important, who will pay a higher price. When the company doesn't find a white knight, and an unfriendly bidder takes it over, its leaders will likely look for new jobs. The takeover process penalizes incompetent or self-serving managers whose actions have lowered the market price of their corporation's stock. Although the process operates with a lag, the forces are strong and persistent. Of course—as a result of economies of scale or other efficiencies—some efficient managers lose their jobs after a takeover through no fault of their own.

This kind of romantic language has been used to offer comic relief, but it contributes to the atmosphere of folklore that surrounds a process fundamental to the corporate world. The resulting myths and misunderstandings distort the public's perception and render a meaningful dialogue impossible.

Folklore: Takeovers harm the shareholders of target companies.
Fact: The pejorative term *raider* used to label the bidding company in an unfriendly takeover suggests that the bidder will buy control of a company, pillage it, and leave the stockholders with only a crumbling shell.

Exhibit I	Abnormal stock price increases from successful takeovers*	
	Target companies	**Bidding companies**
Tender offers	30 %	4 %
Mergers	20 %	0 %
Proxy contests	8 %	N.A.†

*Adjusted to eliminate the effects of marketwide price changes.
†Not applicable.

More than a dozen studies have painstakingly gathered evidence on the stock price effect of successful takeovers (see *Exhibit I* for a summary of the results).[4] According to these studies, companies involved in takeovers experience abnormal increases in their stock prices for approximately one month surrounding the initial announcement of the takeover. (Abnormal stock price changes are stock price changes customarily adjusted by regression analysis to eliminate the effects of marketwide forces on all corporations.)[5] The exhibit shows that target company shareholders gain 30% from tender offers and 20% from mergers.

Because tender offers are often extended for less than 100% of the outstanding shares and because not all takeover announcements result in acquisitions, stock prices do not increase at the announcement of the offer by the full amount of the premium offered. Consequently, average target stockholder returns in takeovers are actually higher than the estimates in *Exhibit I* because the abnormal stock price changes it summarizes generally exclude the purchase premiums shareholders receive when they surrender their shares.

The shareholders of bidding companies, on the other hand, earn only about 4% from tender offers and nothing from mergers. If the much feared raiding has taken place, it seems to be of a peculiar, Robin Hood variety.

When an insurgent group, led by a dissatisfied manager or a large stockholder, attempts to gain controlling seats on the board of directors of a company (thereby taking over the company through an internal proxy fight), shareholders also gain. As *Exhibit I* shows, the stock prices of these companies gain 8% on average.

Because target companies are usually a lot smaller than the bidders, you cannot calculate total returns to both parties from the data in *Exhibit I*. An analysis of more than 180 tender-offer acquisitions, however, indicates statistically significant gains to target and acquiring company shareholders equal to an average 8.4% of the total market value of the equity of both companies.[6]

In sum, contrary to the argument that merger activity wastes resources without benefiting stockholders, stockholders earn substantial gains in successful takeovers. In the Texaco takeover of Getty, for example, Getty Oil shareholders realized abnormal stock price gains of $4.7 billion, or 78.6% of the total equity value, and Texaco shareholders, abnormal returns of $1.3 billion or 14.5%. Gains for both totaled $6 billion, 40% of the sum of their equity values. Gulf stockholders earned abnormal returns of $6.2 billion (79.9%) from the Socal takeover, and Socal stockholders earned $2.8 billion (22.6%). The total gains of $9 billion in this merger represent a 44.6% increase in the total equity values of both companies.

In light of these shareholder benefits, the cries to eliminate or restrain unfriendly takeovers seem peculiar (and in some cases self-serving). In a January 5, 1983 *Wall Street Journal* article, Peter Drucker called for such controls: "The question is no longer whether unfriendly takeovers will be curbed but only when and how." He went on to say:

"The recent shoot-out between Bendix and Martin Marietta has deeply disturbed even the staunchest laissez-faire advocates in the business community. And fear of the raider and his unfriendly takeover bid is increasingly distorting business judgment and decisions. In company after company the first question is no longer: Is this decision best for the business? But, will it encourage or discourage the raider?"

Such arguments may comfort concerned managers and board members who want protection from the discipline of competition in the market for managers. But they are based on false premises. The best way to discourage the competing manager (that's what *raider* means) is to run a company to maximize its value. "Will this decision help us obtain maximum market value?" is the only logically sensible interpretation of "What is best for the business?"

Folklore: Takeover expenditures are wasted.

Fact: Purchase prices in corporate takeovers represent the transfer of wealth from the stockholders of bidding companies to those of target organizations, not the consumption of wealth. In a takeover, the resources represented in the cash received by the target shareholders can still be used to build new plant and equipment or for R&D.

The only resources consumed are those used to arrange the transaction, such as the time and fees of managers, lawyers, economists, and financial consultants. These expenses are often large in dollar terms; the financial fees of the U.S. Steel/Marathon Oil merger were more than $27 million, and those received by four investment banking firms in the Getty take-

over hit a record by exceeding $47 million. But they are a tiny fraction of the dollar value of the acquisition; total financial and legal fees usually amount to only about .7%. More significantly, they help shareholders achieve their much larger gains of 4% to 30%.

In fact, the stock price change is the best measure of the takeover's future impact on the organization. The vast scientific evidence on the theory of efficient markets indicates that, in the absence of inside information, a security's market price represents the best available estimate of its true value.[7] The evidence shows that market prices incorporate all current public information about future cash flows and the value of individual assets in an unbiased way. Stock prices change, of course, in response to new information about individual assets. Because market prices are efficient, however, the new information is equally likely to cause them to decrease or increase, after allowing for normal returns. Positive stock price changes, then, indicate a *rise* in the total profitability of the merged companies. Furthermore, because evidence indicates it does not come from the acquisition of market power, this increased profitability must come from the company's improved productivity.

Folklore: The huge bank credit lines used to carry out large takeovers siphon credit from the financial system and crowd out "legitimate" borrowing for productive investments.

Fact: First, the increases in shareholder wealth I've discussed indicate that takeover activities are productive investments; credit lines are not wasted. Second, companies that make acquisitions with stock or other securities, or with cash on hand or capital acquired from the sale of assets, do not use bank credit.

More important, even when companies accomplish takeovers with bank loans, they do not waste credit because most, if not all, of it is still available for real investment such as new plant and equipment. Let me illustrate the point by using a simple example.

When an acquiring company borrows from a bank for an acquisition, it receives the funds in the form of a credit to its bank account. When target company stockholders deposit receipts from the takeover in their accounts, the bank's total deposits remain unchanged because the acquirer's deposits are reduced by the same amount.

Now, however, the portfolios of the target company shareholders are unbalanced. In response, they can make new investments either directly or by purchasing newly issued shares, and if they do so the credit goes directly into productive real investments. If they take the opposite course of action and reduce their bank debt, the bank will have the same amount of loans and deposits as before the acquisition; total outstanding credit is unchanged and there is no waste.

Alternatively, target company shareholders can purchase securities from other investors, but the sellers then are in the same position as the target company shareholders after the acquisition.

If the recipients of the funds from the takeover don't make new investments or pay down debt, they must increase either their cash holdings or their consumption. If their wealth hasn't changed, they have no reason to change either their cash balances or their consumption, and, therefore, the proceeds will go to make new investments and/or reduce debt. If investor wealth increases, investors will increase their consumption and their cash balances. The value of the consumption and cash balance increases will only be a small fraction of the wealth increase (the capital gains, not the proceeds) from the takeover; the remainder will go for new investments and/or debt reduction. The increase in cash balances and consumption will be the same as that coming from increases in wealth generated by any other cause. Thus, takeovers waste no more credit than any other productive investment.

Folklore: By merging competitors, takeovers create a monopoly that will raise product prices, produce less, and thereby harm consumers.

Fact: The evidence from four studies of the issue indicates that takeover gains come not from the merger's creation of monopoly market power but from its productive economies and synergy.

If the gains did come from the creation of companies with monopolistic powers, industry competitors would benefit, in turn, from the higher prices and would enjoy significant increases in profits and stock prices. Furthermore, the stock prices of rivals would fall if the FTC or the Antitrust Division of the Justice Department cancelled or challenged the merger.

The evidence indicates, however, that competitors gain when two other companies in the same industry merge. But these gains are not related to the creation of monopolistic power or industry concentration. Moreover, the stock prices of competitors do not fall on announcement of antitrust prosecution or cancellation of the acquisition. This evidence supports the hypothesis that takeover gains stem from real economies in production and distribution realized through the takeover and that it signals the availability of similar gains for rival companies.[8]

In fact, the evidence raises serious doubts about the wisdom of FTC or Justice Department policies concerning mergers. The cancellation of an acquisition erases virtually all the stock price increases occurring on its announcement—with no apparent offsetting benefits to anyone.[9]

Folklore: Consolidating facilities after a takeover leads to plant closings, layoffs, and employee dismissals—all at great social cost.

Fact: No evidence with which I am familiar indicates that takeovers produce more plant closings, layoffs, and dismissals than would otherwise have occurred.

This charge raises a serious question, however, about the proper criteria for evaluation of the social desirability of takeovers. The standard efficiency yardstick measures increases in the aggregate real standard of living. By these criteria the wealth gains from takeovers (and their associated effects) are good as long as they do not come from the creation of monopolistic market power. Therefore, even if takeovers lead to plant closings, layoffs, and dismissals, their prohibition or limitation would generate real social costs and reduce aggregate human welfare because of the loss of potential operating economies.

Some observers may not agree that the standard efficiency criterion is the best measure of social desirability. But the adoption of any other criterion threatens to paralyze innovation. For example, innovations that increase standards of living in the long run initially produce changes that reduce the welfare of some individuals, at least in the short run. The development of efficient truck and air transport harmed the railroads and their workers; the rise of television hurt the radio industry. New and more efficient production, distribution, or organizational technology often imposes similar short-term costs.

The adoption of new technologies following takeovers enhances the overall real standard of living but reduces the wealth of those individuals with large investments in older technologies. Not surprisingly, such individuals and companies, their unions, communities, and political representatives will lobby to limit or prohibit takeovers that might result in new technologies. When successful, such politics reduce the nation's standard of living and its standing in international competition.

Folklore: Managers act in their own interests and are in reality unanswerable to shareholders.

Fact: Because executive compensation is related to company size, critics charge that a top officer's desire for wealth and an empire drives merger activity while the stockholders pay the bill. But as *Exhibit I* shows, there is no systematic evidence that bidding company managers are harming shareholders to build empires. Instead, the evidence is consistent with the synergy theory of takeovers. This theory argues that the stock price increases for target companies come from the increase in value obtained by consolidating or altering control of the assets of the companies involved, perhaps because of cost savings from economies of scale or from a highly complementary combination of employees and assets in production and distribution.

The evidence shows that target companies get a large share of the gains; indeed, the gains in mergers go to the target companies while virtually none accrue to bidding companies on the average. Bidding wars such as the DuPont-Seagram-Mobil competition for control of Conoco push up the gain for target companies.

The zero returns to bidders in mergers noted in *Exhibit I* are puzzling. For several reasons, however, this particular estimate has more uncertainty built into it and is probably biased downward. My own assessment is that the returns to bidding companies in mergers are closer to the 4% shown for bidders in tender offers. An examination of the total dollar gains to both bidding and target company shareholders shows that both get about the same amount of dollars but not of percentage gains. The disparity results because bidding companies are generally larger than target companies and the same dollar gains translate into different percentage gains. Because the stock prices of larger companies vary more widely relative to gains in an acquisition than do the stock prices of target companies, their returns cannot be estimated as precisely.

Furthermore, bidders often engage in a prolonged acquisition program. The benefits for target companies from a particular merger occur around the time of the takeover announcement and therefore can be more easily estimated than the bidders' benefits, which may be spread out over several acquisitions.

Often the stock price of a company that seeks several acquisitions reflects the projected benefits of future deals at an early date.[10] When a particular acquisition is announced, the bidder's stock price will change only to the extent that there is a difference between the actual and the previously expected profitability of the merger and on average this will be zero in an efficient market. And because mergers involve negotiations that do not occur in tender offers, more information about the intentions of bidders will leak than will information about the identity of the target; the effect on the bidder's price will therefore be spread out over time.

The record of several large takeovers shows mixed evidence on the returns to acquiring shareholders. In the $13.2 billion takeover of Gulf, Socal shareholders earned $2.77 billion (22.6%) after adjustment for the effects of marketwide price changes (from January 23, 1984 to May 3, 1984). Similarly, in the $10.1 billion takeover of Getty Oil, Texaco shareholders earned $1.3 billion (14.5%, from December 13, 1983 to February 7, 1984). In contrast, Allied shareholders lost $100 million (−8.6%) in the acquisition of Bendix; DuPont lost $800 million (−10.0%) in the takeover of Conoco, while Conoco shareholders realized a gain of 71%, or about $3.2 billion.[11]

On the other hand, Occidental Petroleum shareholders did not lose in Occidental's takeover

of Cities Service, whose shareholders gained about $350 million (12.5%).[12] Mesa Petroleum initiated the Cities Service war with a bid of $45 per share. Cities Service countered with a bid for Mesa Petroleum. Gulf Oil then announced completion of negotiations to merge with Cities Service for $63 per share; Cities Service stock immediately gained over 43%, or $1.25 billion. In contrast, the Gulf stock price fell over 14%, or slightly over $900 million. The $350 million difference between the gain to Cities Service shareholders and the loss to Gulf shareholders measures the market's estimate of the net increase in value from the merger.

Citing antitrust difficulties with the FTC, Gulf cancelled its acquisition of Cities Service seven weeks later. Cities Service countered with a breach of contract suit against Gulf for $3 billion. All the earlier gains in the price of Cities Service stock were eliminated, but only one-third of the Gulf loss was recovered – perhaps because the market forecast that legal action might hold Gulf liable for part of the premium offered to Cities Service shareholders or that Gulf would make more overpriced takeover attempts. Within four weeks of the Gulf cancellation, Cities Service merged with Occidental for a $350 million premium – an amount identical to the estimated value of the net merger gains from the aborted combination of Cities Service and Gulf.

A good way for a company to become a takeover target is to make a series of acquisitions that reduce value but allow the value to be recovered through divestiture. A bidder that realizes it can make money by selling off the pieces at a profit will likely seize the initiative. Victor Posner's attack on Marley Company in 1981 is an extreme example. Marley, which manufactured water-cooling towers and heat exchangers, took control of Wylain, a manufacturer of air conditioning, heating, and pumping systems, for an 87% premium over Wylain's previous market value. Marley's stock price fell 21%. Posner bought 11.2% of Marley during the first six months of 1980. Unable to find a white knight, Marley sold its assets, dissolved, and distributed the proceeds in June 1981. Posner received $21.9 million for his investment of $12.5 million in Marley.[13]

Manager-shareholder conflicts

The interests of managers and shareholders conflict on many, but certainly not all, issues. The divergence intensifies if the company becomes the target of an unfriendly takeover. *Exhibit I* indicates that target shareholders benefit when the bidders offer sub-

Exhibit II	Abnormal stock price changes from unsuccessful bids*	
	Target companies	Bidding companies
Tender offers	−3%	−1%
Mergers	−3%	−5%
Proxy contests	8%	N.A.†

*Adjusted to eliminate the effects of marketwide price changes.
†Not applicable.

stantial premiums over current market value. During a takeover top managers of target companies can lose both their jobs and the value of their talents, knowledge, and income that are particular to the organization. Threatened with these losses, such officers may try to reduce the probability of a successful unfriendly takeover and benefit themselves at the expense of shareholders.

Management struggles

The attempt by Carter Hawley Hale to acquire Marshall Field is an interesting example of a management struggle to retain control. Marshall Field, a high-quality department and specialty store chain, enjoyed less growth than other retailers but consistently rejected merger bids. In early 1978, Carter Hawley Hale, another retailer, offered $42 per share for Marshall Field stock, which was selling for less than $20. Resisting, Marshall Field filed a lawsuit that argued the acquisition would violate securities and antitrust laws. It informed shareholders that the asking price was inadequate and made several defensive acquisitions that aggravated potential antitrust problems and made it less attractive to Carter Hawley. Marshall Field's board authorized top officials to take "such action as they deemed necessary" to defeat the offer. After Carter Hawley withdrew the offer, Marshall Field's stock fell back to $20 per share.

In April 1984, another retailer, The Limited, tried to take over Carter Hawley Hale, whose stock then experienced abnormal gains of 49% in the ensuing conflict. Carter Hawley filed suit against The Limited, claiming securities law violations and antitrust problems, and gave up 33% of its voting rights through the sale of $300 million of convertible preferred stock to General Cinema Corporation. Carter Hawley then gave General Cinema a six-month option to buy the Waldenbook chain, one of its most profitable subsidiaries, and repurchased 51% of its own shares. As a result The Limited withdrew its offer in

May and Carter Hawley stockholders lost $363 million – the entire 49% abnormal stock price gain.

Both of these cases show what happens to stock prices when acquisition bids fail. *Exhibit II* summarizes the general evidence obtained from ten studies on stock price behavior during unsuccessful takeover attempts. The average abnormal stock price changes surrounding unsuccessful takeover bids are uniformly small and negative, ranging from −1% to −5%. The exception is the 8% positive return to shareholders of companies subjected to unsuccessful proxy contests. It is interesting that a proxy contest causes an abnormal stock price gain even when the challengers fail, perhaps because the contest threat motivates incumbent managers to change their strategies.

The uncertainty of the estimates, however, means that only the −5% return for unsuccessful bidders is statistically significantly different from zero. The other negative returns can arise by chance if the true returns from such unsuccessful offers are actually zero. In conclusion, the Marshall Field experience that target company shareholders essentially lose all the offered premiums when an acquisition bid fails, fits the general evidence.

Exhibit II, however, simplifies the story. Sometimes stockholders benefit greatly from opposition to takeover bids.

Uncoordinated, independent decisions by individual shareholders regarding the acceptance or rejection of a tender offer can cause most of the takeover gains to go to bidding company stockholders.[14] If target managers act as the agents for all target shareholders in negotiating with the bidder for a higher price, however, this "free rider" problem can be alleviated.

Empirical evidence also indicates that some managerial opposition benefits target shareholders. For example, on the failure of a tender offer, target stock prices do not on average immediately lose the 30% average increase in price they earned when the offer was made. In fact, they generally stay up, apparently in anticipation of future bids. And target companies that receive at least one more bid in the two years following the failure of a tender offer on average realize another 20% increase in price. Those targets that do not receive another bid, however, lose the entire initial price increase.[15] Apparently, a little opposition in a merger battle is good, but too much can be disastrous if it prohibits takeover of the company.

The corporate charter

Corporate charters specify governance rules and establish conditions for mergers, such as the percentage of stockholders who must approve a takeover. Since constraints on permissible charter rules differ from state to state, changing the state of incorporation will affect the contractual arrangement among shareholders and the probability that a company will be a takeover target. It is alleged that some states desiring to increase their corporate charter revenues make their statutes appealing to corporate management. Allegedly, in doing so they provide management with great freedom from stockholder control and therefore provide little shareholder protection. Delaware, for example, has few constraints in its rules on corporate charters and hence provides much contractual freedom for shareholders. William L. Cary, former chairman of the Securities and Exchange Commission, has criticized Delaware and argued that the state is leading a "movement towards the least common denominator" and "winning a race for the bottom."[16]

But a study of 140 companies switching their state of incorporation reveals no evidence of stock price declines at the time of the change, even though most switched to Delaware.[17] In fact, small abnormal price increases are usually associated with the switch. This evidence is inconsistent with the notion that such charter changes lead to managerial exploitation of shareholders.

Without switching their state of incorporation, companies can amend corporate charters to toughen the conditions for the approval by shareholders of mergers. Such antitakeover amendments may require a "super majority" for approval or for the staggered election of board members and can thus lower the probability that the company will be taken over and thereby reduce shareholder wealth. On the other hand, the amendments can also benefit shareholders by increasing the plurality required for takeover approval and thus enable management to better represent their common interests in the merger negotiations.

Two studies of adoption of antitakeover amendments in samples of 100 and 388 companies reveal no negative impact on shareholder wealth.[18] One exception may arise if the super-majority provisions grant effective power to block mergers to a manager-stockholder. The market value of R.P. Scherer, for example, fell 33.8% when shareholders adopted an 80% super-majority merger approval provision. Because the wife of Scherer's CEO owned 21.1% of the stock, she then had the power to block a proposed takeover by FMC. In fact, FMC withdrew its offer after Scherer stockholders approved the 80% majority provision and the price of Scherer stock plummeted.

Repurchase standstill agreements

Currently available evidence suggests that management's opposition to takeovers reduces shareholder wealth only when it eliminates potential takeover bids. In a privately negotiated or targeted repurchase, for example, a company buys a block of its common stock from a holder at a premium over market price—often to induce the holder, usually an active or a potential bidder, to cease takeover activity. Such repurchases, pejoratively labeled "greenmail" in the press, generate statistically significant abnormal stock price declines for shareholders of the repurchasing company and significantly positive returns for the sellers.[19] These stock price declines contrast sharply with the statistically significant abnormal stock price increases associated with *nontargeted* stock repurchases found in six studies.[20]

The managers of target companies also may obtain standstill agreements, in which one company agrees to limit its holdings in another. Announcements of such agreements are associated with statistically significant abnormal stock price declines for target companies. Because these agreements almost always lead to the termination of an acquisition attempt, the negative returns seem to represent the merger gains lost by shareholders.

Again, however, the issue is not clearcut because closer examination of the evidence indicates that these takeover forays by competing managers benefit target shareholders. Within ten days of an acquisition of 5% or more of a company's shares, the SEC requires the filing of information giving the identity of the purchaser, purpose of acquisition, and size of the holding. The significantly positive increase in stock price that occurs with the initial purchase announcement indicates that potential dissident activity is expected to benefit shareholders even given the chance that the venture will end in a targeted repurchase. Moreover, this is confirmed by the fact that on average during the period from the SEC filing through the targeted repurchase of the shares, target company shareholders earn statistically significant positive abnormal returns.[21]

Thus, when you look at the whole process, repurchase agreements are clearly not "raiding" or "looting" but are profitable for the target shareholders—although not as profitable as a takeover. The stock price decline at repurchase seems due to the repurchase premium that is effectively paid by the nonselling shareholders of the target firm and to the unraveling of takeover expectations with consequent loss of the anticipated takeover premium.

Because, on average, target shareholders lose the anticipated takeover premiums shown in

Exhibit I when a merger or takeover fails for any reason, we cannot easily tell whether they were hurt by a repurchase. If the takeover would have failed anyway and if the target company's stock price would have fallen even more without the repurchase, then the repurchase benefited target company shareholders. Such additional price declines might be caused, for example, by the costs of dealing with a disgruntled minority shareholder.

Although the issue requires further study, current evidence implies that prohibition of targeted large-block repurchases advocated by some may hurt target shareholders. Moreover, since shareholders can amend corporate charters to restrict targeted repurchases, there is little justification for regulatory interference by the state in the private contractual arrangements among shareholders. Such repurchase restrictions might well restrict the vast majority of stock repurchases that clearly benefit shareholders. In addition, by reducing the profitability of failed takeovers, such restrictions would strengthen the position of entrenched managers by reducing the frequency of takeover bids. Doing so would deprive shareholders of some of the stock price premiums associated with successful mergers.

Going private

The phrase *going private* means that publicly owned stock is replaced with full equity ownership by an incumbent management group and that the stock is delisted. On occasion, when going private is a leveraged buy out, management shares the equity with private investors. Some believe that incumbent managers as buyers are exploiting outside shareholders as sellers in these minority freeze outs.

Advocating restrictions on going-private transactions, in 1974 Securities and Exchange Commissioner A.A. Sommer, Jr. argued:

"What is happening is, in my estimation, serious, unfair, and sometimes disgraceful, a perversion of the whole process of public financing, and a course that inevitably is going to make the individual shareholder even more hostile to American corporate mores and the securities markets than he already is."[22]

Study of stockholder returns in 72 going-private transactions, however, reveals that the average transaction offers a premium 56% over market price and that abnormal stock price increases on announcement of the offer average 30%. The gains apparently arise from savings of registration and other public ownership expenses, improved incentives for decision makers under private ownership, and increased interest and depreciation tax shields. Outside shareholders are not harmed in going-private transactions.[23]

Golden parachutes

Some companies provide compensation in employment contracts for top-level managers in the event that a takeover occurs—that is, golden parachutes. Allied agreed, for example, to make up the difference for five years between Bendix CEO William Agee's salary in subsequent employment and his former annual $825,000 salary in the event of a change in control at Bendix. Much confusion exists about the propriety and desirability of golden parachutes, even among senior executives.

But the detractors fail to understand that the parachutes protect stockholders as well as managers. Think about the problem in the following way: top-level managers and the board of directors act as stockholders' agents in deals involving hundreds of millions of dollars. If the alternative providing the highest value to stockholders is sale to another company and the retirement of the current management team, stockholders do not want the managers to block a bid in fear of losing their own jobs. Stockholders may be asking managers to sacrifice position and wealth to negotiate the best deal for them.

Golden parachutes are clearly desirable when they protect stockholders' interests. Like anything else, however, they may be abused. For example, a stockholder doesn't want to pay managers so much for selling the company that they hurry to sell at a low price to the first bidder. But that is a problem with the details of the parachute's contractual provisions and not with the existence of the parachute itself. An analysis of 90 companies shows that adoption of golden parachutes on average has no negative effect on stock prices and provides some evidence of positive effects.[24]

The thing that puzzles me about most golden parachute contracts is that they pay off only when the manager leaves his job and thus create an unnecessary conflict of interest between shareholders and executives. Current shareholders and the acquiring company will want to retain the services of a manager who has valuable knowledge and skills. But the officer can collect the golden parachute premium only by leaving; the contract rewards him or her for taking an action that may well hurt the business. As the bidder assimilates the knowledge that turnover among valuable top-level managers after the acquisition is highly likely, it will reduce its takeover bid. A company can eliminate this problem by making the award conditional on transfer of control and not on the manager's exit from the company.

Selling the 'crown jewels'

Another often criticized defensive tactic is the sale of a major division by a company faced with a takeover threat. Some observers claim that such sales prove that managers will do anything to preserve their tenure, even to the extent of crippling or eliminating major parts of the business that appear attractive to outside bidders. Such actions have been labeled a "scorched earth policy."

Studies of the effects of corporate spin-offs, however, indicate they generate significantly positive abnormal returns.[25] Moreover, when target managers find a white knight to pay more for the entire company than the initial, hostile bidder, shareholders clearly benefit.

In the same way, when an acquirer is interested mainly in a division rather than the whole company, shareholders benefit when target management auctions off the unit at a higher price. Brunswick's sale of its Sherwood Medical Industries division to American Home Products shows how the sale of a crown jewel can benefit shareholders. Whittaker Corporation made a hostile takeover bid for Brunswick in early 1982. In defense, Brunswick sold a key division, Sherwood Medical, to American Home Products through a negotiated tender offer for 64% of Brunswick's shares. American Home Products then exchanged these shares with Brunswick for Sherwood's stock. Because its main interest lay in acquiring Sherwood, Whittaker withdrew its offer.[26]

The value of the Whittaker offer to Brunswick shareholders ranged from $605 million to $618 million, depending on the value assigned to the convertible debentures that were part of the offer. The total value to Brunswick shareholders of the management strategy, selling off the Sherwood division, was $620 million. Moreover, because of the structure of the transaction, the cash proceeds went directly to the Brunswick shareholders through the negotiated tender offer. The $620 million value represents a gain of $205 million (49%) on the total equity value of Brunswick prior to the initial Whittaker offer. The Brunswick shareholders were $2 million to $15 million better off with the management strategy, hardly evidence of a scorched-earth policy.

Takeover artists

Recently, criticism has been directed at corporate takeover specialists who are said to take advantage of a company's vulnerability in the market and thus ultimately harm shareholders. While acting in their own interests, however, these specialists also act as agents for shareholders of companies with entrenched managers. Returning to the Marshall Field story, for example, Carl Icahn launched a systematic campaign to acquire the chain after it had avoided takeover. When it looked as if he would achieve the goal, Marshall Field initiated a corporate auction and merged with BATUS (British American Tobacco Company, U.S.) for $30 per share in 1982. After adjustment for inflation, that price was slightly less than the $20 price of Field's stock in 1977, when it defeated Carter Hawley's $42 offer.

Takeover specialists like Icahn risk their own fortunes to dislodge current managers and reap part of the value increases available from redeploying the assets or improving the management. Evidence from a study of 100 such instances indicates that when such specialists announce the purchase of 5% or more of a company's shares, the stockholders of that company on average earn significantly positive abnormal returns of about 6%.[27]

The effectiveness of the market

The corporation has contributed much to the enhancement of society's living standards. Yet the details of how and why this complex institution functions and survives are poorly understood, due in part to the complexity of the issues involved and in part to the political controversy that historically surrounds it. Much of this controversy reflects the actions of individuals and groups that wish to use the corporation's assets for their own purposes, without purchasing them.

One source of the controversy comes from the separation between managers and shareholders—a separation necessary to realize the large efficiencies in risk bearing that are the corporation's comparative advantage. The process by which internal control mechanisms work so that professional managers act in the shareholders' interest is subtle and difficult to observe. When internal control mechanisms are working well, the board of directors will replace top-level managers whose talents are no longer the best ones available for the job.[28]

When these mechanisms break down, however, stockholders receive some protection from the takeover market, where alternative management teams compete for the rights to manage the corporation's assets. This competition can take the form of mergers, tender offers, or proxy fights. Other organizational forms such as nonprofits, partnerships, or mutual insurance companies and savings banks do not benefit from the same kind of external market.

The takeover market also provides a unique, powerful, and impersonal mechanism to accomplish the major restructuring and redeployment of assets continually required by changes in technology and consumer preferences. Recent changes occurring in the oil industry provide a good example.

Scientific evidence indicates that activities in the market for corporate control almost uniformly increase efficiency and shareholders' wealth. Yet there is an almost continuous flow of unfavorable publicity and calls for regulation and restriction of unfriendly takeovers. Many of these appeals arise from managers who want protection from competition for their jobs and others who desire more controls on corporations. The result, in the long run, may be a further weakening of the corporation as an organizational form and a reduction in human welfare.

Reprint 84609

References

1 For further analysis, see Leo Herzel and John R. Schmidt, "SEC is Probing 'Double Pac-Man' Takeover Defense," *Legal Times,* April 18, 1983, p. 27.

2 For further insight, see Claude W. McAnally, III, "The Bendix-Martin Marietta Takeover and Stockholder Returns," unpublished masters thesis, Massachusetts Institute of Technology, 1983.

3 The only exception is the nonprofit organization, against which there are no residual claims. For a discussion of the critical role of donations in the survival of nonprofits, the nature of the corporation, and competition and survival among organizational forms, see Eugene F. Fama and Michael C. Jensen, "Separation of Ownership and Control," *Journal of Law and Economics,* June 1983, p. 301, and also "Agency Problems and Residual Claims," *Journal of Law and Economics,* June 1983, p. 327.

4 For a summary, see Michael C. Jensen and Richard S. Ruback, "The Market for Corporate Control: The Scientific Evidence," *Journal of Financial Economics,* April 1983, p. 5. The original studies are: Peter Dodd and Richard S. Ruback, "Tender Offers and Stockholder Returns: An Empirical Analysis," *Journal of Financial Economics,* December 1977, p. 351; D. Kummer and R. Hoffmeister, "Valuation Consequences of Cash Tender Offers," *Journal of Finance,* May 1978, p. 505; Michael Bradley, "Interfirm Tender Offers and the Market for Corporate Control," *Journal of Business,* October 1980, p. 345; Peter Dodd, "Merger Proposals, Management Discretion and Stockholder Wealth," *Journal of Financial Economics,* June 1980, p. 1; Michael Bradley, Anand Desai, and E. Han Kim, "The Rationale Behind Interfirm Tender Offers: Information or Synergy?" *Journal of Financial Economics,* April 1983, p. 183; Richard S. Ruback, "Assessing Competition in the Market for Corporate Acquisitions," *Journal of Financial Economics,* April 1983, p. 141; Paul Asquith, "Merger Bids, Uncertainty, and Stockholder Returns," *Journal of Financial Economics,* April 1983, p. 51; Peggy Wier, "The Costs of Antimerger Lawsuits: Evidence from the Stock Market," *Journal of Financial Economics,* April 1983, p. 207; Peter Dodd and Jerold B. Warner, "On Corporate Governance: A Study of Proxy Contests," *Journal of Financial Economics,* April 1983, p. 401;

Paul H. Malatesta, "The Wealth Effect of Merger Activity and the Objective Functions of Merging Firms," *Journal of Financial Economics,* April 1983, p. 155; Paul Asquith, Robert F. Bruner, and David W. Mullins, Jr., "The Gains to Bidding Firms from Merger," *Journal of Financial Economics,* April 1983, p. 121; Katherine Schipper and Rex Thompson, "Evidence on the Capitalized Value of Merger Activity for Acquiring Firms," *Journal of Financial Economics,* April 1983, p. 85; Katherine Schipper and Rex Thompson, "The Impact of Merger-Related Regulations on the Shareholders of Acquiring Firms," *Journal of Accounting Research,* Spring 1983, p. 184; Michael Bradley, Anand Desai, and E. Han Kim, "Determinants of the Wealth Effects of Corporate Acquisitions Via Tender Offer: Theory and Evidence," University of Michigan Working Paper (Ann Arbor: December 1983); Frank H. Easterbrook and Gregg A. Jarrell, "Do Targets Gain from Defeating Tender Offers?" unpublished manuscript, University of Chicago, 1983; Gregg A. Jarrell, "The Wealth Effects of Litigation by Targets: Do Interests Diverge in a Merge?" unpublished manuscript, University of Chicago, 1983.

5 Financial economists have used abnormal price changes or abnormal returns to study the effects of various events on security prices since Eugene F. Fama, Lawrence Fisher, Michael C. Jensen, and Richard Roll used them to measure the impact of stock splits in "The Adjustment of Stock Prices to New Information," *International Economic Review,* February 1969, p. 1. Stephen J. Brown and Jerold B. Warner provide a detailed discussion in "Measuring Security Price Performance," *Journal of Financial Economics,* September 1980, p. 205, and in "Using Daily Stock Returns in Event Studies," *Journal of Financial Economics,* forthcoming.

6 Bradley, Desai, and Kim, "Determinants of the Wealth Effects of Corporate Acquisitions Via Tender Offer."

7 For an introduction to the literature and empirical evidence on the theory of efficient markets, see Edwin J. Elton and Martin J. Gruber, *Modern Portfolio Theory and Investment Analysis* (New York: Wiley, 1984), Chapter 15, p. 375, and the 167 studies referenced in the bibliography. For some anomalous evidence on market efficiency, see the symposia in the *Journal of Financial Economics,* June/September 1978, p. 95.

8 B. Espen Eckbo, "Horizontal Mergers, Collusion, and Stockholder Wealth," *Journal of Financial Economics,* April 1983, p. 241; Robert Stillman, "Examining Antitrust Policy Towards Horizontal Mergers," *Journal of Financial Economics,* April 1983, p. 225; B. Espen Eckbo and Peggy Wier, "Antimerger Policy and Stockholder Returns: A Reexamination of the Market Power Hypothesis," University of Rochester Managerial Economics Research Center Working Paper No. MERC 84-09, (Rochester, N.Y.: March 1984); and B. Espen Eckbo, University of Rochester Managerial Economics Research Center Working Paper No. MERC 84-08, "Horizontal Mergers, Industry Structure, and the Market Concentration Doctrine," (Rochester, N.Y.: March 1984).

9 Wier, "The Costs of Antimerger Lawsuits: Evidence from the Stock Market."

10 Schipper and Thompson, "Evidence on the Capitalized Value of Merger Activity for Acquiring Firms."

11 For a further look, see Richard S. Ruback, "The Conoco Takeover and Stockholder Returns," *Sloan Management Review,* Winter 1982, p. 13.

12 This discussion is based on Richard S. Ruback, "The Cities Service Takeover: A Case Study," *Journal of Finance,* May 1983, p. 319.

13 For a detailed analysis,
see David W. Mullins, Jr.,
*Managerial Discretion and
Corporate Financial Management*,
Chapter 7,
unpublished manuscript,
Harvard Business School, 1984.

14 See S. Grossman and
O. Hart,
"Takeover Bids, the Free-Rider
Problem, and the
Theory of the Corporation,"
Bell Journal of Economics,
Spring 1980, p. 42; and
Michael Bradley,
"Interfirm Tender Offers and the
Market for Corporate Control,"
Journal of Business,
October 1980, p. 345.

15 See Bradley, Desai, and Kim,
"The Rationale Behind Interfirm
Tender Offers."

16 William L. Cary,
"Federalism and
Corporate Law:
Reflections upon
Delaware,"
Yale Law Journal,
March 1974, p. 663.

17 Peter Dodd and
Richard Leftwich,
"The Market for
Corporate Charters:
'Unhealthy Competition'
Versus Federal Regulation,"
Journal of Business,
July 1980, p. 259.

18 Harry DeAngelo and
Edward M. Rice,
"Antitakeover Charter
Amendments and
Stockholder Wealth,"
Journal of Financial Economics,
April 1983, p. 329;
and Scott C. Linn and
John J. McConnell,
"An Empirical Investigation of
the Impact of 'Antitakeover'
Amendments on Common Stock Prices,"
Journal of Financial Economics,
April 1983, p. 361.

19 Larry Y. Dann and
Harry DeAngelo,
"Standstill Agreements,
Privately Negotiated Stock
Repurchases, and the
Market for Corporate Control,"
Journal of Financial Economics,
April 1983, p. 275;
and Michael Bradley and
L. MacDonald Wakeman,
"The Wealth Effects of Targeted
Share Repurchases,"
Journal of Financial Economics,
April 1983, p. 301.

20 Bradley and Wakeman,
"The Wealth Effects of
Targeted Share Repurchases";
Larry Dann,
"The Effect of Common Stock
Repurchase on Stockholder Returns,"
unpublished dissertation,
University of California,
Los Angeles, 1980;
Larry Dann, "Common Stock
Repurchases: An Analysis of
Returns to Bondholders and
Stockholders,"
Journal of Financial Economics,
June 1981, p. 113;
Ronald Masulis,
"Stock Repurchase by Tender Offer:
An Analysis of the Causes of Common
Stock Price Changes,"
Journal of Finance,
May 1980, p. 305;
Ahron Rosenfeld,
University of Rochester,
Managerial Economics Research
Center Monograph and
Theses No. MERC MT-82-01, 1982,
"Repurchase Offers:
Information Adjusted Premiums and
Shareholders' Response";
Theo Vermaelen,
"Common Stock Repurchases and
Market Signalling,"
Journal of Financial Economics,
June 1981, p. 139.

21 Richard S. Ruback and
Wayne H. Mikkelson,
"Corporate Investments
in Common Stock,"
Sloan School of Management
Working Paper #1559-84,
(Cambridge: M.I.T., 1984);
and
Clifford G. Holderness and
Dennis Sheehan,
University of Rochester
Managerial Economics Research
Center Working Paper No. MERC 84-06,
"Evidence on Six
Controversial Investors"
(Rochester: N.Y.: August 1984).

22 A.A. Sommer, Jr.,
" 'Going Private':
A Lesson in Corporate
Responsibility,"
Law Advisory Council Lecture,
Notre Dame Law School,
reprinted in
Federal Securities Law Reports,
Commerce Clearing House, Inc., 1974,
p. 84.

23 Harry DeAngelo,
Linda DeAngelo, and
Edward M. Rice,
"Going Private:
Minority Freezeouts and
Stockholder Wealth,"
Journal of Law and Economics,
October 1984;
and Harry DeAngelo,
Linda DeAngelo, and
Edward M. Rice,
"Going Private:
The Effects of a Change
in Corporate Ownership Structure,"
Midland Corporate Finance Journal,
Summer 1984.

24 Richard A. Lambert and
David F. Larcker,
"Golden Parachutes,
Executive Decision-Making
and Shareholder Wealth,"
Journal of Accounting and Economics,
forthcoming.

25 See Katherine Schipper and
Abbie Smith,
"Effects of Recontracting on
Shareholder Wealth:
The Case of Voluntary Spin-offs,"
Journal of Financial Economics,
December 1983, p. 437;
Gailen Hite and
James Owers,
"Security Price Reactions
Around Corporate Spin-off
Announcements,"
Journal of Financial Economics,
December 1983, p. 409;
J. Miles and J. Rosenfeld,
"The Effect of Voluntary
Spin-off Announcements on
Shareholder Wealth,"
Journal of Finance,
December 1983, p. 1597;
Gailen Hite and
James E. Owers,
"The Restructuring of
Corporate America:
An Overview,"
Midland Corporate Finance Journal,
Summer 1984;
Scott C. Linn and
Michael Rozeff,
"The Effects of Voluntary Spin-offs on
Stock Prices:
The Anergy Hypothesis,"
*Advances in Financial Planning and
Forecasting*,
Fall 1984;
Scott C. Linn and
Michael Rozeff,
"The Corporate Sell-off,"
Midland Corporate Finance Journal,
Summer 1984;
Scott C. Linn and
Michael Rozeff,
"The Effects of Voluntary Sell-offs
on Stock Prices,"
unpublished manuscript,
University of Iowa, 1984;
and Abbie Smith and
Katherine Schipper,
"Corporate Spin-offs,"
Midland Corporate Finance Journal,
Summer 1984.

26 For a further analysis,
see Leo Herzel and
John R. Schmidt,
"Shareholders Can
Benefit from
Sale of 'Crown Jewels,' "
Legal Times,
October 24, 1983, p. 33.

27 For analysis of the effects
of purchases by six so-called
raiders, Bluhdorn, Icahn,
Jacobs, Lindner, Murdock, and
Posner, see Holderness and Sheehan,
"The Evidence on Six
Controversial Investors."

28 For evidence on the relation
between poor performance and
executive turnover, see
Anne Coughlan and
Ronald Schmidt,
"Executive Compensation,
Management Turnover and
Firm Performance: An
Empirical Investigation,"
Journal of Accounting and Economics,
forthcoming.

Eclipse of the Public Corporation

by Michael C. Jensen

The publicly held corporation, the main engine of economic progress in the United States for a century, has outlived its usefulness in many sectors of the economy and is being eclipsed.

New organizations are emerging in its place – organizations that are corporate in form but have no public shareholders and are not listed or traded on organized exchanges. These organizations use public and private debt, rather than public equity, as their major source of capital. Their primary owners are not households but large institutions and entrepreneurs that designate agents to manage and monitor on their behalf and bind those agents with large equity interests and contracts governing the use and distribution of cash.

Takeovers, corporate breakups, divisional spin-offs, leveraged buyouts, and going-private transactions are the most visible manifestations of a massive organizational change in the economy. These

Michael C. Jensen is the Edsel Bryant Ford Professor of Business Administration at the Harvard Business School and founding editor of the Journal of Financial Economics. *His research and writing have figured prominently in the national debate over corporate governance and mergers and acquisitions. This article draws from Mr. Jensen's book,* Organizational Change and the Market for Corporate Control, *to be published by Basil Blackwell in 1990.*

transactions have inspired criticism, even outrage, among many business leaders and government officials, who have called for regulatory and legislative restrictions. The backlash is understandable. Change is threatening; in this case, the threat is aimed at the senior executives of many of our largest companies.

Despite the protests, this organizational innovation should be encouraged. By resolving the central weakness of the public corporation – the con-

> **New organizations resolve the central weakness of the public corporation: the struggle between owners and managers.**

flict between owners and managers over the control and use of corporate resources – these new organizations are making remarkable gains in operating efficiency, employee productivity, and shareholder

The Privatization of Equity

The last share of publicly traded common stock owned by an individual will be sold in the year 2003, if current trends persist. This forecast may be fanciful (short-term trends never persist), but the basic direction is clear. By the turn of the century, the primacy of public stock ownership in the United States may have all but disappeared.

Households have been liquidating their direct holdings and indirect positions (through channels like mutual funds) at an unprecedented rate. Over the last five years, they have been net sellers of more than $500 billion of common stock, 38% of their holdings at the beginning of 1984.

Why have stock prices risen sharply despite this massive sell-off? Because there has been one huge buyer – corporations themselves. LBOs, MBOs, share repurchases, leveraged mergers and acquisitions, and takeovers have been contracting the supply of publicly held equity. In 1988, 5% of the market value of public equity (more than $130 billion) disappeared through these kinds of transactions, even after adding back all of the new issues brought to market during the year.

Of course, the risks and returns from the underlying corporate assets have not disappeared. To some extent they now reside in quasi-equity debt instruments like high-yield bonds, whose total market value exceeds $200 billion. But many of the risks and returns still exist as equity; they just take the form of large positions of privately held equity. The "privatization of equity" is now a central feature of corporate ownership in the United States.

Historically, public stock markets dominated by individual investors developed to a greater extent in the United States than in any other country. Broad public ownership offered managers a reasonably priced source of more or less permanent equity capital that could buffer the company against adversity in a way debt could not. Share ownership allowed individual investors to participate in equity returns and get the benefits of liquidity (because they could sell their shares) and diversification (because they could hold a small number of shares from many corporations).

The virtues of broad public ownership are not what they used to be, for managers or investors. One important factor is the emergence of an active market for corporate control. A capital structure consisting mostly of equity still offers managers protection against the risks of economic downturn. But it also carries substantial risks of inviting a hostile takeover or other threats to management control.

The role of the public market has also changed because investors themselves have changed. For decades, stock ownership has been migrating from direct holdings by millions of individuals to indirect beneficial ownership through large pools of capital – in particular, the huge corporate and governmental pension funds whose total value exceeded $1.5 trillion in 1988. These institutional funds, which now comprise more than 40% of total stock ownership, used to behave like large public investors. They kept diversified by retaining many different investment managers, each of whom traded an array of highly liquid public securities. But their investment philosophy has been evolving in recent years to include participation in a select number of

value. Over the long term, they will enhance U.S. economic performance relative to our most formidable international competitor, Japan, whose companies are moving in the opposite direction. The governance and financial structures of Japan's public companies increasingly resemble U.S. companies of the mid-1960s and early 1970s – an era of gross corporate waste and mismanagement that triggered the organizational transformation now under way in the United States.

Consider these developments in the 1980s:

☐ The capital markets are in transition. The total market value of equity in publicly held companies has tripled over the past decade – from $1 trillion in 1979 to more than $3 trillion in 1989. But newly acquired capital comes increasingly from private placements, which have expanded more than ten times since 1980, to a rate of $200 billion in 1988. Private placements of debt and equity now account for more than 40% of annual corporate financings. Meanwhile, in every year since 1983, at least 5% of the outstanding value of corporate equity has disappeared through stock repurchases, takeovers, and going-private transactions. Finally, households are sharply reducing their stock holdings.[1] (See the insert, "The Privatization of Equity.")

☐ The most widespread going-private transaction, the leveraged buyout, is becoming larger and more frequent. In 1988, the total value of the 214 public-company and divisional buyouts exceeded $77 billion – nearly one-third of the value of all mergers and acquisitions. The total value of the 75 buyouts in 1979 was only $1.3 billion (in constant 1988 dollars), while the 175 buyouts completed in 1983 private illiquid investments and private pools of equity capital. This new investment philosophy makes broad public markets less essential for institutions.

Large pools of capital such as pension funds and endowments don't really need the liquidity the public market offers. Liquidity serves two basic purposes. It allows investors to meet unexpected cash needs and to trade their stocks. Unlike individuals, the large funds can project their cash needs well into the future based on predictable factors such as employee demographics, life expectancies, and health trends. So they can take a long-term view of investment returns and keep their holdings in illiquid assets.

Fund managers are also realizing that trading is a tough discipline in which they hold little comparative advantage. Trading is a zero-sum game played in a fairly efficient market against equally talented rivals. Worse still, large funds face diseconomies of scale when executing trades. The larger a fund, the more difficult it is to trade quickly, based on transient information advantages. The very act of trading moves markets.

Still, these managers remain charged with generating returns in excess of passive benchmarks. Enter the market for private assets such as real estate, venture capital, and, more recently, the market for corporate control and restructurings. Instead of trading a large number of small, liquid positions, the funds can buy and own smaller numbers of large, illiquid positions in a form where they (or, more likely, their agents) participate more actively with management in the control of the assets.

This alternative can be a positive-sum game; real changes in corporate policies can be a route to enhanced value. The very large funds also have a competitive advantage here. The larger their positions, the more actively they can participate in the ownership and management of the underlying assets. In the extreme, as with LBO funds, these changes can be dramatic. The LBO fund itself becomes the managing owner in partnership with company managers. In short, large institutional funds can behave more like owners and less like traders.

The same basic changes are at work in a wide variety of corporate recapitalizations where outside (or related) parties acquire large, relatively nontraded equity positions. Large pools of capital can participate in these private equity positions yet remain diversified by virtue of their own enormous size. Smaller funds and households cannot.

In the short run, this new investment philosophy has been, in the aggregate, a great success. Without the sobering influence of an economic contraction, the returns from these private investments have been very attractive. In the long run, the institutions' new philosophy is ushering in a system of equity ownership dominated by "private positions" that resembles ownership systems in Germany and Japan. Individual investors in this system will increasingly be free riders on the coattails of a small number of very large private investors rather than the central feature of the financial markets.

—JAY O. LIGHT

Jay O. Light is the George Fisher Baker, Jr. Professor of Business Administration at the Harvard Business School.

had a total value of $16.6 billion. This process is just getting started; the $77 billion of LBOs in 1988 represented only 2.5% of outstanding public-company equity. (See the table, "Rise of the LBO.")

☐ Entire industries are being reshaped. Just five years ago, the leading U.S. truck and automobile tire manufacturers were independent and diversified public companies. Today each is a vastly different enterprise. Uniroyal went private in 1985 and later merged its tire-making operations with those of B.F. Goodrich to form a new private company called Uniroyal Goodrich. In late 1986, Goodyear borrowed $2.6 billion and repurchased nearly half its outstanding shares to fend off a hostile tender offer by Sir James Goldsmith. It retained its core tire and rubber business while moving to divest an array of unrelated operations, including its Celeron oil and gas subsidiary,

California-to-Texas oil pipeline, aerospace operation, and Arizona resort hotel. In 1987, GenCorp issued $1.75 billion of debt to repurchase more than half its outstanding shares. It divested several operations, including its General Tire subsidiary, to pay down the debt and focus on aerospace and defense. Last year, Firestone was sold to Bridgestone, Japan's largest tiremaker, for $2.6 billion, a transaction that created shareholder gains of $1.6 billion.

Developments as striking as the restructuring of our financial markets and major industries reflect underlying economic forces more fundamental and powerful than financial manipulation, management greed, reckless speculation, and the other colorful epithets used by defenders of the corporate status quo. The forces behind the decline of the public corporation differ from industry to industry. But its decline is real, enduring, and highly productive. It is not merely a function of the tax deductibility of interest. Nor does it reflect a transitory LBO phase through which companies pass before investment bankers and managers cash out by taking them public again. Nor, finally, is it premised on a systematic fleecing of shareholders and bondholders by managers and other insiders with superior information about the true value of corporate assets.

The current trends do not imply that the public corporation has no future. The conventional twentieth-century model of corporate governance – dispersed public ownership, professional managers without substantial equity holdings, a board of directors dominated by management-appointed outsiders – remains a viable option in some areas of the economy, particularly for growth companies whose profitable investment opportunities exceed the cash they generate internally. Such companies can be found in industries like computers and electronics, biotechnology, pharmaceuticals, and financial services. Companies choosing among a surplus of profitable projects are unlikely to invest systemat-

The public corporation will decline in industries such as aerospace, banking, and food processing.

ically in unprofitable ones, especially when they must regularly turn to the capital markets to raise investment funds.

The public corporation is not suitable in industries where long-term growth is slow, where internally generated funds outstrip the opportunities to invest them profitably, or where downsizing is the most productive long-term strategy. In the tire industry, the shift to radials, which last three times longer than bias-ply tires, meant that manufacturers needed less capacity to meet world demand. Overcapacity inevitably forced a restructuring. The tenfold increase in oil prices from 1973 to 1981, which triggered worldwide conservation measures, forced oil producers into a similar retrenchment.[2]

Industries under similar pressure today include steel, chemicals, brewing, tobacco, television and radio broadcasting, wood and paper products. In these and other cash-rich, low-growth or declining sectors, the pressures on management to waste cash flow through organizational slack or investments in unsound projects is often irresistible. It is in precisely these sectors that the publicly held corporation has

declined most rapidly. Barring regulatory interference, the public corporation is also likely to decline in industries such as aerospace, automobiles and auto parts, banking, electric power generation, food processing, industrial and farm implements, and transportation equipment.

The public corporation is a social invention of vast historical importance. Its genius is rooted in its capacity to spread financial risk over the diversified portfolios of millions of individuals and institutions and to allow investors to customize risk to their unique circumstances and predilections. By diversifying risks that would otherwise be borne by owner-entrepreneurs and by facilitating the creation of a liquid market for exchanging risk, the public corporation lowered the cost of capital. These tradable claims on corporate ownership (common stock) also allowed risk to be borne by investors best able to bear it, without requiring them to manage the corporations they owned.

From the beginning, though, these risk-bearing benefits came at a cost. Tradable ownership claims create fundamental conflicts of interest between those who bear risk (the shareholders) and those who manage risk (the executives). The genius of the new organizations is that they eliminate much of the loss created by conflicts between owners and managers, without eliminating the vital functions of risk diversification and liquidity once performed exclusively by the public equity markets.

In theory, these new organizations should not be necessary. Three major forces are said to control management in the public corporation: the product markets, internal control systems led by the board of directors, and the capital markets. But product markets often have not played a disciplining role. For most of the last 60 years, a large and vibrant domestic market created for U.S. companies economies of scale and significant cost advantages over foreign rivals. Recent reversals at the hands of the Japanese and others have not been severe enough to sap most companies of their financial independence. The idea that outside directors with little or no equity stake in the company could effectively monitor and discipline the managers who selected them has proven hollow at best. In practice, only the capital markets have played much of a control function – and for a long time they were hampered by legal constraints.

Indeed, the fact that takeover and LBO premiums average 50% above market price illustrates how much value public-company managers can destroy before they face a serious threat of disturbance. Takeovers and buyouts both create new value and unlock value destroyed by management through misguided policies. I estimate that transactions associated with the market for corporate control unlocked shareholder gains (in target companies alone) of more than $500 billion between 1977 and 1988 – more than 50% of the cash dividends paid by the entire corporate sector over this same period.

The widespread waste and inefficiency of the public corporation and its inability to adapt to changing economic circumstances have generated a wave of organizational innovation over the last 15 years – innovation driven by the rebirth of "active investors." By active investors I mean investors who hold large equity or debt positions, sit on boards of directors, monitor and sometimes dismiss management, are involved with the long-term strategic direction of the companies they invest in, and sometimes manage the companies themselves.

Active investors are creating a new model of general management. These investors include LBO partnerships such as Kohlberg Kravis Roberts and Clayton & Dubilier; entrepreneurs such as Carl Icahn, Ronald Perelman, Laurence Tisch, Robert Bass, William Simon, Irwin Jacobs, and Warren Buffett; the merchant banking arms of Wall Street houses such as Morgan Stanley, Lazard Frères, and Merrill Lynch; and family funds such as those controlled by the Pritzkers and the Bronfmans. Their model is built around highly leveraged financial structures, pay-for-performance compensation systems, substantial equity ownership by managers and directors, and contracts with owners and creditors that limit both cross-subsidization among business units and the waste of free cash flow. Consistent with

modern finance theory, these organizations are not managed to maximize earnings per share but rather to maximize *value*, with a strong emphasis on cash flow.

More than any other factor, these organizations' resolution of the owner-manager conflict explains how they can motivate the same people, managing the same resources, to perform so much more effectively under private ownership than in the publicly held corporate form.

In effect, LBO partnerships and the merchant banks are rediscovering the role played by active investors prior to 1940, when Wall Street banks such as J.P. Morgan & Company were directly involved in the strategy and governance of the public companies they helped create. At the height of his prominence, Morgan and his small group of partners served on the boards of U.S. Steel, International Harvester, First National Bank of New York, and a host of railroads, and were a powerful management force in these and other companies.

Morgan's model of investor activism disappeared largely as a result of populist laws and regulations approved in the wake of the Great Depression. These laws and regulations – including the Glass-Steagall Banking Act of 1933, the Securities Act of 1933, the Securities Exchange Act of 1934, the Chandler Bankruptcy Revision Act of 1938, and the Investment Company Act of 1940 – may have once had their place. But they also created an intricate web of restrictions on company "insiders" (corporate officers, directors, or investors with more than a 10% ownership interest), restrictions on bank involvement in

Rise of the LBO

Year	Public-Company Buyouts		Divisional Buyouts		Total Value of Buyouts (In billions of 1988 dollars)
	Number	Average Value (In millions of 1988 dollars)	Number	Average Value (In millions of 1988 dollars)	
1979	16	$ 64.9	59	$ 5.4	$ 1.4
1980	13	106.0	47	34.5	3.0
1981	17	179.1	83	21.0	4.8
1982	31	112.2	115	40.7	8.2
1983	36	235.8	139	58.2	16.6
1984	57	473.6	122	104.0	39.7
1985	76	349.4	132	110.1	41.0
1986	76	303.3	144	180.7	49.0
1987	47	488.7	90	144.2	36.0
1988	125	487.4	89	181.3	77.0

Source: George P. Baker, "Management Compensation and Divisional Leveraged Buyouts," unpublished dissertation, Harvard Business School, 1986. Updates from W.T. Grimm, *Mergerstat Review 1988*. Transactions with no public data are valued at the average price of public transactions.

corporate reorganizations, court precedents, and business practices that raised the cost of being an active investor. Their long-term effect has been to insulate management from effective monitoring and to set the stage for the eclipse of the public corporation.

Indeed, the high cost of being an active investor has left financial institutions and money management firms, which control more than 40% of all corporate equity in the United States, almost completely uninvolved in the major decisions and long-term strategies of the companies their clients own. They are almost never represented on corporate boards. They use the proxy mechanism rarely and usually ineffectively, notwithstanding recent efforts by the Council of Institutional Investors and other shareholder activists to gain a larger voice in corporate affairs.

All told, institutional investors are remarkably powerless; they have few options to express dissatisfaction with management other than to sell their shares and vote with their feet. Corporate managers criticize institutional sell-offs as examples of portfolio churning and short-term investor horizons. One guesses these same managers much prefer churning to a system in which large investors on the boards of their companies have direct power to monitor and correct mistakes. Managers really want passive investors who can't sell their shares.

The absence of effective monitoring led to such large inefficiencies that the new generation of active investors arose to recapture the lost value. These investors overcome the costs of the outmoded legal constraints by purchasing entire companies – and using debt and high equity ownership to force effective self-monitoring.

A central weakness and source of waste in the public corporation is the conflict between shareholders and managers over the payout of free cash flow – that is, cash flow in excess of that required to fund all investment projects with positive net present values when discounted at the relevant cost of capital. For a company to operate efficiently and maximize value, free cash flow must be distributed to shareholders rather than retained. But this happens infrequently; senior management has few incentives to distribute the funds, and there exist few mechanisms to compel distribution.

A vivid example is the senior management of Ford Motor Company, which sits on nearly $15 billion in cash and marketable securities in an industry with excess capacity. Ford's management has been deliberating about acquiring financial service companies, aerospace companies, or making some other multibillion-dollar diversification move – rather than deliberating about effectively distributing Ford's excess cash to its owners so they can decide how to reinvest it.

Ford is not alone. Corporate managers generally don't disgorge cash unless they are forced to do so. In 1988, the 1,000 largest public companies (by sales) generated total funds of $1.6 trillion. Yet they distributed only $108 billion as dividends and another $51 billion through share repurchases.[3]

Managers have incentives to retain cash in part because cash reserves increase their autonomy vis-à-vis the capital markets. Large cash balances (and independence from the capital markets) can serve a competitive purpose, but they often lead to waste and inefficiency. Consider a hypothetical world in which companies distribute excess cash to shareholders and then must convince the capital markets to supply

Institutional investors are powerless. Their only option is to vote with their feet.

funds as sound economic projects arise. Shareholders are at a great advantage in this world, where management's plans are subject to enhanced monitoring by the capital markets. Wall Street's analytical, due diligence, and pricing disciplines give shareholders more power to quash wasteful projects.

Managers also resist distributing cash to shareholders because retaining cash increases the size of the companies they run – and managers have many incentives to expand company size beyond that which maximizes shareholder wealth. Compensation is one of the most important incentives. Many studies document that increases in executive pay are strongly related to increases in corporate size rather than value.[4]

The tendency of companies to reward middle managers through promotions rather than annual performance bonuses also creates a cultural bias toward growth. Organizations must grow in order to generate new positions to feed their promotion-based reward systems.

Finally, corporate growth enhances the social prominence, public prestige, and political power of senior executives. Rare is the CEO who wants to be remembered as presiding over an enterprise that makes fewer products in fewer plants in fewer countries than when he or she took office – even when such a course increases productivity and adds hundreds of millions of dollars of shareholder value. The perquisites of the executive suite can be substantial, and they usually increase with company size.

The struggle over free cash flow is at the heart of the role of debt in the decline of the public corporation. Bank loans, mezzanine securities, and high-yield bonds have fueled the wave of takeovers, restructurings, and going-private transactions. The combined borrowings of all nonfinancial corporations in the United States approached $2 trillion in 1988, up from $835 billion in 1979. The interest charges on these borrowings represent more than 20% of corporate cash flows, high by historical standards.[5]

This perceived "leveraging of corporate America" is perhaps the central source of anxiety among defenders of the public corporation and critics of the new organizational forms. But most critics miss three important points. First, the trebling of the market value of public-company equity over the last decade means that corporate borrowing had to increase to avoid a major *deleveraging.*

Second, debt creation *without retention of the proceeds of the issue* helps limit the waste of free cash flow by compelling managers to pay out funds they would otherwise retain. Debt is in effect a substitute for dividends—a mechanism to force managers to disgorge cash rather than spend it on empire-building projects with low or negative returns, bloated staffs, indulgent perquisites, and organizational inefficiencies.

By issuing debt in exchange for stock, companies bond their managers' promise to pay out future cash flows in a way that simple dividend increases do not. "Permanent" dividend increases or multiyear share repurchase programs (two ways public companies can distribute excess cash to shareholders) involve no contractual commitments by managers to owners. It's easy for managers to cut dividends or scale back share repurchases.

Take the case of General Motors. On March 3, 1987, several months after the departure of GM's only active investor, H. Ross Perot, the company announced a program to repurchase up to 20% of its common stock by the end of 1990. As of mid-1989, GM had purchased only 5% of its outstanding common shares, even though its $6.8 billion cash balance was more than enough to complete the program. Given management's poor performance over the past decade, shareholders would be better off making their own investment decisions with the cash GM is retaining. From 1977 to 1987, the company made capital expenditures of $77.5 billion while its U.S. market share declined by 10 points.

Borrowing allows for no such managerial discretion. Companies whose managers fail to make promised interest and principal payments can be declared insolvent and possibly hauled into bankruptcy court.

In the imagery of G. Bennett Stewart and David M. Glassman, "Equity is soft, debt hard. Equity is forgiving, debt insistent. Equity is a pillow, debt a sword."[6] Some may find it curious that a company's creditors wield far more power over managers than its public shareholders, but it is also undeniable.

Third, debt is a powerful agent for change. For all the deeply felt anxiety about excessive borrowing, "overleveraging" can be desirable and effective when it makes economic sense to break up a company, sell off parts of the business, and refocus its energies on a few core operations. Companies that assume so much debt they cannot meet the debt service payments out of operating cash flow force themselves to rethink their entire strategy and structure. Overleveraging creates the crisis atmosphere managers require to slash unsound investment programs, shrink overhead, and dispose of assets that are more valuable outside the company. The proceeds generated by these overdue restructurings can then be used to reduce debt to more sustainable levels, creating a leaner, more efficient and competitive organization.

In other circumstances, the violation of debt covenants creates a board-level crisis that brings new actors onto the scene, motivates a fresh review of top management and strategy, and accelerates response. The case of Revco D.S., Inc., one of the handful of leveraged buyouts to reach formal bankruptcy, makes the point well.

Efficient companies distribute free cash flow to shareholders. So why is Ford sitting on $15 billion?

Critics cite Revco's bankruptcy petition, filed in July 1988, as an example of the financial perils associated with LBO debt. I take a different view. The $1.25 billion buyout, announced in December 1986, did dramatically increase Revco's annual interest charges. But several other factors contributed to its troubles, including management's decision to overhaul pricing, stocking, and merchandise layout in the company's drugstore chain. This mistaken strategic redirection left customers confused and dissatisfied, and Revco's performance suffered. Before the buyout, and without the burden of interest payments, management could have pursued these policies for a long period of time, destroying much of the company's value in the process. Within six months, however, debt served as a brake on management's mistakes, motivating the board and creditors to reorganize the company before even more value was lost.[7]

Developments at Goodyear also illustrate how debt can force managers to adopt value-creating policies they would otherwise resist. Soon after his company warded off Sir James Goldsmith's tender offer, Goodyear chairman Robert Mercer offered his version of the raiders' creed: "Give me your undervalued assets, your plants, your expenditures for technology, research and development, the hopes and aspirations of your people, your stake with your customers, your pension funds, and I will enhance myself and the dealmakers."[8]

What Mr. Mercer failed to note is that Goodyear's forced restructuring dramatically increased the company's value to shareholders by compelling him to disgorge cash and shed unproductive assets. Two years after this bitter complaint, Tom Barrett, who succeeded Mercer as Goodyear's CEO, was asked whether the company's restructuring had hurt the quality of its tires or the efficiency of its plants. "No," he replied. "We've been able to invest and continue to invest and do the things we've needed to do to be competitive."[9]

Robert Mercer's harsh words are characteristic of the business establishment's response to the eclipse of the public corporation. What explains such vehement opposition to a trend that clearly benefits shareholders and the economy? One important factor, as my Harvard Business School colleague Amar Bhide suggests, is that Wall Street now competes directly with senior management as a steward of shareholder wealth. With its vast increases in data, talent, and technology, Wall Street can allocate capital among competing businesses and monitor and discipline management more effectively than the CEO and headquarters staff of the typical diversified company. KKR's New York offices and Irwin Jacobs' Minneapolis base are direct substitutes for corporate headquarters in Akron or Peoria. CEOs worry that they and their staffs will lose lucrative jobs in favor of competing organizations. Many are right to worry; the performance of active investors versus the public corporation leaves little doubt as to which is superior.

Active investors are creating new models of general management, the most widespread of which I call the LBO Association. A typical LBO Association consists of three main constituencies: an LBO partnership that sponsors going-private transactions and counsels and monitors management in an ongoing cooperative relationship; company managers who hold substantial equity stakes in an LBO division and stay on after the buyout; and institutional investors (insurance companies, pension funds, and money management firms) that fund the limited partnerships that purchase equity and lend money (along with banks) to finance the transactions.

Much like a traditional conglomerate, LBO Associations have many divisions or business units, companies they have taken private at different points in time. KKR, for example, controls a diverse collection of 19 businesses including all or part of Beatrice, Duracell, Motel 6, Owens-Illinois, RJR Nabisco, and Safeway. But LBO Associations differ from publicly held conglomerates in at least four important respects. (See the illustration, "Public Company vs. LBO Association.")

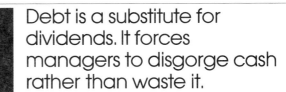

Debt is a substitute for dividends. It forces managers to disgorge cash rather than waste it.

Management incentives are built around a strong relationship between pay and performance. Compensation systems in LBO Associations usually have higher upper bounds than do public companies (or no upper bounds at all), tie bonuses much more closely to cash flow and debt retirement than to accounting earnings, and otherwise closely link management pay to divisional performance. Unfortunately, because these companies are private, little data are available on salaries and bonuses.

Public data are available on stock ownership, however, and equity holdings are a vital part of the reward system in LBO Associations. The University of Chicago's Steven Kaplan studied all public-company buyouts from 1979 through 1985 with a purchase price of at least $50 million.[10] Business-unit chiefs hold a median equity position of 6.4% in their unit. Even without considering bonus and incentive plans, a $1,000 increase in shareholder value triggers a $64 increase in the personal wealth of business-unit chiefs. The median public-company CEO holds only .25% of the company's equity. Counting *all* sources of compensation—including salary, bonus, deferred compensation, stock options, and dismissal penalties—the personal wealth of the median public-company CEO increases by only $3.25 for a $1,000 increase in shareholder value.[11]

Thus the salary of the typical LBO business-unit manager is almost 20 times more sensitive to performance than that of the typical public-company manager. This comparison understates the true differences in compensation. The personal wealth of managing partners in an LBO partnership (in effect, the CEOs of the LBO Associations) is tied almost exclusively to the performance of the companies they control. The general partners in an LBO Association typically receive (through overrides and direct equity holdings) 20% or more of the gains in the value of the divisions they help manage. This implies a pay-for-performance sensitivity of $200 for every $1,000 in added shareholder value. It's not hard to understand why an executive who receives $200 for every $1,000 increase in shareholder value will unlock more value than an executive who receives $3.25.

LBO Associations are more decentralized than publicly held conglomerates. The LBO Association substitutes compensation incentives and ownership for direct monitoring by headquarters. The headquarters of KKR, the world's largest LBO partnership, has only 16 professionals and 44 additional employees. In contrast, the Atlanta headquarters of RJR Nabisco employed 470 people when KKR took it private last year in a $25 billion transaction. At the time of the Goldsmith tender offer for Goodyear, the company's Akron headquarters had more than 5,000 people on its salaried payroll.

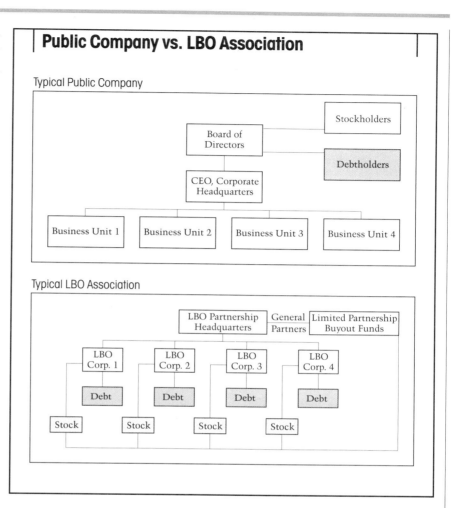

Public Company vs. LBO Association

Typical Public Company

Typical LBO Association

It is physically impossible for KKR and other LBO partnerships to become intimately involved in the day-to-day decisions of their operating units. They rely instead on stock ownership, incentive pay that rewards cash flow, and other compensation techniques to motivate managers to maximize value without bureaucratic oversight. My survey of 7 LBO partnerships found an average headquarters staff of 13 professionals and 19 nonprofessionals that oversees almost 24 business units with total annual sales of more than $11 billion. (See the table, "LBO Partnerships Keep Staff Lean.")

LBO Associations rely heavily on leverage. The average debt ratio (long-term debt as a percentage of debt plus equity) for public companies prior to a buyout is about 20%. The Kaplan study shows the average debt ratio for an LBO is 85% on completion of the buyout.

Intensive use of debt dramatically shrinks the amount of equity in a company. This allows the LBO general partners and divisional managers to control a large fraction of the total ownership without requiring huge investments they would be unable to make

or large grants of free equity. For example, in a company with $1 billion in assets and a debt ratio of 20%, management would have to raise $80 million to buy 10% of the equity. If that same company had a debt ratio of 90%, management would have to raise only $10 million to control a 10% stake. By concentrating equity holdings among managers and LBO partners, debt intensifies the ownership incentives that are so important to efficiency.

High debt also allows LBO Associations and other private organizations to tap the benefits of risk diversification once provided only by the public equity market. Intensive use of debt means much of it must be in the form of public, high-yield, noninvestment-grade securities, better known as junk bonds. This debt, which was pioneered by Drexel Burnham Lambert, reflects more of the risk borne by shareholders in the typical public company. Placing this public debt in the well-diversified portfolios of large financial institutions spreads equitylike risk among millions of investors, who are the ultimate beneficiaries of mutual funds and pension funds – without requiring those risks to be held as equity. Indeed, high-yield debt is probably the most important and productive capital market innovation in the last 40 years.

LBO Associations have well-defined obligations to their creditors and residual claimants. Most buy-out funds are organized as limited partnerships in which the partners of the sponsoring LBO firm serve as general partners. The buyout fund purchases most of the equity and sometimes provides debt financing. The limited partnership agreement denies the general partner the right to transfer cash or other resources from one LBO division to another. That is, all returns from a business must be distributed to the limited partners and other equity holders of that business. Such binding agreements reduce the risk of unproductive reinvestment by prohibiting cross-subsidization among LBO units. In effect, the LBO sponsor must ask its institutional investors for permission to reinvest funds, a striking difference from the power of public-company managers to freely shift resources among business units.

The management, compensation, and financial structures of the LBO Association square neatly with the rebirth of active investors. Institutional investors delegate the job of being active monitors to agents best qualified to play the role. The LBO partnerships bond their performance by investing their own resources and reputations in the transaction and taking the bulk of their compensation as a share in the companies' increased value.

To be sure, this delegation is not without its tensions. The fact that LBO partnerships and divisional managers control the LBO Association's small equity base but hold little of the debt creates incentives for them to take high-risk management gambles. If their gambles succeed, they reap large rewards by increasing their equity value; if their gambles fail, creditors bear much of the cost. But the reputational consequences of such reckless behavior can be large. As long as creditors behave rationally, an LBO partnership that tries to profit at the expense of its creditors or walks away from a deal gone sour will not be able to raise funds for future investments.

To date, the performance of LBO Associations has been remarkable. Indeed, it is difficult to find any systematic losers in these transactions, and almost all of the gains appear to come from real increases

Wall Street allocates capital more effectively than public-company CEOs do.

in productivity. The best studies of LBO performance reach the following conclusions:

☐ LBOs create large gains for shareholders. Studies estimate that the average total premium to public shareholders ranges from 40% to 56%.[12] Kaplan finds that in buyouts that go public again or are otherwise sold (which occurs on average 2.7 years after the original transaction), total shareholder value increases by an average of 235%, or nearly 100% above market-adjusted returns over the same period.[13] These returns are distributed about equally between pre-buyout shareholders and the suppliers of debt and

LBO Partnerships Keep Staff Lean

LBO Partnership	Year Started	Number of Professionals	Number of Nonprofessionals	Number of Business Units	Combined Annual Revenues (In billions of dollars)
Berkshire Partners	1986	14	6	15	$ 1
Butler Capital	1979	8	14	33	2.3
Clayton & Dubilier	1976	10	11	8	4.8
Gibbons Green van Amerongen	1969	6	7	12	5.3
Kohlberg Kravis Roberts	1976	16	44	19	58.7
Thomas H. Lee Co.	1974	15	12	25	8
Odyssey Partners	1950	19	39	53	N.A.

equity to the transaction. Prebuyout shareholders earn average market-adjusted premiums of 38%, while the total return to capital (debt plus equity) for buyout investors is 42%. This return to buyout investors is measured on the total purchase price of the LBO, not the buyout equity. Because equity returns are almost a pure risk premium, and therefore independent of the amount invested, they are very high. The median nominal return on buyout equity is 785%, or 135% per year.

☐ Value gains do not come at the expense of other financial constituencies. Some critics argue that buyout investors, especially managers, earn excessive returns by using inside information to exploit public shareholders. Managers do face severe conflicts of interest in these transactions; they cannot simultaneously act as buyer and agent for the seller. But equity-owning managers who are not part of postbuyout management teams systematically sell their shares into LBOs. This would be foolish if the buyout were significantly underpriced in light of inside information, assuming that these nonparticipating insiders have the same inside information as the continuing management team. Moreover, LBO auctions are becoming common; underpriced buyout proposals (including those initiated by management) quickly generate competing bids.

No doubt some bondholders have lost value through going-private transactions. By my estimate, RJR Nabisco's prebuyout bondholders lost almost $300 million through the downgrading of their claims on the newly leveraged company. This is a small sum in comparison to the $12 billion in total gains the transaction produced. As yet, there is no evidence that bondholders lose on average from LBOs. Evidence on LBOs completed through 1986 does show that holders of convertible bonds and preferred stock gain a statistically significant amount and that straight bondholders suffer no significant gains or losses.[14]

New data may document losses for bondholders in recent transactions. But the expropriation of wealth from bondholders should not be a continuing problem. The financial community is perfecting many techniques, including poison puts and repurchase provisions, to protect bondholders in the event of substantial restructurings. In fact, versions of these loss-prevention techniques have been available for some time. In the past, bondholders such as Metropolitan Life, which sued RJR Nabisco over the declining value of the company's bonds, chose not to pay the premium for protection.

☐ LBOs increase operating efficiency without massive layoffs or big cuts in research and development. Kaplan finds that average operating earnings increase by 42% from the year prior to the buyout to the third year after the buyout. Cash flows increase by 96% over this same period. Other studies document significant improvements in profit margins, sales per employee, working capital, inventories, and receivables.[15] Those who doubt these findings might take a moment to scan the business press, which has chronicled the impressive postbuyout performance of companies such as Levi Strauss, A.O. Scott, Safeway, and Weirton Steel.

Importantly, employment does not fall systematically after buyouts, although it does not grow as quickly as in comparable companies. Median employment for all companies in the Kaplan study, including those engaged in substantial divestitures, increased by nearly 1%. Companies without significant divestitures increased employment by 5%.

Moreover, the great concern about the effect of buyouts on R&D and capital investment is unwarranted. The low-growth companies that make the best candidates for LBOs don't invest heavily in R&D to begin with. Of the 76 companies in the Kaplan study, only 7 spent more than 1% of sales on R&D before the buyout. Another recent study shows

LBO performance: dramatic gains in profit margins, cash flow, sales per employee, and working capital.

that R&D as a fraction of sales grows at the same rate in LBOs as in comparable public companies.[16] According to Kaplan's study, capital expenditures are 20% lower in LBOs than in comparable non-LBO companies. Because these cuts are taking place in low-growth or declining industries and are accompanied by a doubling of market-adjusted value, they appear to be coming from reductions in low-return projects rather than productive investments.

☐ Taxpayers do not subsidize going-private transactions. Much has been made of the charge that large increases in debt virtually eliminate the tax obligations of an LBO. This argument overlooks five sources of additional tax revenues generated by buyouts: capital gains taxes paid by prebuyout shareholders; capital gains taxes paid on postbuyout asset sales; tax payments on the large increases in operating earnings generated by efficiency gains; tax payments by creditors who receive interest payments on the LBO debt; and taxes generated by more efficient use of the company's total capital.

Overall, the U.S. Treasury collects an estimated 230% more revenues in the year after a buyout than it would have otherwise and 61% more in long-term present value. The $12 billion gain associated with the RJR Nabisco buyout will generate net tax revenues of $3.3 billion in the first year of the buyout; the company paid $370 million in federal taxes in the year before the buyout. In the long term, the transaction will generate total taxes with an estimated present value of $3.8 billion.[17]

☐ LBO sponsors do not have to take their companies public for them to succeed. Most LBO transactions are completed with a goal of returning the reconfigured company to the public market within three to five years. But recent evidence indicates that LBO sponsors are keeping their companies under private ownership. Huge efficiency gains and high-return asset sales produce enough cash to pay down debt and allow LBOs to generate handsome returns as going concerns. The very proliferation of these transactions has helped create a more efficient infrastructure and liquid market for buying and selling divisions and companies. Thus LBO investors can "cash out" in a secondary LBO or private sale without recourse to a public offering. One recent study

---

High debt creates incentives to avoid bankruptcy. Troubled companies are reorganized quickly.

---

finds that only 5% of the more than 1,300 LBOs between 1981 and 1986 have gone public again.[18]

Public companies can learn from LBO Associations and emulate many of their characteristics. But this requires major changes in corporate structure, philosophy, and focus. They can reduce the waste of free cash flow by borrowing to repurchase stock or pay large dividends. They can alter their charters to encourage large investors or experiment with alliances with active investors such as Lazard Frères' Corporate Partners fund. They can increase equity ownership by directors, managers, and employees. They can enhance incentives through pay-for-performance systems based on cash flow and value rather than accounting earnings. They can decentralize management by rethinking the role of corporate headquarters and shrinking their staffs.

Some corporations are experimenting with such changes—FMC, Holiday, and Owens-Corning—and the results have been impressive. But only a coordinated attack on the status quo will halt the eclipse of the public company. It is unlikely such an attack will proceed fast enough or go far enough.

Who can argue with a new model of enterprise that aligns the interests of owners and managers, improves efficiency and productivity, and unlocks hundreds of billions of dollars of shareholder value? Many people, it seems, mainly because these organizations rely so heavily on debt. As I've discussed, debt is crucial to management discipline and resolving the conflict over free cash flow. But critics, even some who concede the control function of debt, argue that the costs of leverage outweigh the benefits.

Wall Street economist Henry Kaufman, a prominent critic of the going-private trend, issued a typical warning earlier this year: "Any severe shock—a sharp increase in interest rates in response to Federal Reserve credit restraint, or an outright recession that makes the whole stock market vulnerable, or some breakdown in the ability of foreign firms to bid for pieces of U.S. companies—will drive debt-burdened companies to the government's doorstep to plead for special assistance."[19]

The relationship between debt and insolvency is perhaps the least understood aspect of this entire organizational evolution. New hedging techniques mean the risk associated with a given level of corporate debt is lower today than it was five years ago. Much of the bank debt associated with LBOs (which typically represents about half of the total debt) is done through floating-rate instruments. But few LBOs accept unlimited exposure to interest rate fluctuations. They purchase caps to set a ceiling on interest charges or use swaps to convert floating-rate debt into fixed-rate debt. In fact, most banks require such risk management techniques as a condition of lending.

Critics of leverage also fail to appreciate that insolvency in and of itself is not always something to avoid—and that the costs of becoming insolvent are likely to be much smaller in the new world of high leverage than in the old world of equity-dominated balance sheets. The proliferation of takeovers, LBOs, and other going-private transactions has inspired innovations in the reorganization and workout process. I refer to these innovations as "the privatization of bankruptcy." LBOs do get in financial trouble more frequently than public companies do. But few LBOs ever enter formal bankruptcy. They are reorganized quickly (a few months is common), often under new management, and at much lower costs than under a court-supervised process.

How can insolvency be less costly in a world of high leverage? Consider an oversimplified example. Companies A and B are identical in every respect except for their financial structures. Each has a going-concern value of $100 million (the discounted value of its expected future cash flows) and a liquidation or salvage value of $10 million. Company A has an equity-dominated balance sheet with a debt ratio of 20%, common for large public companies. Highly leveraged Company B has a debt ratio of 85%, common for LBOs. (See the illustration, "The Privatization of Bankruptcy.")

Now both companies experience business reversals. What happens? Company B will get in trouble with its creditors much sooner than Company A. After all, Company B's going-concern value doesn't have to shrink very much for it to be unable to meet its payments on $85 million of debt. But when it does run into trouble, its going-concern value will be nowhere near its liquidation value. If the going-concern value shrinks to $80 million, there remains $70 million of value to preserve by avoiding liquidation. So Company B's creditors have strong incentives to preserve the remaining value by quickly and efficiently reorganizing their claims outside the courtroom.

No such incentives operate on Company A. Its going-concern value can fall dramatically before creditors worry about their $20 million of debt. By the time creditors do intervene, Company A's going-concern value will have plummeted. And if Company A's value falls to under $20 million, it is much more likely than Company B to be worth less than its $10 million salvage value. Liquidation in this situation is the likely and rational outcome, with all its attendant conflicts, dislocations, and costs.

The evolving U.S. system of corporate governance and finance exhibits many characteristics of the postwar Japanese system. LBO partnerships act much like the main banks (the real power center) in Japan's *keiretsu* business groupings. The keiretsu make extensive use of leverage and intercorporate holdings of debt and equity. Banks commonly hold substantial equity in their client companies and have their own executives help them out of difficulty. (For years, Nissan has been run by an alumnus of the Industrial Bank of Japan, who became CEO as part of the bank's effort to keep the company out of bankruptcy.) Other personnel, including CFOs, move frequently between banks and companies as part of an ongoing relationship that involves training, consulting, and monitoring. Japanese banks allow companies to enter formal bankruptcy only when liquidation makes economic sense—that is, when a company is worth more dead than alive. Japanese corporate boards are composed almost exclusively of insiders.

Ironically, even as more U.S. companies come to resemble Japanese companies, Japan's public companies are becoming more like U.S. companies of 15 years ago. Japanese shareholders have seldom had any power. The banks' chief disciplinary tool, their power to withhold capital from high-growth, cash-starved companies, has been vastly reduced as a result of several factors. Japan's victories in world product markets have left its companies awash in profits. The development of domestic and international capital markets has created ready alternatives to bank loans, while deregulation has liberalized corporate access to these funds. Finally, new legal constraints prevent banks from holding more than 5% of the equity of any company, which reduces their incentive to engage in active monitoring.

Many of Japan's public companies are flooded with free cash flow far in excess of their opportunities to invest in profitable internal growth. In 1987, more than 40% of Japan's large public companies had no net bank borrowings—that is, cash balances larger than their short- and long-term borrowings. Toyota, with a cash hoard of $10.4 billion, more than 25% of its total assets, is commonly referred to as the Toyota Bank.[20]

In short, Japanese managers are increasingly unconstrained and unmonitored. They face no effective internal controls, little control from the product markets their companies already dominate, and fewer controls from the banking system because of self-financing, direct access to capital markets, and lower debt ratios. Unless shareholders and creditors discover ways to prohibit their managers from behaving like U.S. managers, Japanese companies will make uneconomic acquisitions and diversification moves, generate internal waste, and engage in other value-

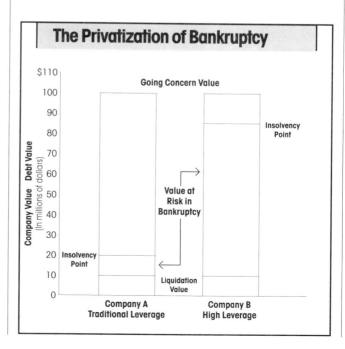

destroying activities. The long-term result will be the growth of bureaucracy and inefficiency and the demise of product quality and organizational responsiveness—until the waste becomes so severe it triggers a market for corporate control to remedy the excesses.

The Japanese remedy will reflect that country's unique legal system and cultural practices. But just as hostile takeovers, LBOs, and other control transactions went from unacceptable behavior in the United States to a driving force in corporate restructuring, so too will they take hold in Japan—once the potential returns outweigh the costs and risks of challenging the corporate status quo.

Meanwhile, in the United States, the organizational changes revitalizing the corporate sector will create more nimble enterprises and help reverse our losses in world product markets. As this profound innovation continues, however, people will make mistakes. To learn, we have to push new policies to the margin. It will be natural to see more failed deals.

There are already some worrisome structural issues. I look with discomfort on the dangerous tendency of LBO partnerships, bolstered by their success, to take more of their compensation in front-end fees rather than in back-end profits earned through increased equity value. As management fees and the fees for completing deals get larger, the incentives to do deals, rather than good deals, also increases. Institutional investors (and the economy as a whole) are best served when the LBO partnership is the last member of the LBO Association to get paid and when the LBO partnership gets paid as a fraction of the back-end value of the deals, including losses.

Moreover, we have yet to fully understand the limitations on the size of this new organizational form. LBO partnerships are understandably tempted to increase the reach of their talented monitors by reconfiguring divisions as acquisition vehicles. This will be difficult to accomplish successfully. It is likely to require bigger staffs, greater centralization of decision rights, and dilution of the high pay-for-performance sensitivity that is so crucial to success. As LBO Associations expand, they run the risk of recreating the bureaucratic waste of the diversified public corporation.

These and other problems should not cloud the remarkable benefits associated with the eclipse of the large public corporation. What surprises me is how few mistakes have occurred thus far in an organizational change as profound as any since World War II.

References

1. Equity values based on trends in the Wilshire Index. Private-placement data from IDD Information Services as published in Sarah Bartlett, "Private Market's Growing Edge," New York Times, June 20, 1989.

2. For more analysis of the oil industry, see my article, "The Takeover Controversy: Analysis and Evidence," in Corporate Restructuring and Executive Compensation (Cambridge, Mass: Ballinger, 1989).

3. Calculated from Standard & Poor's Compustat file.

4. Kevin J. Murphy, "Corporate Performance and Managerial Remuneration," Journal of Accounting and Economics, 1985, vol. 7, no. 1-3.

5. Federal Reserve Board, Balance Sheets of U.S. Economy.

6. G. Bennett Stewart III and David M. Glassman, "The Motives and Methods of Corporate Restructuring: Part II," Journal of Applied Corporate Finance, Summer 1988.

7. Stephen Phillips, "Revco: Anatomy of an LBO that Failed," Business Week, October 3, 1988.

8. "A Hollow Victory for Bob Mercer," Industry Week, February 23, 1987.

9. Jonathan P. Hicks, "The Importance of Being Biggest," New York Times, June 20, 1989.

10. Steven Kaplan, "Sources of Value in Management Buyouts," Journal of Financial Economics, forthcoming.

11. Michael C. Jensen and Kevin J. Murphy, "Performance Pay and Top Management Incentives," Journal of Political Economy, forthcoming.

12. Yakov Amihud, "Leveraged Management Buyouts and Shareholders' Wealth," in Leveraged Management Buyouts: Causes and Consequences (Homewood, Ill.: Dow Jones-Irwin, 1989).

13. That is, returns net of the returns that would normally be earned on these securities, given their level of systematic risk (beta) and general market returns.

14. L. Marais, K. Schipper, and A. Smith, "Wealth Effects of Going Private for Senior Securities," Journal of Financial Economics, 1989, vol. 23, no. 1.

15. In addition to Kaplan, see Abbie Smith, "Corporate Ownership Structure and Performance," unpublished paper, University of Chicago, 1989. See also Frank R. Lichtenberg and Donald Siegel, "The Effects of Leveraged Buyouts on Productivity and Related Aspects of Firm Behavior," National Bureau of Economic Research, 1989.

16. Lichtenberg and Siegel, NBER, 1989.

17. Michael C. Jensen, Steven Kaplan, and Laura Stiglin, "Effects of LBOs on Tax Revenues of the U.S. Treasury," Tax Notes, February 6, 1989.

18. Chris Muscarella and Michael Vetsuypens, "Efficiency and Organizational Structure: A Study of Reverse LBOs," unpublished paper, Southern Methodist University, April 1989.

19. Henry Kaufman, "Bush's First Priority: Stopping the Buyout Mania," Washington Post, January 1, 1989.

20. Average (book value) debt ratios fell from 77% in 1976 to 68% in 1987. Given the 390% increase in stock prices over this period, market-value debt ratios fell even more dramatically. Figures calculated from the NEEDS Nikkei Financials file for all companies on the First Section of the Tokyo Stock Exchange.

Reprint 89504

T. Boone Pickens, Jr.

Professions of a short-termer

It is no coincidence that the two largest acquisitions in history had essentially the same ingredients. In each case, management had compiled a miserable long-term operating record. Equally important, a disenchanted shareholder stepped forward to serve as a catalyst for change.

> *"It is questionable how much more long-term planning shareholders can stand. What many managements seem to be demanding is more time to keep making the same mistakes."*

In 1983 Gordon Getty and the trusts for which he had fiduciary responsibility represented the largest single block of Getty Oil stock. Dissatisfied with the meager returns received by the company's shareholders and the continuing depletion of oil and gas reserves, he orchestrated the $10 billion acquisition of Getty Oil by Texaco in early 1984.

I represented an investor group that became Gulf Oil's largest shareholder. Rather than consider the group's proposals to enhance shareholder value, Gulf ran into the arms of Chevron for $13 billion.

Before they lost their independence, Getty Oil and Gulf were case studies in unsuccessful long-term planning. Unable to find as much new oil and gas as they produced, they had entered a state of gradual liquidation. During the five years ending in 1983, Gulf depleted the equivalent of 400 million barrels of oil, or 22% of its domestic reserve base. Getty Oil lost 250 million barrels, or 14% of its domestic re-

Boone Pickens is founder, chairman, and chief executive officer of Mesa Petroleum in Amarillo, Texas.

serve base, during the same period. The two companies' costs of adding new domestic reserves averaged more than $14 per barrel, higher than for all but one of their competitors.[1]

Like other major oil companies, Getty Oil and Gulf plowed a substantial portion of the excess cash flow generated by OPEC oil price increases into marginal investments and disappointing diversifications. Gulf poured its money into unprofitable refineries, uranium, and coal. Getty bought a portion of the ESPN cable network, which Texaco later unloaded.

The common stock of Gulf and Getty Oil sold at a fraction of the value of their underlying assets. In short, they had no viable long-term strategies, and their shareholders were paying the price.

Yet public perceptions of these two megadeals were much different. No one called Gordon Getty a raider, a pirate, or a predator, although his insurrection ended Getty Oil's independence.

I was called all those things and more.

The reason for the name-calling? Unlike Getty, who had inherited his holdings long ago, we in the Gulf Investors Group had bought our shares in late 1983. We were short-term shareholders with short-term objectives. Or so our critics claimed.

An appealing theory...

I raise the contrast between the Getty Oil and the Gulf cases because it underscores a fundamental issue affecting the future accountability of corporate America. After decades of near sovereign autonomy, the professional managers of many large, publicly held corporations are finding themselves on the firing line. They are being asked to justify lackluster performance and questionable strategies. They are being called on to address the chronic undervaluation of their securities. In some cases, their indifference or antipathy gives rise to hostile tender offers or activist shareholders' proxy fights.

As often as not, these besieged managers decry their detractors as short-termers. Consider the following comments:

☐ "The vast majority of unfriendly acquisitions reflect strategies for short-term gain at the expense of long-term values." (Raymond Plank, chairman, Apache Corporation, and founder, Stakeholders in America)[2]

☐ "Today, equity is valued in the marketplace in relationship to its current, or immediate past, or immediate future earnings....This translates to a tremendous pressure on every corporation that is owned by these people for short-term performance." (Andrew C. Sigler, chairman and CEO, Champion International, and spokesman, Business Roundtable)[3]

☐ "Can you run America with a fairly large percentage of your investors being casino gamblers? That's the problem you've got with all of your managers of your pension funds and foundation funds....You know they trade on a tenth of a point. They'll sell and buy your stock twice in one day. They have no wait, no holding periods, no taxes to pay...it's entirely fast buck." (Fred Hartley, chairman, Unocal Corporation)[4]

☐ "It's not just the oil companies. A majority of the *Fortune* '500' companies are susceptible....If this persists, American industry will move into a short-term strategy of decision making. With a short-term strategy, who's going to do the research for tomorrow?" (Charles Kittrell, executive vice president, Phillips Petroleum Company)[5]

These sentiments appear throughout corporate America. In 1985 the Conference Board surveyed the attitudes of nearly 300 chief executive officers in the United States and abroad. On the question of accountability, the respondents acknowledged their responsibility to the owners of their companies. Yet the Conference Board's report noted that allegiance to shareholders is waning:

"In the United States particularly, shareholders, as such, do not command the esteem they used to....The changing structure of equity holdings evokes a bit of cynicism among some CEOs about shareholders. A U.S. CEO complains: 'A year from now, 70% of my stockholders will have changed. On that basis, I put my customers, and my employees, way ahead of them.'"[6]

In recent months comments like these have become the rallying cry of entrenched managements. Many CEOs and their lobbying organizations have seized on a new philosophical rationale for insulating themselves from the expectations of owners and explaining away the undervaluation of their securities.

This new argument against shareholder activism has come to be known as the short-term theory. It is based on the premise that achieving value for shareholders within a reasonable time frame is incompatible with pursuing future growth. When confronted with a perceived threat to their sovereignty, managers have learned to portray themselves as long-term visionaries and their dissident stockholders as short-term opportunists.

Increasing acceptance of the short-term theory has freed executives to scorn any shareholders they choose to identify as short-termers. Executives aim their contempt not only at the initiators of takeover attempts but at the arbitrageurs and the institutional investors who frequently trade in and out of stocks.

Armed with this argument, growing numbers of corporations are erecting potent new takeover defenses. These corporations are subdividing shareholders into categories based solely on seniority. Those that management determines have been on the shareowners' roster a sufficient length of time are accorded increased voting rights, preferential treatment, and much more respect. Those who have climbed on board more recently are seated at the back of the bus or disenfranchised altogether.

An example of this indentured shareholder concept is the creation of dual classes of stock, with one class bestowing "super" voting rights on its holders. Another is the adoption of waiting periods before new shareholders are entitled to vote on an equal basis with other shareholders. One variation on the separate-and-unequal theme is the selective self-tender. This tactic, recently employed against Mesa by Unocal, excludes a specified shareholder from participating in a corporate stock repurchase. Like other discriminatory defensive tactics, the tactic allows companies, on the basis of their perceived objectives, to deny full rights of ownership to selected shareholders.

Although they take different forms, these strategies to differentiate classes of owners are alike in one respect: they effectively cast aside the traditional tenet of stockholder equality and give managements the ability to categorize, divide, and conquer.

. . . that's pure hokum

On a rational level, the short-term theory attracts support because it seems plausible to those not closely involved with takeover activity. On an emotional level, the theory appears to embrace basic American values such as patience, perseverance, and faith in future rewards.

In reality, the short-term theory is pure hokum. Any observer who believes in even a modicum of market efficiency should be able to see through the smoke.

"No wonder prices are slightly higher north of the Himalayas."

There is a virtual vacuum of empirical evidence to indicate that sound planning for tomorrow depresses today's stock prices and increases vulnerability to takeovers. In fact, recent research indicates that the opposite relationship may exist.

In a 1985 study Gregg Jarrell and Kenneth Lehn of the Securities and Exchange Commission compared the relative levels of research and development expenditures among 324 companies representing a cross-section of 19 research-intensive industries. The SEC economists found no evidence that increasing stock ownership of performance-oriented institutional investors has coerced managements to forgo long-term expenditures such as those for R&D. As average institutional ownership of the 324 companies grew from 1980 to 1983, average ratios of R&D expenditures to corporate revenues also rose.

In 217 companies that had been targets of takeover attempts, average R&D expenditures were measurably lower than for other rivals in their industries. It's interesting that institutional investors owned an average of only 19% of the takeover targets but an average of nearly 34% of the nontarget businesses.

"The evidence strongly refutes the proposition that the stock market values only short-term earnings, and not expected future earnings," the SEC economists concluded. "A logical inference to be drawn from this evidence is that it is futile for corporate managers to try to forestall a hostile takeover by pumping up short-term earnings at the expense of investing in long-term projects with positive net present values."[7]

Preliminary findings from another 1985 study, undertaken on behalf of the Investor Responsibility Research Center (IRRC), indicate that the objects of unfriendly takeover attempts do not have superior financial characteristics. Yale University researcher John Pound determined that target companies have neither higher levels of cash flow and capital expenditures than nontarget companies nor superior returns on equity and rates of earnings growth. The targets in Pound's sample also tend to have as much or more debt on their balance sheets, a finding in conflict with the contention that "stronger" companies are often targets of acquisition offers.[8]

In a separate study also commissioned by the IRRC, Pound corroborates the SEC's earlier finding that a high level of institutional ownership does not appear to increase vulnerability to takeovers. He found that institutional ownership averaged only 22% among 100 companies that were takeover targets from 1981 through 1984, whereas for the market as a whole it averaged 35%.[9]

The findings of the SEC and the IRRC researchers illustrate the fallacy of the short-term theory. To those who understand the fundamentals of stock market valuation, the inherent contradiction of this theory has been obvious all along.

The market price of any common stock represents the investing public's collective judgment of the value of underlying assets and the anticipated results of corporate strategies. If investors have good reason to believe that current strategies will yield superior returns, they will gladly pay a premium to participate. If they are convinced that current strategies will yield inferior returns, they will undervalue the stock. The securities of a corporation expected to generate average returns will be priced in the market at a level approximating the underlying asset value.

In projecting a company's performance, only a fool would ignore its past. In many cases, undervaluation reflects the market's recognition that previous long-term planning has not panned out. Without apparent change in corporate strategies or industry economics, the future is unlikely to appear much brighter.

In the oil industry, the undervaluation of many companies stems largely from corporate strategies that have yielded dismal returns on recent investments. For years, many oil companies poured funds into marginal exploration programs, underutilized refineries, and unsuccessful diversification efforts. These investments continued despite ominous economic signals such as excess supply, diminished demand, declining prices, and low inflation.

A 1985 study by Bernard J. Picchi, a petroleum analyst with the investment firm of Salomon Brothers, documented the subpar returns achieved by 30 large oil companies on their exploration expenditures. From 1982 through 1984, Picchi reported, the companies' expenditures on exploration far exceeded the discounted present value of their added oil and gas reserves. His findings indicate that every dollar invested yielded new oil and gas reserves with a present value of only $.80.[10]

"Very few companies really have very much to crow about," Picchi told a group of drilling contractors in November 1985. "Most firms' exploration expenditures, in my estimation, have achieved such poor rates of return as to constitute a waste of the shareholders' assets."[11]

Despite clear indications of declining industry fundamentals, America's major oil companies spent approximately $105 billion on exploration and development from 1982 through 1984. Extrapolating from Picchi's findings, we see that the major oil companies lost as much as $200 billion in present value during this period.

The oil companies' ill-conceived attempts to diversify have compounded their problems. In the late 1970s and early 1980s, the majors rushed headlong to acquire companies engaged in unfamiliar undertakings. Exxon bought Reliance Electric. Mobil bought Montgomery Ward. Atlantic Richfield and Standard of Ohio bought into the minerals business at the top of the cycle. Gulf invested in uranium, and Getty became a broadcaster. The list goes on.

Many of these acquisitions have caused huge write-downs in recent months, and some have been sold at substantial losses. The assets the majors are writing down and selling off today are the legacy of their long-term strategies of five years ago.

Judging from the experience of the oil industry, it is questionable how much more long-term planning America's shareholders can stand. What many managements seem to be demanding is more time to keep making the same mistakes.

In defense of owners— all of them

If the confidence of America's investing public is to be maintained in the years ahead, the short-term theory must be exposed for what it really is: a weak argument advanced by weak managements. Companies are not punished for taking the long view; they are applauded. Investors are not impressed by efforts to embellish the near term; they question the impact on future returns.

Perhaps proponents of the short-term theory have lost sight of the commitment they or their predecessors made when their companies went public. Corporations issue stock to the public to acquire capital for financing future growth. The market provides those funds with the expectation that management will strive to achieve competitive returns. Management's failure to do so invites undervaluation and, ultimately, acquisition offers.

In many cases, the professional managers of mature or declining corporations seem to feel little affinity for shareholders. It may have been decades since their companies last went to the equity markets for capital. Today's stockholders may bear little resemblance to the investors who helped bankroll company growth. Why should shareholders' interests take precedence over relationships with employees, customers, and other corporate constituencies?

Because shareholders own the companies. In any public corporation they bear the ultimate financial risk for management's actions. The exposure is no less for the investors who bought their stock 5 days ago than for those who inherited their stock 50 years earlier. There is no initial grace period during which new shareholders are shielded from the effects of corporate blunders. No money-back guarantee protects the recently arrived from unexpected earnings declines. When it comes to allocating risk, length of ownership is not a factor.

The same standards should apply to the rights of ownership. Companies that invite public investors to participate in their glory years should not selectively ignore them once growth slows and performance turns sluggish. Their decision to go public encumbers them with a continuing obligation to serve the interests not only of the initial equity owners but of their successors as well. After all, short-termers would not exist if it weren't for long-termers who were ready to sell. If managements fail to earn competitive returns, they must stand equally accountable to all owners, not just to those who have suffered the longest.

Finally, I encourage investors, managers, and policymakers to think twice before endorsing antitakeover devices based on unequal treatment of investors. These strategies not only fail to advance any corporate purpose other than management tenure, but they also undermine a basic democratic tradition. America's publicly owned corporations should not selectively abrogate the one-person, one-vote principle inherent in any representative form of governance.

As I observe an increasing number of corporate executives embrace the short-term theory, I am reminded of remarks made by Gulf's chairman James E. Lee. In early 1984 I met with Lee to discuss Gulf's future. Another major oil company, which Chevron subsequently outbid, had offered to pay $70 per share to acquire Gulf.

As Gulf's operating decline became apparent, the price of its stock receded from an oil boom high of $54 in 1980 to about $37 in the fall of 1983. The stock was trading at roughly a third of the intrinsic value of Gulf's assets, estimated by analysts at about $114 per share.

Still, Lee wanted to talk long term.

"Boone, you're our largest shareholder. Would you be willing to give me two or three years more?" he asked.

"Why would you want two or three more years?" I replied.

"Because I think we can get the stock up to $60 or $65 by then."

"Jimmy, why would we want to wait two or three years to get the price up to $60 or $65 when you have an offer on the table for $70?"

"Boone, I was afraid you would say that."

As an unrepentant short-termer, I offer a final suggestion to the 47 million other shareholders who have placed their funds at risk in America's public corporations: beware the manager who proclaims to the world he is a long-termer, beginning today.

Reprint 86311

References

1 *Oil and Gas Reserve Disclosures, Survey of 375 Public Companies 1980-1983* (Houston: Arthur Andersen & Co., 1984).

2 "Corporate Coalition Formed to Counter Hostile Takeovers," press release (Minneapolis: Stakeholders in America, November 19, 1985).

3 "Rules for the Takeover Game," *Financier*, March 1985, p. 15.

4 Remarks to Association of Petroleum Writers, San Francisco, November 17, 1985.

5 "Phillips Not Off Guard, Says Kittrell," *The Journal Record* (Oklahoma City), April 25, 1985.

6 *Chief Executives View Their Jobs: Today and Tomorrow,* Report No. 871 (New York: Conference Board, 1985).

7 *Institutional Ownership, Tender Offers, and Long-Term Investments* (Washington, D.C.: Office of the Chief Economist, Securities and Exchange Commission, April 19, 1985).

8 *Are Takeover Targets Undervalued? An Empirical Examination of the Financial Characteristics of Target Companies* (Washington, D.C.: Investor Responsibility Research Center, 1985).

9 *The Effects of Institutional Investors on Takeover Activity: A Quantitative Analysis* (Washington, D.C.: Investor Responsibility Research Center, November 1985).

10 Bernard J. Picchi, *The Structure of the U.S. Oil Industry: Past and Future* (New York: Salomon Brothers, July 1985).

11 Remarks to the International Association of Drilling Contractors, Houston, November 12, 1985.

Raiders and LBOs:
Not What Adam Smith
Intended

*Q: What's the difference between
current stock price and maximum share price?
A: Maybe your job.*

Corporate Raiders: Head 'em Off at Value Gap

by WILLIAM E. FRUHAN, JR.

CEOs of large publicly held companies are confronting a new and imposing challenge—managing the "value gap." The stakes are huge. Those who meet the test get to keep their jobs. Those who don't face unemployment, as new owners who don't want their services acquire their companies.

The value gap is the difference between the market price of a share of a company's common stock and the value of that share if the company were managed as though the current owners were the only constituency that mattered—that is, managed for the maximum share price possible at this time. For most companies, the size of the value gap is a function of three factors:

1. Opportunities for improved operations.

2. Untapped capacity for high-wire financial acrobatics.

3. Potential economic benefits to new owners of company assets that are less valuable to the current company owners.

Corporate chieftains like to blame Wall Street for the takeover battles that are shaking up their companies. But raiders and arbitrageurs aren't the cause of hostile tender offers; they are a symptom of the large value gaps that persist throughout corporate America. Raiders are messengers whose impact ebbs and flows; the message endures.

That message is: public companies must become more efficient and more focused, and they must put incentives directly into the hands of people who will make the enterprise more enterprising. Shareholders may tolerate short-term gaps, cyclical gaps, or one-time setbacks in stock prices. But a large, sustained discount between actual and potential share price

represents an engraved invitation to an unsolicited takeover. The value gap measures how much needs to be done.

Of course, much is already being done—whether CEOs like it or not. The dollar value of mergers and acquisitions between 1985 and 1987 exceeded $520 billion—ten times the value of mergers between 1975 and 1977. Put another way, businesses representing 5.5% to 7% of the total market value of all U.S.

> The size of the value gap is a measure of how much management needs to do.

companies have disappeared through acquisitions in each of the past four years, as the first table shows.

And the pace of takeover activity seems destined to accelerate. There is now at least $17 billion of equity capital in leveraged buyout funds—capital that can be expanded by a factor of four through borrowing, which lifts the buyout potential to $85 billion. This pool of funds doesn't include the vast amount of capital available to big corporations on the prowl for merger partners. Nor does it include foreign investors with currencies that have appreciated enormously versus the dollar. In short, an unprecedented amount of money is searching for targets of oppor-

William E. Fruhan, Jr. is professor of business administration at the Harvard Business School, where he teaches corporate finance. In recent years, his research has concentrated on how companies restructure and build value as a result. His books include Financial Strategy *(Richard D. Irwin, 1979). He has written four other HBR articles.*

tunity—which helps explain why mergers and take-overs valued at nearly $75 billion were announced in the first three months of 1988.

The search is intensifying all the time. Wall Street analysts are working day and night to identify companies with the largest value gaps. In November 1986, a prominent analyst ranked 40 large retailers by an index that measured the spread between current and potential share price. For 10 of them, the value gap ranged from 60% to 25% (see the second table).

Within 16 months, at least half of these companies had engaged in some form of restructuring or anti-takeover maneuvering—voluntary or otherwise. Dayton-Hudson, Stop & Shop, and Supermarkets General all came under attack from the same raider, the Dart Group. Of the three, only Dayton-Hudson avoided a change of ownership, largely as a result of

U.S. Corporate Equity Disappearing Through Acquisitions

Year	Total Purchase Price Paid (in billions of dollars)	Total Market Value of Corporate Equity on December 31 (in billions of dollars)	Acquisition Price as Percentage of Total Market Value of Corporate Equity
1967	$ 18.0	$ 824	2.2%
1968	43.0	981	4.4
1969	23.7	866	2.7
1970	16.4	859	1.9
1971	12.6	1,004	1.3
1972	16.7	1,138	1.5
1973	16.7	901	1.9
1974	12.5	642	1.9
1975	11.8	850	1.4
1976	20.0	1,006	2.0
1977	21.9	950	2.3
1978	34.2	983	3.5
1979	43.5	1,180	3.7
1980	44.3	1,572	2.8
1981	82.6	1,505	5.5
1982	53.8	1,721	3.1
1983	103.2	2,022	5.1
1984	122.2	2,022	6.0
1985	179.6	2,584	7.0
1986	176.6	2,948	6.0
1987	165.8	3,008*	5.5*

*Estimated.

Sources: W.T. Grimm & Company and Board of Governors of the Federal Reserve System.

tough antitakeover laws passed by a special session of the Minnesota legislature. Best Products issued preferred shares as a "poison pill" to ward off hostile bids, while Kroger spun off divisions in management-led buyouts.

As the pool of available capital grows, and the number of easy targets declines, acquirers will turn their attention to companies with smaller and smaller value gaps. No one is immune.

The graph, "Value Gap of a Hypothetical Company," tracks the eight-year stock performance of a fictitious company ripe for a forced restructuring. The current share price is $50. If management streamlined operations (by aggressively reducing corporate overhead, for example), profits would increase and the share price might climb to $60. If management also borrowed heavily (say, creating a debt structure similar to that in a leveraged buyout), the share price might rise to $80. Finally, if the company sold any of its business units to buyers willing to pay more than what the assets are worth now, the share price might jump to $90. The value gap is the 80% difference between the market price of $50 and the potential price of $90.

This example may be hypothetical, but it more or less represents many companies' stock performance for years. And in plenty of real-world cases, going back some time, value gaps of this size or wider have been closed within weeks or months.

Recall the actions of Donald Kelly during his tenure as CEO of Esmark, Inc. In early 1980, Esmark traded at about $24. The company had three significant business units: Swift & Company, Playtex, and a modest oil and gas operation. Analysts were describing the company as an undervalued asset situation. Indeed, Esmark's equity in its oil and gas business alone was estimated to be worth more than the market value of the entire company. The value gap was huge, and Esmark was clearly vulnerable to a takeover.

So Kelly moved decisively. He announced plans to: (1) repair and divest a low-profit business (fresh meats); (2) lever up the company by using borrowed funds to repurchase half the outstanding shares; and (3) sell the oil and gas reserves to a buyer (Mobil) that was willing to pay a premium for these assets to avoid exploring at an even higher cost.

Kelly's plan remains one of the most striking examples of a company quickly closing the gap between its stock's market price and potential value. Esmark's share price *doubled* to $48 during the five-week period surrounding the plan's unveiling. Before the announcement, the common stock market value was $660 million. After the announcement, the value of repurchased and outstanding shares totaled

Estimated Value Gap for Ten Selected Retailers
(November 1986)

Company	1 Price per Share	2 Value per Share (based on restructuring)	2−1=3 Value Gap per Share	3÷2=4 Value Gap (in percentage)
Best Products	$11.75	$29.14	$17.39	60%
Oshman's Sporting Goods	13.75	33.26	19.51	59
Service Merchandise	11.00	22.55	11.55	51
Great Atlantic & Pacific	22.50	38.27	15.77	41
Kroger	32.63	52.84	20.21	38
Dayton-Hudson	43.00	65.61	22.61	34
Stop & Shop	54.25	76.68	22.43	29
Supermarkets General	28.25	39.19	10.94	28
May Department Stores	36.13	48.22	12.09	25
Gordon Jewelry	19.63	26.14	6.51	25

Source: Stuart M. Robbins, "Retailing: Breaking Up That Old Gang of Ours," Donaldson, Lufkin & Jenrette, November 17, 1986.

nearly $1.3 billion. This $636 million value gap reduction substantially lessened Esmark's vulnerability to a takeover.

The cases and data that follow are meant to illuminate simple truths about a phenomenon that has been shrouded in needless complexity and confusion. New capital market forces make it imperative for CEOs to monitor the gap between what shareholders might be able to get for their stock and what they can realize now. Understanding what needs to be done is straightforward, but CEOs have a limited menu of options from which to choose.

Improve Operations

As Donald Kelly's moves at Esmark demonstrate, when management attacks all three elements of the value gap simultaneously, it can make enormous strides in closing it. But in many situations it is not necessary, or even possible, to address the three factors at once.

Improvement in internal operations is usually the readiest element to address. The targets include revenue enhancement, cost reductions, and more effective use of existing assets, of which the easiest is reduction in overhead. Progress in other areas tends to come more slowly.

It's important to understand that the financial effect of cost cutting goes beyond the savings themselves. Generating millions of dollars in additional profits not only adds value by increasing per-share earnings but also creates potential for leveraging the

company. When interest rates are at 10%, a company that cuts $10 million in overhead can borrow $100 million, use the money to boost dividends or repurchase stock (either way immediately raising the market price), and pay the interest out of the overhead savings. Wasteful spending of $10 million per year amounts to a value gap of $100 million.

Recent events at Beatrice Companies illustrate this leveraging potential. In April 1986, all outstanding Beatrice stock was acquired in a $6.1 billion hostile tender offer. The price represented a premium of $1.7 billion above what the shares had been selling at just 30 days earlier. Within 12 months, the new owner-managers slashed corporate and business-unit overhead from $190 million to $90 million, including millions of dollars spent on corporate-image advertising and sponsoring auto races. The $100 million annual saving was enough to service the $800 million of junk bonds issued to help finance the deal. (The entity that acquired Beatrice issued $800 million of subordinated debt at an interest rate of 12.5%.) Had Beatrice's former management acted on this excess overhead, it could have boosted profits and the share price (perhaps by borrowing against the cash flows and repurchasing stock) and thereby eliminated about half the takeover premium.

Use Leverage

The second important element of the value gap is the use of leverage in the capital structure. The assumption of high levels of debt can add to shareholder value in at least three ways. First, debt generates tax benefits through the deductibility of interest payments. Second, debt has a disciplining effect on corporate executives. As one authority argues, a highly leveraged capital structure "motivate[s] managers to disgorge...cash rather than invest it at below the cost of capital or waste it through organizational inefficiencies."[1] Finally, the use of extreme leverage is often accompanied by top management's acquisition of a higher fraction of the remaining stock, which creates incentive effects that work to close the value gap.

The opportunity to use extreme leverage in a healthy business's capital structure is a fairly recent phenomenon, sparked by the mushrooming junk bond market in the United States. The volume of junk bond financing and the pace of LBO activity have grown in parallel since 1982. Annual new issues of junk bonds in 1977 were $600 million, compared with $28.6 billion in 1987. Leveraged buyout transactions were worth $600 million in 1979, compared with $22.1 billion in 1987. In turn, the rising volume of leveraged buyout activity has sharply focused attention on the failure of companies to lessen the value gap by the aggressive use of leverage. LBO transactions have delivered big premiums to selling shareholders, as the list of the 20 largest LBOs shows. The principals in these transactions have often realized even more remarkable returns for themselves.

A handful of corporations has recognized the desirability of achieving leverage ratios comparable to those of leveraged buyouts, without completely

1. Michael C. Jensen, "Takeovers: Their Causes and Consequences," *Journal of Economic Perspectives*, Winter 1988, p. 21.

changing their equity ownership structures. These enterprises, the largest of which include Multimedia, FMC, Owens-Corning, Holiday Corporation, and Harcourt Brace Jovanovich, have executed what are called leveraged recapitalizations.

Perhaps the most dramatic example of the value gap associated with untapped borrowing capacity is the leveraged recapitalization that Colt Industries engineered. In July 1986, Colt announced that it would distribute more than $1.5 billion in cash to shareholders, a plan that required borrowing about $1.4 billion. Approximately $800 million came from commercial banks and $550 million from junk bond sales. Each Colt share, which sold at just under $67 before the announcement, was entitled to receive $85 in cash and one new share of a highly leveraged Colt Industries. The new Colt share was estimated to

Value Gap Exposed in the 20 Largest LBOs

Year	Company	Estimated Purchase Price (in billions of dollars)	Premium Price Paid over Market (in percent)
1987	Borg-Warner	$3.8	31%
	Southland Corporation	3.7	14
	Burlington Industries	2.1	45
	Supermarkets General	1.8	34
	Taft Broadcasting	1.4	1
	Singer	1.1	50
	Charter Medical	1.0	−3
1986	Safeway Stores	4.2	44
	Owens-Illinois	3.6	36
	Viacom International	1.6	28
	Revco D.S.	1.2	22
1985	Beatrice Companies	5.8*	44
	R.H. Macy	3.5	54
	Storer Communications	1.6	30
	National Gypsum	1.3	50
	Jack Eckerd	1.2	10
	Levi Strauss	1.1	42
1984	Northwest Industries	1.0	−8
	ARA Services	.9	56
1983	Metromedia Broadcasting	1.5	140

*Not including $300 million of acquisition-related expenses.

Source: W.T. Grimm & Company.

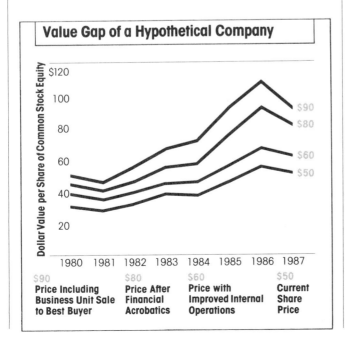

Value Gap of a Hypothetical Company

Dollar Value per Share of Common Stock Equity

$120, 100, 80, 60, 40, 20

1980 1981 1982 1983 1984 1985 1986 1987

$90
$80
$60
$50

$90	$80	$60	$50
Price Including Business Unit Sale to Best Buyer	**Price After Financial Acrobatics**	**Price with Improved Internal Operations**	**Current Share Price**

Selling Business Units to the Best Buyer—the Beatrice Example

Business Group Sold	Sale Price (in billions of dollars)	Sale Completed	Purchaser
Avis	$ .3	July 1986	Management-Led LBO
Playtex	1.3	December 1986	Management-Led LBO
Webcraft	.2	December 1986	Management-Led LBO
Americold	.5	December 1986	Management-Led LBO
International Foods	1.0	November 1987	Management-Led LBO
Subtotal	$3.3		
Various Consumer Products	$1.5	July 1987	Spin-off or Public Sale
Coca-Cola Bottlers	1.0	September 1986	Coca-Cola
Dairy Companies	.3	December 1986	Borden
Bottled Water Businesses	.4	July 1987	Perrier
U.S. Food Companies	2.8*	Up for Sale	?
Subtotal	$4.5*		Form of Financing (in billions of dollars)
Total Proceeds	$9.3*	Debt	$4.8
Less Acquisition Cost	6.1	Preferred Stock	.9†
Total Profit	$3.2*	Common Stock	.4
Allocation of Profit	$ .7	Debt-Raising Intermediary	
	2.2	Common Stock Providers and Intermediary	
	.3	Beatrice Management	
Total	$3.2		

Sources: James Sterngold, "Shaking Billions from Beatrice," *New York Times*, September 6, 1987 and Beatrice Companies proxy statements.

*Estimated.

†Issued to public shareholders of old Beatrice Companies as part of purchase price of shares.

be worth more than $10, based on the performance of the "stub" share left over after the earlier FMC recapitalization. Colt's stock price rose to $93.50 the day after the announcement.

Shares held in the Colt Retirement Savings Plan received an equivalently valued package of new shares. This increased the retirement plan's overall stake from 7% to 30% of Colt's outstanding shares. By insuring a "substantially disproportionate redemption" for them, this plan allowed other shareholders to report capital gains rather than ordinary gains, further enhancing the transaction's value.

Colt's balance sheet after the leveraged recapitalization looks rather curious. Its long-term debt rose by 400%, and Colt has a negative net worth in excess of $1 billion. Obviously, interest coverages will be tight for some time. In 1985, Colt's earnings before interest and taxes (EBIT) were 16 times greater than its debt-service charges. EBIT for 1989 are projected to be only 1.6 times interest charges.

Nonetheless, Colt's management closed a value gap in the area of financial acrobatics equal to 40% of

the company's total equity. It thus removed a dangerous source of takeover vulnerability, allowing management and other employees to contend with a different but presumably more acceptable threat—a higher probability of financial distress in the future. In March 1988, Colt announced a plan to purchase the company's remaining public shares at $17 to complete a full-scale LBO.

Few companies have engaged in leveraged recapitalizations as drastic as Colt's, although we can expect the strategy to become more popular. Far more companies have opted for a watered-down version by repurchasing significant amounts of their stock. A sample of the 25 largest common stock share repurchases in 1986 includes: Union Carbide's equaling $3.3 billion; Goodyear Tire & Rubber's, $2.6 billion; IBM's, $2.1 billion; and SmithKline Beckman's, $1.4 billion. Repurchases ratchet up the leverage in a company's capital structure, but not enough to qualify as a leveraged recapitalization. Companies often take this more measured shift in leverage in response to a real or imagined threat of takeover, although with some huge businesses it is simply a convenient way to deal with excess liquidity. Stock buybacks are a partial yet effective step in managing the size of a company's value gap.

Sell to the Best Buyer

The third big factor contributing to the value gap stems from the fact that business units operated by a *new* owner may have more economic value than they do in the hands of the *existing* owner. This additional value may come from many sources, including: (1) higher cash flows as a result of tax advantages; (2) scale economies from combining operations with the new owner's related operations; or (3) incentive effects from more focused ownership. To the extent that a potential buyer must share the benefits of its enhanced economies with the existing owner (in the form of the price paid), a value gap will exist as long as the business unit continues to be owned by the less-than-best owner.

Here too, events at Beatrice show what can be done (see the table, "Selling Business Units to the Best Buyer—the Beatrice Example"). Within three months of the takeover, the new owners began selling off its parts to the "best buyers"—i.e., the highest bidders. Management partitioned the company into ten business groups. Nine units found buyers within 20 months of the acquisition, and the final unit is now on the block. Five units, representing one-third of the estimated disposition proceeds, went to management-led buyout groups. Another group, comprising one-sixth of the estimated proceeds, was spun off and brought public. The remaining four groups, representing one-half of the estimated disposition proceeds, have been or are expected to be sold to "synergy buyers," where the efficiencies associated with combined operations should be rewarding.

In all, the sale of these businesses will generate $9.3 billion—$3.2 billion more than the cost of acquiring the entire company. This enormous value gap represented about 50% of what the new owners paid for Beatrice. Had the former executives recognized and addressed the financial penalties connected with maintaining this collection of businesses, Beatrice might not have been a sitting duck to a hostile bid.

What are the lessons for top management? First, it must measure and track the company's value gap periodically. The size of a gap is always changing, based on the business's stock market performance, interest rates, overall corporate liquidity, the health of the junk bond market, the vigor of antitrust enforce-

ment, and other factors. Measuring the gap is the easy part. (If you don't want to do it, Wall Street analysts will do it for you.) Managing it is much harder—not because it is conceptually challenging but because it may hurt executives, workers, and communities. Yet in virtually all instances, the costs of complacency are much higher.

CEOs face three choices. First, they can close their value gap by taking all or some of the same value-enhancing actions potential acquirers would. Put simply, CEOs can start thinking and acting like raiders. This pill is less bitter today than it was a few years ago; employees are beginning to accept the necessity of some of these changes. Top management can say "the devil made me do it" and be both honest and credible. Moreover, if management acts before the company attracts outsiders' attention, it can adopt less painful measures than if it must defend itself against an actual takeover attempt. Early action to reduce the value gap by a material amount, say 30% or 40%, may be enough to convince hostile suitors to look elsewhere. But once a company is in play, every dollar of additional value matters. Remaining independent after a hostile bid usually requires steps painful in the extreme.

A second tactic is to throw legal hurdles in the path of potential acquirers. Poison pills, dual-class shares with different voting rights, and reincorporation in a state with tough antitakeover provisions can all be implemented. These hurdles may raise the cost of an acquisition above a sensible acquirer's ceiling or make an unfriendly acquisition simply impossible.

A third option involves coordinated lobbying in Washington. A significant portion of the value gap at many companies is tax related, and lobbying at the national level can help shrink the gap. The elimination of mirror-image subsidiaries for business units that an acquirer will sell immediately and the abolition of the General Utilities doctrine have already reduced the value gap for many businesses. A proposal now circulating in Washington to remove the deductibility of interest expenses on debt incurred to finance acquisitions would also help close the gap. Ironically, perhaps, more vigorous antitrust enforcement against combinations that enhance product market shares (and thereby create economies of scale) would also narrow the gap.

Or CEOs can adopt an ostrich strategy and continue business as usual, harnessed to their yet unopened golden parachutes. Who knows, their companies may well remain unnoticed for a year or two while they reach retirement unscathed. But their successors can rest assured that subpar stock market performance will not be tolerated indefinitely.

A corporation is more than its stock

Warren A. Law

Dr. Samuel Johnson once noted that man is seldom as innocently occupied as when in pursuit of money. Why then do most corporate raiders justify their actions by claiming that social welfare is thereby enhanced? You would hope that an $18 million bonus, plus ego gratification from countless magazine cover appearances and television interviews, would be enough. Instead, we must submit to lectures about the inadequacies of American managers, from whose ineptitude the fortunate stockholders of target companies are rescued by a few daring takeover artists.

Carl Icahn believes "these managements need shaking up—they're horrendous." T. Boone Pickens asserts that "chief executives, who themselves own few shares of their companies, have no more feeling for the average stockholder than they do for baboons in Africa."[1] Even the *1985 Economic Report of the President* from the Council of Economic Advisers claims that takeovers "improve efficiency, transfer scarce resources to higher valued uses, and stimulate effective corporate management. They also help recapitalize firms so that their financial structures are more in line with prevailing market conditions."

In a recent HBR article, Ralph S. Saul countered with the observation, "It is hard to imagine the power—or the tyranny—of the argument that takeover activity enhances shareholder wealth and returns on corporate assets. Few question it."[2] I not only question the argument but—more important—I want to emphasize a fundamental disparity between the attitudes of stockholders and managers with which neither financial theory nor laws of corporate governance has dealt satisfactorily.

Managers are more averse than stockholders to the risk that the higher leverage incurred during a takeover fight brings. Less concerned with the immediate price of its stock, management is locked into the fortunes of the company and has an enormous investment in its human capital. Stockholders, in contrast, worry more and more about the short-term impact of stock price fluctuation on the financial capital invested in their portfolios.

The chiaroscuro of science

No matter what the CEA contends, it is impossible to apply some Benthamite calculus to reach a scientific conclusion about the ultimate impact of our takeover binge. Observation of a few facts, for example, can often obscure the clarity of this kind of science:

☐ Stockholders in target companies gain greatly from takeovers, but the record of their counterparts on the acquiring side is less distinct. A recent study of 78 mergers and takeovers in the years 1976 through 1981 concluded that three years later the price of the acquirers' stock was much lower than if it had continued to perform as it had before the acquisition.[3] You might argue that three years is the wrong period to use as a benchmark or point out that the stock had probably changed hands several times. But, in any event, you would weaken the overall argument of enhanced stockholder welfare.

☐ There is no proof that target companies are mismanaged. A study of 56 hostile tender offers initiated from 1975 through 1982 found that the targets, as a group, had significantly higher ROEs than the bidders; 39 of the 56 had outperformed their bidders over the preceding two years.[4]

☐ The extent of corporate leverage has risen dramatically. In 1984 and 1985, nonfinancial corporations had a *net* retirement of $150 billion of equity—an amount greater than the total net issuance of equity by nonfinancial companies between the Korean War and 1984. While not all this restructuring was due either to takeovers or to fear thereof, the climate was surely an important cause. One result has

Mr. Law is Edmund Cogswell Professor of Banking and Finance at the Harvard Business School. A director of several American companies, he has participated in both sides of the takeover battle.

been the downgrading of previously blue-chip bonds. Unocal's rating, for example, dropped from AA + to Bbb after the Pickens attack; more than one-fourth of Moody's downgrades last year were associated with takeovers.

☐   An equally dramatic shift has occurred in the executive ranks of acquired companies. One recent survey of senior executives whose companies were acquired found that almost half left within one year and another quarter planned to leave within the next two years.

☐   Many takeovers are feasible only because of the tax benefits they generate. On the assumption that someone must eventually pay the taxes, the social cost-benefit equation becomes confused.

Only time will tell what all this means for society, and even then a conclusion may be elusive. The basic argument for most raids on oil companies, for example, is that they waste their assets (the cash flows from previous discoveries) in high-cost exploration for new reserves instead of passing this cash to shareholders as a return on capital. While the stock market apparently agrees, managers in target oil companies contend that the argument is myopic and that we will someday regret the reduction in exploration. History will determine who is right.

Is the market too short-run oriented? I find it difficult to conclude otherwise when 100-million-share days are commonplace, many mutual funds turn their portfolios over more than once a year, and the floating supply of some stocks changes hands as often as every six months. A "now generation" of portfolio managers has emerged who, under pressure to outperform their counterparts each quarter, look for near-instant results from their investments.

"The corporation is not a piece of paper and should not be bought and sold in that way."

A large body of academic work demonstrates that stock prices fluctuate much more than changes in the rationally formed expectations of shareholders can justify. As a consequence, prices are pushed to unsustainable levels—in both directions. A recent study found that, over the past half-century, hypothetical portfolios of "loser" stocks (NYSE stocks that had declined sharply over a test period) subsequently outperformed portfolios of "winners" by 25% when held three more years, even though the prior winners had been much more risky.[5]

Why then do so few contrarians exist in the market? One answer is that, to a mutual fund manager, three years are an eternity. A half-century ago, Keynes put it succinctly: "The game of professional investment is intolerably boring and over-exacting to anyone who is entirely exempt from the gambling instinct." Moreover, he noted, a real long-term investor appears eccentric to others. "Worldly wisdom teaches that it is better for reputations to fail conventionally than to succeed unconventionally." He predicted that as investment markets become liquid we can scarcely avoid an outcome in which "enterprise becomes the bubble on a whirlpool of speculation." Keynes concluded, "It is usually agreed that casinos should, in the public interest, be inaccessible and expensive. And perhaps the same is true of Stock Exchanges."[6]

The truth of Keynes's assertions is mirrored by the top executives studied by Gordon Donaldson and Jay Lorsch.[7] They were less concerned about their stock prices and considered professional money managers hostile to the interests of their corporations. I wonder what a survey of their attitudes today would reveal. T. Boone Pickens claims that, as a result of takeovers, "managements are going to be a hell of a lot more interested in the price of stock in the marketplace," and contends that the only duty of management is to maximize that price.

The human factor

If only it were that easy! How *does* a manager raise a company's stock price? The vague advice of takeover apologists is to "be a better manager." (Pickens asserts that 80% of America's top executives are incompetent.) Pressed for specifics, they usually advise management to "restructure the firm," a euphemism for "use more leverage." Unfortunately, managers are taking this advice, although often under duress. Phillips Petroleum, under attack from Carl Icahn, for example, bought back half its shares and more than doubled its debt.

If higher leverage is the criterion of good management, why have managers resisted debt until prodded by takeover fears? The answer is found in the fundamental conflict between management and stockholders, one version of the short- versus long-run argument. Managers are probably more risk averse than their stockholders because of their self-interest, their different view of the company, and their unique time horizon.

Financial theorists recognize that stockholders may prefer high leverage because they receive all the upside return but share the downside risk (bankruptcy) with creditors or the state (if it bails out the company to avoid bankruptcy). Moreover, stockholders can offset risk by diversifying their portfolio and can usually liquidate a position quickly if they perceive a downturn that would threaten their position.

In contrast, managers have invested *human* capital, usually in the form of many years of loyal service. Although they may hope to share the upside potential of higher leverage via bonuses, managers cannot easily diversify this "investment." They are locked in, and the downside risk (unemployment) is obvious.

The argument is still more complex. The perceived risk of leverage may not be a fear of bankruptcy but the eventual need to liquidate assets or fire people to service debt. Managers understandably feel some responsibility for employees who have also "invested" human capital in the company. You could argue that, contrary to the opinion of Boone Pickens or financial theorists, the stockholder is not the only bearer of residual risk.

This argument clearly applies to highly leveraged takeovers. Top management has learned to protect itself with golden parachutes, but there weren't enough to provide a soft landing for the 10,000 employees scheduled to lose their jobs in Chevron's takeover of Gulf. You could easily be skeptical of Boone Pickens's contention that few jobs would have been lost in his attempted takeover of Unocal: "The only change

would have been at the very top, which would be a change for the better."

Pickens has said, "I'm amused by people who say that if an arbitrageur bought a stock an hour ago, he should not have the right to decide what happens to 40,000 employees." Many managers fail to see the reason for amusement. Those studied by Donaldson and Lorsch felt committed to enhancement of corporate wealth, including the company's human as well as financial assets. Takeover apologists argue that some unemployment is the price society must pay for greater efficiency. (I am intrigued by the ease with which tenured academics discuss unemployment.)

But others contend that today's takeovers are changing the rules of the game; that there has always been an implicit contract between employees and shareholders under which dismissal was the expected penalty only of personal incompetence or deterioration in a company's profitability. Today dismissal may simply result from a junk-bond takeover. While Boone Pickens sees only the responsibility of employees and managers to stockholders, others see a two-way street.[8]

What we have is simply two different ways of viewing the world. In discussing takeovers, Andrew C. Sigler, chairman and CEO of Champion International, said, "Things that affect free enterprise affect the whole society, so that the underlying issue

is not the shareholders of the business—it is the society." In response, Pickens was almost apoplectic: "You think this guy understands free enterprise? That's pure crap...the shareholders own the company. If you operate under a free market, the shareholders decide. That's all there is to it."

All is fair in such arguments, but others have pointed out that our "free" market is really one of man-made regulations in which interest on debt is deductible for taxes while dividends are not, in which pension funds need not pay taxes, and in which six months is the definition of "long term."

The battle is clearly over the line between the rights of shareholders and the discretion of managers. But a broader constituency is interested in the outcome of the battle. This constituency is not only employees. Chevron closed Gulf's Pittsburgh headquarters, dismissing or transferring 5,800 people. Some 50 Pittsburgh institutions got partial support from Gulf's charitable contributions, and countless local companies supplied it and its employees. While the optimal degree of leverage is not the only issue in this battle, it helps to focus the discussion.

Until recently the courts have given boards of directors great latitude in settling the question. You might expect outside directors to be even more risk averse than managers. After all, they share little of the upside potential of higher leverage, and in a world where litigation against directors is almost endemic and their liability insurance rapidly disappearing, directors have considerable downside risk if leverage leads to financial distress. But the courts have put directors' actions under greater scrutiny, and parties attempting a takeover more often file suits against them.

In GAF's recent raid on Union Carbide, it was reportedly Carbide's outside directors who, against management's wishes, decided to retire more than half the company's equity and sell off the consumer products division, for which management had long-run plans. One investment banker noted that the directors had apparently decided that "unrecognized value in the company should go to the shareholders, and everything they did carried out that. I think it's laudable." Boone Pickens would undoubtedly agree. Creditors, employees, and other Danbury companies were not interviewed.

Financial theorists are wrong; there is no scientific answer to the dilemma. Oscar Wilde was right: truth is never pure and rarely simple. There is a fundamental conflict between managers and shareholders that neither financial theory nor the courts has resolved. Legal orthodoxy has always said that directors owe unswerving loyalty only to the shareholders. Yet managers rarely hold this attitude, nor is it enforced by the courts.

Fifty years ago Professor E.M. Dodd described the difficulties in rigid adherence to a rule that has lost contact with public opinion: "If trusteeship for absentee investors, in addition to having little emotional appeal for managers, is an ideal that is losing ground in the community generally,...the prospect of its effective enforcement as an interim legal rule of conduct is not encouraging. Abandon it, as yet, we dare not—enforce it with more than moderate success, it is to be feared we cannot."[9] Little has changed since then; our present takeover mania has merely dramatized the dilemma.

The legendary innocent bystander might listen to this debate with bemused detachment and even find the antics of various participants in takeover battles innocently diverting. But Andrew Sigler is right: the public interest is involved. Yet in choosing sides we have little to guide us but visceral intuition. Thinking of a corporation's assets as a portfolio that can be diverted to "higher valued uses" and leveraged to meet "prevailing market conditions" is a useful classroom exercise but dangerous when it leads to a belief that human and physical capital is no more real than pieces of paper in a stock portfolio.

It is undeniable that managers and employees have responsibilities to shareholders. But is it also inconceivable that shareholders have responsibilities to them?

Reprint 86308

References

1 All quotes of T. Boone Pickens are from interviews in *Barron's*, September 23, 1985, and *Chief Executive*, Fall 1985.

2 "Hostile Takeovers: What Should Be Done?" HBR September-October 1985, p. 5.

3 Ellen B. Magenheim and Dennis C. Mueller, "On Measuring the Effect of Acquisitions on Acquiring Firm Shareholders," presented at the Conference on Takeovers and Contests for Corporate Control, Center for Law and Economic Studies, Columbia University, November 13-15, 1985 (hereafter, Columbia Takeover Conference).

4 Edward S. Herman and Louis Lowenstein, "The Efficiency Effects of Hostile Takeovers: An Empirical Study," Columbia Takeover Conference.

5 W.F.M. DeBondt and Richard Thaler, "Does the Stock Market Overreact?" *Journal of Finance*, July 1985, p. 793.

6 John Maynard Keynes, *The General Theory of Employment, Interest, and Money* (New York: Harcourt, Brace, 1936), Ch. 12.

7 Gordon Donaldson and Jay W. Lorsch, *Decision Making at the Top* (New York: Basic Books, 1983).

8 I am indebted for the idea of an implicit stockholder-manager contract to John C. Coffee, Jr., "Shareholders Versus Managers: The Strain in the Corporate Web," Columbia Takeover Conference.

9 E.M. Dodd, Jr., "Is Effective Enforcement of the Fiduciary Duties of Corporate Managers Practicable?" *Chicago Law Review*, 2:194 (1935), p. 207.

From the Boardroom

Joseph G. Fogg, III

Takeovers: last chance for self-restraint

Private sector reform could forestall government intervention in the takeover arena

The battle over hostile takeovers is not only heating up—it is also becoming destructive. Split interests among management, boards of directors, groups of shareholders, and the perceived public interest threaten to undermine the fundamental precepts of corporate governance that have evolved over the years. If management does not take the initiative to make the needed reforms, the action will shift to Congress—with the prospect of even more infighting.

There still is time, however, for the private sector to show enough self-restraint to forestall government intervention. An agenda for private sector reform can rebalance the interests of the parties involved and restore their confidence in the relationship between management and shareholders. To speak to the concerns of each interest, such an agenda would have to deal with the concerns of each interest— paying directors in stock, providing more and better information to shareholders, and creating a new class of stock that would place value on continued ownership. At the core would be the idea of a voting concentration charter provision that would make any potential change in corporate control a more rational, informed, and fair decision-making process.

Mr. Fogg is a managing director at Morgan Stanley & Company and has had extensive experience in defending clients against hostile takeover bids, including Carter Hawley Hale, St. Regis Corporation, Continental Group, Phillips Petroleum, and CBS.

The passage of the securities acts of 1933 and 1934 ushered in the modern era of the large widely held and publicly traded American corporation. For more than 50 years, the system of public stockholder ownership of most of the United States' productive resources has resulted in unparalleled growth and prosperity. The system of governance of our large publicly owned corporations that has evolved over this period is based on a complex balancing of federal, state, and private sector regulation. The courts have played an important role, too, in interpreting our corporate and securities laws and in providing a forum for resolving disputes that arise among interested parties.

Above all, the system has worked well because of a presumption of mutual confidence that all concerned—shareholders, boards of di-

rectors, and management—want to preserve and enhance shareholder values while respecting the legitimate rights of other constituents such as customers, employees, and the community. Today, that confidence shows signs of fading.

The strain that has developed in the relationship among shareholders, boards, and management shows up most clearly in the takeover arena. For many years, something called "the business judgment rule" has governed the deliberations of boards of directors of public companies in initiating and responding to takeover proposals. This is a judicial rule developed over the years whereby the courts will not second-guess directors exercising their business judgment in making important decisions unless there is significant evidence of gross negligence, bad faith, or conflict of interest. In other words, in takeover battles courts afford boards of directors a clear presumption that their actions, even if extreme, will be considered as being in the best interests of the shareholders. This has been a fundamental principle of American corporate governance.

In recent takeover battles, however, legislators, business commentators, and thoughtful executives have questioned the quality, if not the motivation, of some of the tactics of certain boards. Similarly, some companies and wealthy individuals have used aggressive acquisition tactics to pursue their own takeover objectives, which have raised equally serious questions about the fairness of the rules that govern the takeover process.

What is most disturbing, the debate is becoming increasingly polarized. As a consequence, the prospect of government intervention has grown. It is up to the private sector to reform itself. Otherwise, it will invite the heavy hand of government.

Opposing voices

Respected observers on both sides have weighed in with their opinions. Peter F. Drucker, a noted business

---

Editor's note: All references are listed at the end of the article.

consultant and professor, for example, recently argued that the "fiduciaries" (pension funds, endowments, trust departments), which actually vote shares in large public companies and make decisions on tender offers, will accept takeover bids at virtually any market premium, regardless of their view of the long-term value of the company. Drucker has expressed the interesting view that "a good many experienced business leaders now hold takeover fear to be a main cause of the decline in America's competitive strength in the world economy."[1]

Andrew C. Sigler, chairman and chief executive officer of Champion International Corporation and chairman of the Business Roundtable task force on hostile takeovers, recently told a Securities and Exchange Commission hearing that the wave of hostile takeovers is "threatening the nation's economy."[2] Martin Lipton, one of the foremost takeover lawyers in the country, the inventor of the famous "poison pill," and a professional with wide-ranging experience on both sides of the takeover process, has taken a similar public policy stand against the "abusive tactics" of the "front-end-loaded, bootstrap, bust-up, junk-bond-financed hostile takeover."[3] Finally, Felix Rohatyn, senior partner of Lazard Frères & Company and veteran merger adviser, believes that there is a "growing feeling today that the capital markets have become the property of insiders and speculators, of raiders and other professionals to the detriment of the general public."[4]

On the other hand. An entirely opposite point of view, however, can be found in the 1985 *Annual Report of the Council of Economic Advisers*. In a remarkable free market dissertation, the council takes the position that "while the recent exposure of …many of the largest publicly traded corporations…to the discipline of the market for corporate control has caused substantial controversy and has stimulated calls for legislation that would deter hostile takeovers,…the evidence suggests that abusive practices in the market for corporate control are limited largely to tactics employed by target managements" and that "further federal regulation of the market for corporate control would be premature, unnecessary, and unwise."

Some empirical support for this position comes from the retired chairman of ITT—now a private investor—Harold Geneen. In a recent *Fortune* article, he offered a cynical observation that boards of directors of large public corporations do not generally consider investors' interests as paramount and usually vote to support management whenever there is any conflict.[5] Whether this observation is accurate or even applicable to a cross section of publicly owned companies is obviously debatable. The point is that responsible people are raising serious questions about the actions of outside directors in takeover contexts, questions just as serious as those the critics of the takeover process raise.

In a recent letter to the editor of the *Harvard Business Review*, Professor Warren A. Law of the Harvard Business School has contributed a thoughtful analysis to the debate. He points out that the problem of maximizing shareholder values in the context of takeover bids is complicated by the fact that a public company faced with a bid is likely to have at least three very different sets of shareholders. The first group is long-term holders, probably including many past and present employees; the second is the institutional holders; the third is the arbitrageurs. Law asks the obvious question: Even with the best of good faith intentions, how do you act in the best interests of these different sets of shareholders?[6]

The conclusion of directors that a takeover bid is not in the best interests of stockholders does not automatically signal a desire motivated by a conflict of interest to maintain the status quo. In fact, an analysis prepared by *Forbes* shows that of 39 hostile takeover bids that have been successfully defended over the past ten years, the shareholders have been better off keeping their shares in 44% of the cases on a time/value-adjusted basis.[7]

Sleeping giants. Finally, the sleeping giants, the institutional shareholders—who collectively own 50% of American industry—are awakening. The recent formation of the Council of Institutional Investors, an umbrella organization composed of approximately 20 state and local pension funds, with the stated intention of playing a more inquisitive and activist

role in contests for corporate control, signals a potent new countervailing lobbying power to the heretofore more organized management-oriented interests.

Concern about these corporate governance issues has, of course, found its way to Washington. Many legislators are convinced that the system is not working as it is supposed to. In the past Congress, there were at least 11 hearings in the House and Senate relating to these questions and no fewer than 25 pieces of legislation, including a moratorium on oil mergers, anti-greenmail and anti-golden-parachute legislation, and a bill that would have required each director of a publicly held corporation to own 1,000 shares of the company's common stock. The current Congress appears to be at least as interested in these issues.

The SEC is also actively participating in this debate and last year sponsored a blue ribbon commission of experts in the area to study these questions. Subsequently it proposed its own agenda of reform measures. State legislators, meanwhile, are recovering from federal preemption of their own takeover laws and are proceeding to devise second-generation antitakeover measures, some of which may prove to be surprisingly effective.

Of course, all the affected vested interests, including those of bankers, lawyers, and corporations, have been actively lobbying on these issues, often from the narrow perspective of self-interest. The sound of the grinding of many axes is in the air, and a dangerous confrontation is building between the owners and stewards of the nation's productive assets.

Theory vs. practice

Underlying all this debate is the feeling that the presumption of good faith that is supposed to characterize the relationship among stockholders, boards of directors, and managements of public corporations may no longer exist. In theory, the system should work well. The board of a public company is elected by the stockholders and expected to act as a proxy for the shareholders in matters affecting their interests. The management of a public company serves at the pleasure of the board and is expected to manage the business professionally and to maximize values for the shareholders. Individual shareholders, in turn, have an opportunity to express their views in two ways: through their right to vote for directors and through their ability to sell their shares and select alternative investments. Management would like to presume that shareholders who have determined to remain investors support management and the board that they have elected and look at their investment as a long-term proposition.

In practice, each of these three groups has its own set of problems with the current state of affairs. From the shareholders' perspective, there is the concern (voiced repeatedly by important institutional investors) that in too many recent cases the boards of public companies have not governed their actions by the test of what is, in fact, in the best interests of the shareholders. As evidence, they cite the wave of "shark repellent" measures, such as the poison pill warrant hundreds of corporations have adopted, the payment of greenmail to ransom potentially threatening blocks of shares acquired by unwelcome investors, and the granting of lucrative golden parachute contracts to top managers.

Shareholders have also expressed concern that outside directors often serve at the pleasure of chief executives rather than the other way around and often have little, if any, equity interest in the companies on whose boards they serve.

A matter of perspective.
From management's perspective, a different set of issues exists. Many chief executives of major public corporations are concerned about the institutionalization of the stock market and what they perceive to be the very short-term perspective of today's investors. Some CEOs even go so far as to express the belief (at least privately) that investors with the shortest perspective—that is, arbitrageurs who invest in companies' stock only after it is under the threat of takeover—deserve no recognition or consideration as shareholders at all.

As the competitive edge of American business has diminished in comparison with that of competitors abroad, managers have made the case that the short-term orientation of the stock market has forced them, in turn, to make investment decisions based on a short-term rather than a long-term perspective, to the overall detriment of their enterprises over time. Since the job of management is to orchestrate the corporation's relationships, not only with its stockholders but also with its employees, its customers, and the communities in which it operates, management naturally feels compelled to consider the interests of these other constituencies in balancing its reaction to a takeover. Those interests can sometimes, however, be in serious conflict with what is best for the shareholders alone.

Management generally also feels that the takeover rules are tilted in favor of the aggressive acquirer, who may be able to take advantage of high-pressure takeover tactics in the stock market to acquire a business at less than its long-term value.

Finally, boards of directors (at least the outside members) feel most directly the tension between management and shareholders when a takeover comes up for consideration. Members can be torn between a sense of loyalty to the management, to whom they have entrusted the well-being of the corporation, and the legal advice they invariably receive, which is that they must place the interests of shareholders well above those of all others.

The lack of confidence in our system of corporate governance that has developed out of the takeover wave of the past five years and the corollary tendency for special interests to seek relief for problems in Washington has resulted in a keen awareness of these issues in Congress. Unfortunately, this is precisely the type of issue with which Congress is ill-equipped to deal. It inevitably will, however, unless the private sector takes some initiative.

Shooting down parachutes.
The rules under which our major public corporations are governed, based primarily on trial and error and the marketplace, have evolved over a long time. Any changes in these rules or in the balance of power between shareholders and corporations or between raider corporations and target corporations can upset the system and have serious, unintended consequences.

An example is the anti-golden-parachute provisions, which were tacked onto the Deficit Reduction Act of 1984. These provisions, which generally limit golden parachute compensation to three times average compensation for the executive concerned during the past five years, were added on the floor of the Senate and were not the subject of any hearings on either side of Congress. While they may sound reasonable, their blanket application would, for example, prevent the management of a company from providing an incentive compensation arrangement to the management of a subsidiary that might be for sale.

The golden parachute limitation would apply, notwithstanding the fact that the selling corporation might well find it in its best interest to give the management of the subsidiary a higher payment if, for instance, certain price expectations were fulfilled for the business in the sale. It is difficult to find a public policy purpose in limiting the legitimate flexibility of management to design incentive compensation arrangements of this nature.

Even more disturbing is the premise under which Congress acted to preempt the rights and prerogatives of boards of directors. The premise underlying the golden parachute legislation is that, at least in cases of executive compensation where change of control is concerned, a board of directors may not be presumed to be able to act in an unbiased fashion and in the best interests of the shareholders.

If this premise is admitted in the case of golden parachutes, it can, of course, give rise to virtually unlimited application of federal law into other areas of corporate governance. Many legislators are headed in this direction. Some even seek the adoption of a federal securities code.

Voluntary reform

In my view we need some thoughtful, voluntary reform in the private sector to forestall federal intrusion into an area where its competence is in question. This is precisely the invitation the administration extends in the section of the 1985 *Annual Report of the Council of Economic Advisers* dealing with takeover legislation. Making the point that this area is a complex one in which regulation can have unforeseen consequences, the council states that "it is preferable to allow individual companies to decide whether and how they want to protect themselves than to have the federal government dictate an inflexible nationwide policy."

To stimulate discussion of private sector initiatives, I have a few suggestions. First, the concerns of shareholders: we could strengthen the presumption that directors should represent a proxy for the shareholders by encouraging directors to become significant shareholders. One way to do so is to pay directors in common stock rather than cash and to require that these shares be retained during the individual's tenure on the board. Over time, senior outside directors of a corporation would become significant shareholders of the corporation or at least have a significant portion of their own wealth invested in the company's shares. Another step that many companies practice is to limit inside directors to one or two and to make the chairman of the board a nonexecutive director.

Taking a page from the proxy statement of most educational institutions, companies could also require would-be directors to include in each

proxy a short statement setting forth their views on their role as trustees of the stockholders' interests — in effect, to present a platform by which stockholders could judge directors' qualifications and their perspectives on corporate policy.

Communication with and accountability to shareholders might get serious if directors decided to furnish all stockholders with the same projections they regularly receive (in most companies they would be in the form of three- to five-year plans). The SEC has already promulgated safe-harbor rules for the provision of forecasts to shareholders. If directors have performed with the diligence expected of them, they should carefully evaluate arguments for not disclosing this kind of information in light of the need to restore confidence in the board's relationship with shareholders.

As for management's concerns, one way to encourage long-term investors in the company would be to create two classes of stock. Class A shares could be freely traded and carry a dividend equal to the current dividend rate. A newly created Class B share, into which the A shares could be converted and vice versa, would have to be registered directly in the name of the actual owners and would pay dividends that would increase over time at a higher rate than that of the A shares. For example, the dividend rate might reach a premium of 50% over the A share rate by the time the shares had been held for ten years or more. B shares could not be sold or transferred (except by gift or bequest) but could be freely converted into A shares for sale. The dividend premium, however, would be lost in the hands of the new owner.

Another measure management would find beneficial to both shareholders and management would be to establish an ESOP plan with the objective of placing approximately 20% ownership of the corporation in the hands of management and employees.

Clearly, the most useful measure would address the concern that takeover rules are stacked in favor of corporate raiders and short-term investors and would also preserve the possibility for shareholders to consider legitimate takeover bids. A good place

to start would be to assess what is troublesome about the current system.

Certainly, many commentators and economists have taken the position that, on balance, there is nothing wrong with the present system or at least nothing that new federal or state regulation should change. Those taking this position believe that the threat of a takeover acts as a healthy stimulus to management. They fear that additional regulation would only serve to entrench incumbents.

Some of these people would even argue that the only appropriate defense against a takeover bid at a market premium is to solicit a higher bid. They argue that two-tier offers are not coercive inasmuch as nothing about a two-tier offer prevents the making of a competing higher offer. The Office of the Economist of the SEC, for example, has reported in its own study of takeover bids that, statistically, two-tier offers are not more likely to succeed than "any and all" offers and that the "blended premiums" associated with two-tier offers are not lower than other kinds.

This analysis, however, ignores a basic proposition: whether the point at which a raider chooses to make a bid is an advantageous or even an appropriate time to sell the company at all. As I have noted, statistics show that when takeover bids have been defeated many target companies' stock prices have subsequently risen to levels far above bid prices adjusted for the time value of money. Therefore, it does not follow that the decision to accept a takeover bid at any market premium is necessarily right. Rational investors acting in their own interest and given a free choice would accept some bids and reject others.

The obvious problem with front-end-loaded, two-tier offers is that even investors who determine that an offer is inadequate cannot afford to refrain from tendering in order to protect themselves from receiving the lower "back-end" price for all their shares if the bid succeeds. Not only does the process substitute coercive market pressures for objective judgment, but the short time during which an offer is required to remain outstanding also hardly affords shareholders the benefit of an informed public discussion of such important issues as values, alternatives, reputation of bidder management, and reliability of finance (especially if "junk-bond" financing is involved).

Just as troublesome are the defensive actions of target companies. Standard takeover defense strategy today calls for resort to the courts as well as to the state legislatures and Congress to delay, if not ultimately to thwart, an unwelcome bid.

Target companies today are also apt to resort to "structural defenses," particularly if management considers the terms of a bid inadequate and especially if they involve a front-end-loaded, two-tier structure. Defensive tactics have included issuing poison pill securities, issuing voting securities to friendly parties, locking up voting control in friendly hands, and making defensive acquisitions of questionable business merit. Just as managements have felt that the tender offer rules are biased in favor of bidders, so shareholders—some of them increasingly vocal—are upset about structural defenses, which in their view simply disenfranchise the stockholders.

Rebalance the equities

Many objective practitioners would probably agree privately that at least three aspects of the framework of takeover regulation are unfair to a greater or lesser extent. These are the front-end-loaded, two-tier offer, the short period allotted to the target company and its shareholders to react to a bid, and the court-sanctioned ability of target managements to create severe structural barriers to takeovers without shareholder approval. Indeed, unlike the British system governing takeover bids, in which an offer is the subject of an active and informed debate about the merits of the proposal and the values of the company, the American system seems to work on the principle that any bid, at any premium, regardless of its merits in terms of value or business sense, will succeed unless blocked, legally or structurally.

There is one simple way to deal with these imbalances that builds on existing mechanisms: to subject the takeover process to the proxy rules. If two companies choose to combine, they can do so through either the ten-

der offer process or the merger process. The latter requires a shareholder vote, which can be obtained only after a proxy statement describing the deal has been filed with the SEC, approved, and distributed to shareholders. This same process and all the well-developed rules and procedures governing it can be employed to rebalance the equities in the hostile takeover process.

The way for companies to put this solution into practice is to amend their charters through shareholder action so as to make it impossible for a third party to acquire more than 5% of the voting power of a corporation without the approval of a majority of the company's shareholders. The principle on which such a charter provision would be based is that the modern publicly held corporation exists and operates on the premise of widespread, diffuse, and ever-changing public ownership. The accumulation of a significant voting block (5% or more) of the shares of a company would thus constitute a fundamental change in the investment and operating characteristics of the company.

Under such circumstances an array of new considerations and market forces comes into play and the company's stock can no longer be valued purely as a passive investment opportunity. Takeover speculation begins to govern the trading of the company's securities (even though the accumulation of a large block of voting stock could either presage a takeover or preclude one, depending on the objectives of the party accumulating the block).

The emergence of such a potential control group must also affect the ability of management to focus on operating the business for the long-term benefit of the corporation. Other questions, such as the arm's-length nature of any business dealings between the company and the new investor, could also arise. All these considerations suggest that a mechanism to allow shareholders to make a rational, deliberate, informed decision about whether to subject a company to a change of control should benefit both management and the shareholders.

A charter provision, which I call a "voting concentration charter provision," would accomplish these objectives through five key features:

1 A person or a group (an interested party) would be permitted to vote no more than 5% of the outstanding voting power of the company unless such voting concentration had been approved by a majority of the shareholders entitled to vote. Shares owned by an interested party in excess of 5% of the outstanding voting power could not be voted for this or any other purpose until approved.

2 On the request of any interested party seeking to obtain shareholder approval for any level of voting concentration above 5%, the company would be required to call a shareholder meeting promptly. The interested party and the company would be free to solicit proxies for or against the approval of the voting concentration at their own expense. An interested party making a tender offer for voting shares could condition the offer on approval of a specified voting concentration but could not condition acceptance of tenders of shares on the receipt of proxies for the shares.

3 Once approved, a specified level of voting concentration could not be exceeded except by a new approval; could be attained and could then be regained if lost through dilution, sales of shares, or other means within a period of six months; and could not be transferred except by gift or bequest.

4 Voting concentration restrictions would apply to third-party purchases of existing shares and to shares newly issued by the company.

5 Repurchases of voting securities by the company in excess of 5% of the outstanding voting power (or greenmail) would also be subject to shareholder approval of a majority of the outstanding voting shares.

According to independent legal counsel, a charter provision of this nature would be legal under the laws of Delaware, provided that it was adopted by shareholders. Various parts of it have precedent in long-standing provisions of corporate law that restrict voting rights under certain conditions—for example, foreign ownership of regulated companies such as those engaged in defense production or broadcasting. As far as the issue of the likelihood of shareholder approval of this type of plan is concerned, the plan represents a reasonable balancing of interests.

There is no question that it would reduce a company's vulnerability to takeover tactics that were primarily designed to benefit the raiders by bringing time and market pressure on a target company and its shareholders. It would, for example, make it more difficult for a raider who is unable to arrange firm financing or to make an "any and all" bid to put a company "in play." It should not affect, however, and indeed could be argued to make more likely, the type of bid that is designed to appeal to shareholders on a fundamental economic basis.

This reduced vulnerability is a small price for shareholders to pay in return for the protection the plan offers against the new generation of takeover defense measures (including greenmail payments, large voting-block share issuances, and poison pills), which are designed to prevent shareholders from even considering bids and have increasingly frustrated and alienated shareholders. Indeed, this type of private initiative represents a reasonable balancing of the interests of shareholders and managements and may represent the best chance to progress toward eliminating some of the more disturbing offensive and defensive tactics that have caused so much concern. It may also interrupt the call to subject reform of the takeover process to the uncertain outcome of additional federal legislation.

These are examples of measures that corporations could adopt either directly or pursuant to shareholder vote to begin to address some of the concerns I have discussed. Not all these proposals are suitable for every corporation, and some may seem unworkable for most. The point is that if the private sector does not take some initiative along these lines to restore confidence in our system of corporate governance, there is no question that reform, probably unwise and ineffective, will come from Washington.

Reprint 85605

References

1 "Taming the Corporate Takeover,"
Wall Street Journal,
October 30, 1984.

2 "Business Says 'Stop' to the Raiders,"
New York Times,
April 14, 1985.

3 "Takeover Abuses Mortgage the Future,"
Wall Street Journal,
April 5, 1985.

4 "Junk Bonds and Other Securities Swill,"
Wall Street Journal,
April 18, 1985.

5 Harold S. Geneen,
"Why Directors Can't
Protect the Shareholders,"
Fortune,
September 17, 1984, p. 28.

6 "Corporate Takeovers" in
"Letters to the Editor,"
HBR January-February 1985, p. 172.

7 Allan Sloan,
"Why Is No One Safe?"
Forbes,
March 11, 1985, p. 134.

From the Boardroom

Ralph S. Saul

Hostile takeovers: What should be done?

For directors and management, the main question is whether the proposed combination makes economic sense

HBR published a sweeping defense of hostile takeovers ("Takeovers: Folklore and Science" by Michael C. Jensen) in the November-December 1984 issue. The one-sidedness of the argument and the nature of the underlying assumptions made the editors uneasy, but they decided that the reasoning deserved attention and would indeed invite rebuttal. In a discussion that HBR hopes will continue, a well-known corporate executive takes a different view of the most dramatic development of the long-standing merger and acquisition movement.

The author identifies the reasons for the surge in takeovers, the rise of the belief that a takeover enhances shareholder wealth, and what he considers to be the fallacies of the argument. He finds that the activities of the major participants in the takeover market create a feverish atmosphere that makes careful board and shareholder deliberation impossible. To investment bankers and boards of would-be acquirers, he proposes restraint and recommends that the SEC become concerned about the speculative excesses of takeover entrepreneurs and arbitrageurs.

Mr. Saul is chairman of the board of Peers & Company, a merchant bank. He was chief executive

officer of INA Corporation from 1975 to 1982 and remained as chairman for two years after the 1982 merger of INA with Connecticut General to form CIGNA Corporation. He has held a number of executive posts, including director of the Division of Trading and Markets of the SEC and chairman of the management committee of the First Boston Corporation.

The recent dramatic rise in hostile corporate takeover activity has excited strong feelings and sharp differences of opinion among businesspeople, investors, politicians, and the public. Since 1984, the volume of mergers and acquisitions has soared to record levels. Designing strategies for mergers and acquisitions and planning defenses against hostile takeovers now preoccupy many corporate managements. Critics fear that this preoccupation is blinding managements to the long-term interests of their enterprises. Congress and the public sometimes see takeovers as predatory moves that

Editor's note: Mr. Saul's article is based on a lecture delivered at the Wharton School of the University of Pennsylvania in November 1984.

destroy honest companies and deprive families and communities of jobs.

After several years of mounting debate, we have no clear consensus on what, if anything, should be done to control hostile takeovers. Last year, the Business Roundtable told the SEC that no legislation should be adopted until we understand "what's driving the change" and "how the system really works."

The reasons for the increase in mergers and acquisitions are complex. Several developments account for the surge in both friendly and unfriendly takeovers:

☐ International competition, a strong dollar, high interest rates, and declining inflation are driving the restructuring of many older U.S. industries. Mergers and acquisitions enable these industries to become competitive by bringing down costs and increasing productivity.

☐ The legal and business climate permits corporate combinations to take place with little risk of government interference and public criticism. Moreover, our tax policies subsidize debt over equity, thus encouraging the use of debt financing for acquisitions.

☐ Financial markets have facilitated merger and acquisition activity, and, in some cases, stimulated it.

In this article, I hope to provide some answers to the questions posed by the Roundtable by first exploring these developments and then suggesting some steps toward creating a takeover policy.

Industrial restructuring

In the face of a major recession, manufacturing employment in the United States fell from 21 million in 1979 to 18.2 million in 1982. This decline was particularly severe in older industries like steel, agricultural equipment, textiles, and automobiles. Even with the recovery since 1982, manufacturing employment remains below its 1979 level. A strong dollar handicaps manufacturers, making it difficult for them to sell abroad and to compete domestically with imports. In 1984, the U.S. trade deficit in manufactured goods was $87 billion, and our overall trade deficit reached an astronomical $123 billion – a massive loss of markets here and overseas for U.S. business.

This downsizing of our older manufacturing industries has occurred through mergers and acquisitions, through write-downs and partial liquidations, or, in extreme cases, through bankruptcy reorganizations. Without a recovery of America's international competitive position, the shrinking of our older industrial base will continue. For these industries, survival depends on changing their cost structures.

Older industries are not the only ones restructuring. Those commodity businesses that thrived in an inflationary environment can no longer simply meet higher costs through higher prices. Energy, for example, was the growth industry of the 1970s. Indeed, concern arose that energy absorbed too much capital. Now, with the decline in crude oil prices, the industry is changing: domestic refining and marketing capacity is shrinking, employment is declining, and the huge capital flows characteristic of the 1970s have slowed. Mergers and acquisitions, combined with asset write-offs and stock repurchases, are slowly decapitalizing this industry. The growth industries of the past decade, such as computers and semiconductors, now face the need to restructure because of foreign competition and overcapacity.

These shifts in capital and labor reflect the efficiency of our free markets. In Europe, such adjustments are inhibited by rigid controls on labor costs, plant closings, and employee layoffs. We should applaud our ability to move resources from older industries to technology or service sectors where employment is rising and returns on investment are growing. Shareholders of companies receiving cash in acquisitions assist in this process by reinvesting in businesses where returns are higher.

Much merger and acquisition activity has little or nothing to do with industrial restructuring to meet market changes. Some of it reflects Wall Street's negative views about the benefits of diversification or changes in management strategies to improve returns on assets. Companies may, for example, rationalize their businesses by selling units that no longer fit a new corporate strategy. As their markets become more competitive, companies may find it difficult to manage effectively a diverse group of businesses and so sell off subsidiaries to establish a firmer grip on businesses they know best. Or they may sell subsidiaries to liquefy their balance sheets. Induced in part by fear of hostile takeovers, managements are under greater pressure to demonstrate they are using assets more aggressively.

Proponents of the hostile takeover argue that it forces "entrenched management" to take action that market forces dictate. The real issue, however, is whether the hostile corporate takeover accelerates an adjustment to market forces or whether it creates or threatens to create combinations that serve primarily to enrich aggressors and market professionals.

A favorable climate

International competition has weakened the old arguments for restraints on company size and industrial concentration. And since many takeovers lead to deconglomeration, it is difficult to argue that takeovers represent a trend toward industrial concentration. Thus the enforcement of antitrust laws has been benign, emphasizing economic efficiency over social and political objectives.

Deregulation policies encourage merger and acquisition activity to reduce the overcapacity that regulation fosters. As price competition replaces regulated rates, companies merge to become more competitive in costs or to improve market position.

Tax policies subsidize the use of debt to finance mergers and acquisitions. The full deductibility of interest encourages tax arbitrage. Acquiring companies may write up the assets of the acquired company and use accelerated depreciation schedules that may bear little relation to the economic life of the assets. Finally, tax credits are available for certain classes of property.

With this combination of subsidies generating additional cash flow, it is little wonder that aggressors have made liberal use of credit to finance takeovers. These subsidies also help explain why aggressor companies and takeover entrepreneurs do not use exchange offers, much less proxy contests. Junk financings accelerate the takeover process by permitting entrepreneurs to get cash quickly without the delays of an exchange offer or a bank loan.

Another key factor spurring hostile takeover activity is its new-found intellectual respectability. The idea of a hostile tender offer was alien a decade ago. Managements respected the other fellow's right to manage his business. In the late 1960s, when takeovers were effected through exchange offers with "Chinese money" (that decade's version of junk bonds), aggressors were primarily smaller, little-known companies challenging established corporations.

Today, managements are rarely inhibited in making unfriendly tender offers. Moreover, economists, business journalists, and Wall Street leaders justify these actions as a form of "market discipline" of lackluster managements. The 1985 Economic Report of the President contains the most elaborate defense of the hostile takeover. Marshaling the range of market-oriented arguments, it rejects the need for any further federal regulation of the market for corporate control. But like all arguments of this sort, it goes much too far.

It is hard to imagine the power – or the tyranny – of the argument that takeover activity enhances shareholder wealth and returns on corporate assets. Few question it. Its proponents attribute attempts to limit or restrict takeover activity to managements that want to protect their jobs or to members of the business establishment who want to preserve the status quo.

As SEC Chairman John Shad has pointed out, this justification of corporate takeovers overlooks the fact that corporations are ongoing institutions with their own history and momentum. Past decisions to borrow at times of low interest rates, to acquire cheap reserves or real estate, to overfund pension plans, to invest in improved plant and equipment, or to enter new and growing businesses may create undervalued assets. But these values may signal management's competence – not its incompetence. Management has not necessarily failed because a company's stock price is temporarily low and does not yet reflect its improved prospects. Carried to an extreme, the marketplace argument would lead to partial or complete liquidations of companies so as to yield immediate benefits to shareholders.

Furthermore, this argument confuses transient stock market prices with long-term values. A corporation represents far more than its current stock price; it embodies obligations to employees, customers, suppliers, and communities.

In well-run corporations, careful attention to these obligations builds a storehouse of goodwill that doesn't always show up in stock prices. A company may decide, for example, not to merge or pursue a major acquisition to avoid rupturing long-established relationships with employees or destroying a carefully nurtured corporate culture. A parent corporation may decide not to sell a subsidiary commanding a higher market multiple because of its importance to the parent's long-term strategy.

Current stockholders would benefit, of course, if a company pumped up its stock price to realize immediate values. Such a move, however, might jeopardize the long-term interests of the enterprise.

Finally, the market discipline argument ignores the subsidy for debt that helps drive takeover activity. When the cost of debt is below the cost of equity, it makes sense in the short term for a raider to substitute debt for equity. The target company is thus left in a position where it must leverage itself to fend off a takeover or let the aggressor do the same thing. It is dismaying to see companies with strong balance sheets take on debt and shrink their equity.

Those who see the takeover as a vehicle for creating wealth rarely point out that it may leave the survivor top-heavy with debt and thus handicapped in making future investments. Takeover proponents see debt burdens only as forcing managements to be more careful in making capital expenditures and diversifying. What is left unsaid is that high debt-equity ratios increase the risks for creditors, the common shareholders, and the enterprise itself if cash flows fall short of expectations.

Role of financial markets

The major participant in the takeover market is the institutional investor. Institutions tend to favor corporate breakups and mergers that might enhance the value of their portfolios and to oppose proposals that might forestall takeovers or entrench management. In many cases, they have marshaled the votes necessary to defeat such measures.

Although they are legal owners, they are rarely asked to consider the long-term interests of portfolio companies. As fiduciaries, they believe they must achieve the highest immediate return on funds under their direction. Facing intense competitive pressures, portfolio managers seek short-term results. Their investment policies reappear in the trading markets as volatile stock prices.

Merger and acquisition specialists in investment banking and law firms have become essential intermediaries in facilitating the restructuring and reshuffling of corporate assets. With great imagination and skill, they have helped takeover entrepreneurs and managements devise acquisition and defense strategies.

The field of mergers and acquisitions has attracted many talented young people. Under pressure to generate fees, M&A specialists must constantly come up with new takeover ideas. Financial innovation is the watchword. Unfortunately, we will not know its consequences until these innovations are tested through a declining business or market cycle.

Competitive pressures may also result in merger or acquisition proposals that cater to the vanity or insecurity of corporate managements more than they aid in the execution of well-planned strategies. When these proposals are prepared under extreme time pressures, it is unlikely they will reflect a deep understanding of the client company. All too frequently, such proposals result in placing a company "in play." By putting a company in play, Wall Street whets the appetite of arbitrageurs, speculators, and takeover entrepreneurs.

Takeover entrepreneurs are a new phenomenon on the financial scene. Embracing the market discipline argument, they justify their tactics as a battle against "entrenched" management. They exploit the greed and gullibility of speculators and the appetite of the financial press for excitement. They devote much effort to the artful use of public relations. If they have track records, they receive capital from institutions and wealthy individuals. They may join forces with other takeover entrepreneurs in shell companies whose only business is assuming equity positions in takeover candidates. They may also enlist the help of risk arbitrageurs who become shareholders with the sole objective of seeing the company sold.

We have a classic example of placing a company in play in the recent Avco takeover. Leucadia National, a much smaller company, took a position in Avco and then announced a tender offer. It withdrew when Avco paid it off in what amounted to a greenmail transaction. The *Wall Street Journal* reported that the arbitrageurs were upset by this turn of events and some, expecting another tender offer, decided to hold their positions in Avco.

In quick succession, the Irwin Jacobs group took a 12% position in Avco, Ivan Boesky, the arbitrageur, bought 8% of Avco's shares in the open market, and Textron announced a tender offer. Under its agreement with Avco, Leucadia received the benefits of Textron's premium price to Avco shareholders. Thus three groups of takeover entrepreneurs and the arbitrageurs received millions in quick profits while Textron loaded itself with debt.

Damaging consequences

Short-term debt on the balance sheets of American corporations has risen sharply, surging 40% in 1984 after three years of no growth. After improving in 1983, debt-equity ratios are deteriorating even though we are in the third year of economic expansion. Much of this deterioration reflects the financing of takeovers and leveraged buyouts in which debt is substituted for outstanding equity.

Some businesses and even entire industries are decapitalizing themselves by taking on debt and shrinking their equity bases. Even conservatively capitalized companies, fearing takeovers, may leverage themselves by repurchasing their own shares. Net equity retirements skyrocketed to $90 billion in 1984, or 4.5% of total equity outstanding – by far the largest reduction in any one year. Corporate repurchases constituted more than $25 billion of this amount.

Many of these stock repurchase programs may prove in retrospect to have achieved little. If assumptions about prices and earnings growth used to rationalize the investment in their own stock prove unfounded, corporate repurchasers may be left in a more leveraged and vulnerable position.

Prior to takeovers or leveraged buyouts, companies generally have large borrowing capacity because of low debt-equity ratios. The shares of many sound, well-managed companies trade below the market values of their assets and at low multiples of cash flows. Once these companies are taken over or bought out by their managements, as John Shad observes, debt-equity ratios increase, undervalued assets are sold off or written up, and cash flows are dedicated to debt service rather than investment in future business growth.

Even if the target company maintains excellent financial ratios, the acquirer's credit rating may cause a downgrading of the subsidiary. A good example is the sad story of Cities Service Gas, a former subsidiary of Cities Service, which had a rating of AA (higher than its parent). After Occidental Petroleum acquired Cities Service, it sold Cities Service Gas to Northwest Energy, the parent of Northwest Pipeline – rated BBB. With a weaker parent, the rating of Cities Service Gas fell to A. When it was sold again to Williams Companies, which was rated below investment grade by Standard & Poor's, its rating fell to BB +. In the brief course of a year, with no significant change in financial ratios, the rating of Cities Service Gas dropped from AA to BB +.

As this example shows, takeovers and leveraged buyouts can suddenly change the credit rating of older bond issues. Investors receive little or no warning that high-grade bonds can swiftly become junk bonds.

There are other consequences of hostile takeovers that in the long run may be as damaging as the financial consequences. The race for corporate control compels quick decisions by managements and boards. In the heat of a takeover battle, boards are presented with proposals that they must act on immediately. Although this pace of events may excite advisers, consultants, lawyers, market professionals, and speculators, it is hardly conducive to making multibilliondollar decisions that can have a profound impact on jobs, pension rights, and communities. Indeed, decision making in this heated atmosphere may make a mockery of careful corporate strategic planning. It contrasts sharply with the time and attention devoted to review of a company's annual budget or an internal investment decision.

Moreover, a wide-open market for corporate control encourages a business climate in which companies are treated as trading chips rather than as vehicles for creating wealth. This market stimulates management to think more about self-aggrandizement than about the interests of shareholders and employees. It undermines the role of the board. Over time it may engender strong cynicism about the ethics of American business.

Toward restraint

Do current takeover practices encourage careful deliberation by boards and shareholders on the issues surrounding changes in corporate control? In my view, no. Rather, they have created a feverish atmosphere that promotes market speculation, undue reliance on outside professionals, and hastily improvised defense measures.

Fortunately, concerned corporate executives, business thinkers, and lawyers are beginning to speak out. Martin Lipton, a prominent corporate lawyer, has stated there may be no defense against a "two-tier, front-end loaded, bust-up, junk bond takeover." He has recommended a package of legislative proposals aimed at eliminating two-tiered offers. Peter Drucker has warned that "business had better think through what the policies [on takeovers] should be instead of waiting for the 'scandal' that pushes the politicians into demagoguery."

As so frequently happens with market manias of this sort, it is possible that the speculative bubble will burst. Declining oil prices, effective corporate defense measures, greater risks for arbitrageurs, and a scarcity of good targets may all contribute toward making the unfriendly takeover less appealing. The prospect of fewer takeovers, however, does not lessen the need for change.

In my view, control over takeovers should lie within the boardrooms of American business, on Wall Street, and in the law firms that advise these enterprises. On its part, the SEC could recommend changes in the rules of the takeover game that would allow more time for careful board and shareholder deliberation, thus making the takeover game more risky for raiders and speculators.

Directors must develop a more hard-nosed attitude toward proposals for mergers or acquisitions – whether hostile or friendly. Boards of acquiring companies must probe deeply to determine whether a proposal will help create long-term values for shareholders. Will it, for example, result in economies of scale or product or marketing synergies? Will it provide a balance of earnings contracyclical to the company's business? They should also concentrate on the consequences of the acquisition for their balance sheets. In general, does the board have adequate information to judge the wisdom of the acquisition? Boards should have as much – if not more – information on acquisitions as they have on internal investments.

One irony of the corporate takeover debate is that few talk about the loss of wealth to the bidding shareholders if the takeover is ill-conceived. A McKinsey survey of 400 acquisitions shows that only half of them worked; in the other half, shareholders of the acquiring companies lost value.

To avoid being pushed into a hurried takeover defense, the board of a potential target company should inquire about management's defense strategy long before any emergency arises. In the heat of a takeover battle, key decisions are all too often made in a few weeks or even days and on the basis of limited information. While perhaps saving the company from an unwanted suitor, a board is generally not happy about having to adopt a "poison pill'' defense or rush to a ''white knight.'' Careful planning allows the board time to better exercise its business judgment.

Institutional investors should not take for granted that all defense proposals are designed to protect incompetent managements or that they will hurt the value of their portfolio investments. The issues are not that simple. Some takeover defenses permit a competent management to focus on the long-term interests of the enterprise without being preoccupied by a possible takeover. Others ensure fairness to all shareholders. It has yet to be proven that takeover defenses will, in the long run, reduce the market value of a well-run company.

Of course, institutional investors have legitimate concerns about the impact of some defense measures on the rights of shareholders. My gripe is that too many institutional investors fail to distinguish between measures that seek to protect shareholders from those that undermine shareholder rights.

Asset managers are often hired by trustees and directors of institutions and corporations critical of corporate takeovers. Yet these same trustees and directors will often fire asset managers for poor or mediocre short-term performance. I suggest that responsible trustees and directors shift their emphasis from short-term performance to the creation of long-term values and that they encourage their asset managers to do the same.

Restraint must come from Wall Street as well. The financial community should stop talking about market discipline and consider that companies subject to hostile takeovers might be undervalued precisely because of superior management. Every undervalued asset on or off the balance sheet does not have to be written up, sold, or spun off. In fact, it is not always clear that these undervalued assets carry the market values assigned to them.

Investment bankers have a responsibility to curb the youthful zeal generating takeover proposals that have not been thoroughly researched and financial innovations that may disregard long-term consequences. Older and wiser partners in investment banking firms should ask, for example, whether the firm's plan incorporates a solid understanding of the client company's markets, products, and history and whether a new financial instrument could harm the company in a period of market decline or financial stress.

A long-term perspective may be a lot to ask of a highly competitive business like investment banking. Yet most other businesses must be concerned about whether their products and services offer long-term customer satisfaction. Since the financial community will have to live with the new enterprises it helps create, a long-term perspective is certainly in order.

Changing the rules

Finally, the SEC has a role to play. As the agency entrusted by Congress to regulate the securities markets, it should determine whether takeover practices are consistent with its mandate to protect investors and maintain fair and orderly markets. The SEC should seek ways to give boards and shareholders more time to deliberate proposed changes in corporate control through changes in tender offer and proxy rules. It should also examine the practices of takeover entrepreneurs and market professionals to ensure consistency with the Exchange Act and the rules of the exchanges.

The Business Roundtable has made a proposal that would increase board involvement and deliberation in takeover decisions. It would require the board to approve or disapprove a tender offer when a raider reaches a threshold number of shares. If the board were to disapprove, the matter would go before the shareholders through a proxy contest in which each side would present its case. An orderly takeover process would lessen the need for takeover defenses and calm fears about unfair treatment of shareholders. Greater board involvement at an earlier stage would also focus the board's attention on management's plans and strategies for building shareholder wealth.

The SEC should try to control the speculative excesses that accompany the hostile takeover by examining the practices of takeover entrepreneurs. Are they acting as market professionals? Should they be subject to some or all of the restraints applied to brokers? The SEC should further examine whether the trading of risk arbitrageurs is excessive. To ensure fair and orderly public markets, the Exchange Act and the rules of the exchanges long ago imposed limitations on a firm's trading for its own account. We risk losing public confidence if we don't get back to some of the fundamentals governing our securities markets.

I would recommend that the SEC study the impact of takeover activity on fair and orderly markets and investors' rights and make recommendations to Congress. The study should be done promptly, before Congress, relying on limited information, proposes legislation that may exacerbate rather than solve the problem.

All parties now involved—corporate boards, institutional investors, Wall Street, and the SEC—must begin to examine their individual roles in the takeover game. After all, these institutions determine the style in which the game is played and what its outcome will be. If something goes wrong, they will bear the responsibility. The time isn't too late for wisdom and restraint. ▽

Reprint 85511

From the Boardroom

Taken over, turned out

Paul O. Gaddis

In the ongoing debate about whose interests corporate takeover truly serves, both raider and raided defend the purity of their motives. But in my view from the boardroom, neither pays enough attention to one of the most important ramifications of takeover: the massive destruction it can wreak on a raided organization's capacity to achieve.

After being involved in the takeover of a company I served as director, I believe I have some insight into the magnitude of this loss and its ethical dimension. The moral responsibility of the board of directors is far more extensive in takeover than usually assumed.

For almost a decade, I had the privilege of sitting on the board of one of the larger U.S. independent oil and gas companies, headquartered in Kansas. This board had gone through the full energy cycle, from the years of euphoria—which began to fade in 1981—to the tough years thereafter.

In good times and bad, the heart of the company was its young pro-

Paul O. Gaddis is professor of management and former dean of the School of Management at the University of Texas at Dallas. He consults and lectures on multinational corporate strategy and has served on numerous boards in the United States and Europe. He is the author of Corporate Accountability *(Harper & Row, 1964) and many articles, several of them in HBR.*

fessional management team, which we had worked hard and long to assemble. The CEO was educated as both a geologist and a lawyer and had more than 20 years' experience in the oil fields. The chief operating officer was an entrepreneur and a lawyer who had spent his entire career in the energy industry. The chief of exploration had a Ph.D. in geology and many years of senior experience. Throughout the ranks, the qualifications of the company's executives were impressive. This management strength continually attracted the best new petroleum engineer graduates to the company, even though many other companies aggressively sought them out.

Heavy weather

In early 1982, however, our board faced a difficult situation. The falling prices of oil and gas threatened the value of our company as a going concern. Oil at $40 a barrel had yielded a far more attractive projected stream of future revenues than oil at $15 a barrel, and the estimated value of the company began a long fall. In addition, the stock markets began to take a negative view of all independent exploration and production companies, and the price-earnings multiple on our common shares dropped accordingly. We began to realize that we would have to become

familiar with the kind of valuation known as the breakup (or terminal or liquidation) value of the company.

By now, the calculation of a company's liquidation value has become a basic part of corporate economics, but at the time, our older directors had little experience with this concept. We had to seek out and interpret a set of none-too-reliable data—indications of whether and when our company was going to be "in play." We had to separate sound information about who was buying our shares and why from rumors about various "vulture capitalists" who might try to gain from liquidating our reserve assets in the ground.

If one of these raiders offered a price above any reasonable projection of the company's value as a going concern, we knew we would have to take it to protect the interest of our shareholders.

The decisions we faced were troubling because the future for companies like ours was so uncertain. Experts' opinions about how much oil prices would change and when fluctuated dramatically, and our long-term projections

The real cost of takeovers is the loss of company productivity.

oscillated like aircraft instruments during heavy weather. The company's changing mix of shareholders during this period was another dimension of uncertainty. We still had a group of loyal, long-term holders, albeit shrinking, but there were also arbitrageurs looking for a short ride on the stock and buyers who had the look of raiders but motives we couldn't make out. We keenly realized the difficulty in determining the best interests of this diverse and changing group.

As directors, we felt a moral obligation to serve the best interests of another group, too—the highly capable managers and supervisors who had remained loyal to the company during the boom years when energy professionals were receiving numerous offers to jump ship. Their record of efficiency in finding new oil and gas reserves, to

Commentaries on this case from
three executives appear at the
end of the article.

cite just one of their achievements, was
one of the best in the industry. We began to believe that the effectiveness of
this management team of 40 men and
women was the essence of our corporation's value to society.

Yet counsel reminded us,
and we agreed, that once the company
appeared to be on the block, its management expertise would become
irrelevant. Then we would have to go
through that fateful moment when we
would be no longer stewards charged
with overseeing the company's operations but auctioneers charged with
seeking the highest price for the company's so-called real assets.

The time came when we had
to take a cold look at the raiders hover-
ing around the company. At least five
were acquiring large amounts of stock,
for reasons ranging from a desire to emulate Carl Icahn to a desire to recover
losses they had incurred when the
company's stock dropped. Moreover,
several large corporations, some of
them multinationals based overseas,
were interested in everything from the
short-term breakup of our company to
its long-term operating assimilation.

As we analyzed the manage-
ment, resources, and intentions of our
potential acquirers, we came to classify
them as either "Type A," those who
recognized the value of an effectively
functioning management organization,
or "Type B," those who did not recognize management effectiveness or care
about preserving it.

Each of these motivations
for stock acquisition called for a different response from us. One person, for
example, had held some of our shares
for years and was now rapidly acquiring
additional blocks. When our management questioned him, he was candid
about his Type B motives. Spurred by
his need for liquidity, he was hustling
our company in financial centers
around the country and hoping to gain
even a minimal premium over the market price of the stock.

When he offered to sell his
stock to the company for such a pre-

mium, our board vigorously debated
the wisdom of accepting his terms,
which would be essentially engaging in
greenmail. Accepting his proposal
would not be illegal, of course, but
would it be ethical – if we considered
our shareholders at large – to buy out
this one holder's shares? At first, the entire board was opposed to any response
to his proposal, but then we came up
against the advice of our array of impressive counselors, all of whom urged
us to accept the proposal. In the opinion
of our two prestigious law firms, a major investment banking firm, and our
commercial bankers, if this shareholder continued trying to auction our
company, his efforts could compromise
the amount of premium our shareholders could get later on in the depressed
market.

After considerable legal
counseling, our company bought the
investor out and halted his efforts to
sell the company anywhere he could.
As we expected, a few shareholders
filed a suit on the grounds that the buyout had injured the shareholders. This
skirmish was minor, however, because
we had received excellent counsel and
done our homework. The plaintiffs
quickly settled out of court for a very
nominal sum, which offset their legal
fees.

It was reassuring to our directors to note that subsequent events
clearly vindicated our decision to buy
these shares. We were able to sell the
company at a price substantially more
beneficial to our shareholders.

After this matter was re-
solved, our board turned its attention
to the corporate investors that had
shown interest in our company. One
conglomerate promised us complete
autonomy after the merger, but in our
view the company already had indiges-
tion from all the companies it had tak-
en in. Later developments confirmed
our judgment, for the conglomerate
divested and spun off acquisition after
acquisition. Our company would have
been spit out almost before it had been
swallowed.

We were somewhat more
open to overseas companies because of
the widely held belief that European
and Japanese executives "think long-
term." A chemical giant based in West
Germany was a persistent suitor and
clearly Type A in its appreciation of
our management. That company's ex-

ecutives, however, were among the
world's most deliberate reviewers, and
we estimated that it would take a year
or two to close a deal with them. We
did not think we had the luxury of that
much time for reflection.

In late 1983, we centered our
attention on an Australian corporation,
a heavy-industry group with worldwide operations in mining, petroleum,
and steel. We had met the company's
executives through our investment
bankers in New York the year before
and, over the course of several business
and social encounters, had developed a
certain rapport.

As the reason for their interest in our company, the executives
cited their corporation's strategic need
to increase its petroleum activity in
North America. They explained that
an energy depression was the most favorable time for them to make a large
petroleum investment, given their highly liquid balance sheet. (They might
also have mentioned that they themselves were being pursued by a profi-
cient acquirer and needed to reduce
their liquidity through an acquisition
or two.)

In talking with the Austra-
lian executives, we sensed none of the
fast-turnover, quick-buck, liquidate-
the-organization thinking so prevalent
in the United States. From the beginning, they emphasized their interest in
the character, competence, and depth
of our management team. They not
only reviewed our financial status and
our headquarters management thor-

oughly but also visited our key field locations to assess our exploration and production managers. Their intensive review supported the claim that they were interested in North American petroleum operations for the long term. They appeared to be Type A all the way.

This is not to say that we had no qualms about our suitor from down under. We had no experience with Australian management, and we wondered how merging operations from two different cultures would go. On the one hand, we saw the Australians as forthright and easy to work with. On the other, we were concerned about the reservations some of our associates had expressed about the state of Australian corporate business. Australians in general, one business veteran told me, did not see management as a profession. They looked down on management education and were unfamiliar with current managerial philosophies and methods. In a word, he said, as managers they were unsophisticated compared with their peers in other industrialized nations. And this difference might be one factor contributing to Australia's continuing slippage in economic growth.

Generalizations like these, coming from several sources, worried us, but it was clear that our operating managers enjoyed working with the Australian group's managers. The rapport between them boded well for a merger.

Smooth sailing

By late autumn 1984, our suitors had completed their reviews and our investment banker had appraised our company. The valuation told us that we would be acting prudently and in our shareholders' interest if we sold the company at the price we had negotiated with the Australians.

Our board voted unanimously to recommend that our stockholders accept the tender offer, and the deal was soon consummated: cash for 100% of our common shares. The Australians paid about 75% over the market value, a premium that underscored the point they had often made that they were "buying management." We had acquitted ourselves well in tending to our fi-

duciary duties, and now we sat back to see how our operating management would perform when given access to our acquirers' financial and managerial resources.

The Australians reiterated their intention to run our former company as an autonomous subsidiary with its own directorate, although in form we would initially operate under the group's San Francisco-based mining subsidiary. Our board retained its former composition with only minor changes, including the addition of three of the acquirer's representatives—one from group headquarters in Melbourne and two from the offices in San Francisco.

Our acquirers *said* they were buying management.

A period of resourceful and gratifying collaboration between American and Australian managers at the business-unit level followed. Our managers and geologists played a key role in planning an international exploration project to be directed from Melbourne. As chairman of our board's long-range planning committee, I was excited about the competitive advantages that could accrue from a well-designed worldwide plan—one so extensive that an independent company could never have even contemplated it. In the boardroom in these early months, we occasionally heard references to a "honeymoon" period, but the analogy seemed inappropriate—honeymoons, after all, last only about a year.

During this time, the Australians gave us more indication of the direction in which they wanted to take the company. A U.S. consulting firm had studied the Australian group and recommended that it be divided into three subsidiary operating companies—steel, headquartered in Australia; petroleum, headquartered at a world petroleum center in some U.S. city; and mining, headquartered at the San Francisco office. (A fourth company with diversified products might also be formed, the consultant had said, to

lessen the group's dependence on basic industries.) The companies would operate multinationally and autonomously so that each would have the management experience needed to compete successfully in the three different industries.

Holding to our course

The Australians informally invited us to help refine the concept of the world petroleum organization, and we gladly joined in, expecting our view from Kansas to have some impact.

As the world-exploration plan developed, however, we began to notice problems arising from the structure of the megacorporation we had joined. The lines of authority were unclear. Those of us who were on the long-range planning committee felt an uncomfortable ambiguity because we could not tell who was to review our unit's strategic plans. We also noted divergent advice from our Australian board member and the San Francisco board members, all of whom supposedly represented our parent organization.

Still, our top managers in Kansas continued to work on fleshing out the skeletal concept of a world petroleum organization. It was a good time to buy producing assets and exploration properties at bargain prices, and our engineers knew where the best bargains were in both North and South America.

Our chairman entered discussions with a large U.S. chemical corporation and confirmed that its Houston oil and gas subsidiary was for sale. The subsidiary was almost as large as our company had been when acquired, and our management believed its operations meshed well with the master plan for growth that our new corporation was developing. It would represent a second building block for the North American petroleum organization.

Two months later, after the Australian-American teams had conducted another painstaking review, our executives in Kansas recommended to our board that the parent group acquire the oil and gas subsidiary. Our managers expected us to add our approval to their recommendation, which would then pass up the ladder of reviewing authority.

We deemed the proposed acquisition sensible but hesitated to make a recommendation on it for several reasons. First, we were not sure that our recommendation, coming from a subsidiary board, would be meaningful. We hoped our doubt was simply a reflection of the ambiguity in the role of subsidiary boards in general, whose prerogatives and responsibilities are usually defined imprecisely.

Second, we again had the nagging thought that we didn't know where in our multinational superstructure such strategic issues were decided. Middle and senior managers from Melbourne evaluated the proposed acquisition and had presumably communicated with the parent company about the wisdom of the investment. We noticed, however, that the board-level managers from the San Francisco mining subsidiary had been silent throughout the project analysis. Did their silence indicate their tacit acceptance of the acquisition or merely their confusion?

Third, and most troubling, we wanted to know more about the management structure that would be put in place after the acquisition. Our managers in Kansas had told us how they would manage the combined petroleum operation, and we were unwilling to endorse the acquisition if some other management team was to be chosen.

With all these misgivings, we were reluctant to bless the project, especially since it would take an investment of more than a half billion dollars from our parent group. After much debate, however, we finally responded to the enthusiasm of our management in Kansas and their Australian counterparts. We recommended, for the benefit of whatever body would decide on the proposal, that the acquisition proceed.

Coming apart

Now all the hidden agendas we had sensed but not fully discerned during our eight months as a subsidiary board came into play. The parent company proceeded with the acquisition. It gave the leadership to Kansas and at this point owned about a billion dollars' worth of petroleum assets in the two operations in North America. The combined petroleum organization was now as large as the mining organization in San Francisco.

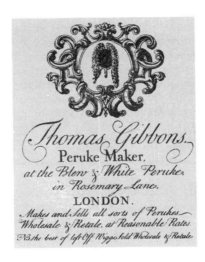

It was clear that the three proposed worldwide companies—petroleum, steel, and mining—represented a natural course of evolution for the parent group. Evidence of this came from the managing director of the group's Melbourne petroleum operations, who let it be known that he would welcome an invitation to sit on our board of directors. Unexpectedly, his overture provoked a negative reaction from the San Francisco subsidiary.

This turn of events suddenly made the shape of the situation apparent to me: our Kansas operation was caught in a conflict between turf and market. Clearly, in their strategic plans, our senior colleagues in Melbourne viewed the world in terms of market segments—and, in view of the disparities among their major markets, it was a most rational view. But our colleagues in San Francisco viewed the world in terms of geographic areas, or turf. They apparently felt that every operating unit in America, whatever its business, should report to them. They saw their company as the North American headquarters.

This was a humbling experience for our board. With an average of 40 years' management experience each, we five outside directors now found ourselves in an organizational schism that any good MBA student would have pinpointed in a case study. It was time to see whether we could exert our influence to preserve the effective business entity we had kept together for more than a decade.

It took almost exactly one year from the time our company was acquired for the smoldering turf war to burst into flames. In December 1985, our chairman tried to negotiate with San Francisco and Melbourne to maintain the autonomy of the North American oil companies. But he got no help. San Francisco was like a stone wall, and the executives from Melbourne with whom we had enjoyed such a constructive collaboration receded into inaccessibility.

On a bitter cold day in January, I arrived in Kansas for a board meeting the next day. Our chairman had phoned me earlier to warn that a "drastic reorganization" might be forthcoming. He was not more specific during the call because, as I later learned, he was then still engaged in talks with his superiors in San Francisco and would not learn all the details of the changes himself until after midnight that night.

All the hidden agendas were coming into play.

In the hotel lobby at around 7 the next morning, I happened on the chairman of the group's San Francisco mining corporation. He invited me to breakfast, and I accepted in the hope that he might let me know something about his strategic plans for his new energy business in North America. If he had plans in mind, however, he did not share them, and we passed the breakfast discussing items from the morning's *Wall Street Journal*.

The board meeting started promptly at 8. Our chairman, obviously tired from his late sessions the previous night, turned the meeting over to the chairman of the mining corporation, who proceeded to explain the "reorganization." It was a tentative performance, especially when he set forth his rationale for the changes. One of our directors interrupted with the question, "Are you trying to say that we are all fired? If so, let's get it over with."

During the preceding weeks, we had all come to realize that our subsidiary was in jeopardy. But only now did we realize how drastic and how rapid the changes would be.

The mining executives from San Francisco had proposed that the corporation consolidate all North American operations, and they had prevailed with the parent group. The Kansas subsidiary would be dissolved, the Kansas headquarters eliminated, our board disbanded. A new division headquarters for oil and gas would be established in San Francisco. All the operations of the chemical company's oil and gas subsidiary, so recently acquired that the ink was barely dry on the merger papers, would be folded into the new U.S. division.

From this point on, our organization unraveled at a remarkable rate.

From this point on, our former company's organization unraveled at a remarkable rate. Our chairman, who had been one of the best CEOs of a medium-size corporation in the country, was named head of just another division in the San Francisco operation. Only a few of the Kansas staff officers followed him to the new headquarters. After reflecting on his first few conferences with top management in San Francisco, our president struck out on his own in an entrepreneurial venture. After seeing his recommendations ignored and being put into a reporting relationship he could not accept, our production chief—whose wisdom had contributed so much to our earlier success in Kansas—departed into premature retirement. Our brilliant exploration chief felt out the situation for a month and then left for another position in the petroleum industry. Many members of his staff, spread throughout the western states, followed his lead.

The harmful effects of the dismantling did not end there. The dissolution of yet another company's home office in Kansas, a state already hard hit by receding fortunes in energy, farming, and general aviation, had a predictably disastrous impact on the local economy. It meant, of course, the layoff of many employees.

Assessing the damage

What we as a board had tried so hard to avoid—the destruction of a highly developed, finely tuned operation—had happened. After that last board meeting broke up awkwardly, we ex-directors left for our home bases without even the time to say good-bye. Although we were never to sit around the same table again, we realized that we needed time for reflection and analysis and over the next year talked by phone and in meetings of two or three. What had we done wrong? What had we done right?

On the plus side, we knew we had fully discharged our fiduciary obligations to our former shareholders. From the loyal widows to the quick-buck arbs, all had done well when we sold. Nor had the company's executives and managers suffered great losses in their personal fortunes. We had negotiated reasonable terms for their separations. While many of their careers were sharply diverted, their solvency was not threatened, at least in the short term.

Since we had fully met our obligations to our stockholders, we knew that the narrow constructionists like Milton Friedman of the old school and T. Boone Pickens of the new school would highly approve our decision to accept the Australians' offer. After all, in the final analysis, our board had responded to price as its chief criterion in selling our shareholders' company.

Merger-watchers might say that the demise of our operation in Kansas was Darwinian, an inevitable response to the forced downsizing of the nation's oil industry. We rejected this argument, however, because our exploration and production company had been one of the fittest—a business that had been strong enough to survive because its managers had understood its

markets and known how to respond to them. It had not been run by the kind of managers Mr. Pickens has vowed to turn out of office.

Even with the approbation of the traditionalists, we went through months of self-doubt. The loss of this business and its management team was a loss for the whole economy, and some of us blamed ourselves for the damage. Those who say that this kind of team can be rebuilt quickly do not even begin to understand the difficulty of recruiting, assembling, and developing the human resources needed to carry out the demanding professional tasks of such a group.

We were also chagrined that we had not seen the potential for a common turf war. And we resented the ungracious way our senior directors had been treated during the reorganization. Progressively managed corporations have begun to recognize and even codify their obligations to long-term directors, and we felt that directors who had served a company through good times and bad for ten years, as we had, might at the very least get a handshake when they left.

Our resentment was minor because we all realized that the surviving company had no legal obligations to any of our former directors. Yet one of our former company's most accomplished young managers thought our resentment was justified. The main reason he had decided to leave the reorganized concern, he told us, was the way it had treated our board during the crucial deliberations. He further noted that not one of our directors had been asked to sit on the surviving board in San Francisco. This conduct was symptomatic of the San Francisco operation's managerial philosophy, he said, and had convinced several other key managers to leave.

What did we learn from all this? First, we realized that premerger discussions bring no guarantees. The Australian managers who had discussed the merger with us did believe enthusiastically in the future they were preaching. They did not foresee any conflict arising from it. But we should have realized that the premerger statements of acquiring company managers are at best merely informed judgments. They are not commitments. They are usually not even relevant, because they are not conveyed to the senior executives who will make the implementation decisions later. Moreover, acquiring managers are rarely in a position to inform acquirees about organizational problems that could threaten a company's future.

In this regard, I looked back uncomfortably on my earlier role as an acquisitions officer for a *Fortune* "500" company. I had never felt compelled to tell the "lambs" sitting opposite me about the various power shifts and factions brewing within our corporation, some of which had had the potential to destroy the benefits that could have resulted from the acquisitions.

AT the Old Collier *and* Cart, *at* Fleet-Ditch, *near* Holborn-Bridge, *Are good* Coals, Deals, Wainfcote *and* Beach, &c. *fold at reafonable* Rates, *by* **John Edwards.**

Second, we learned not to let alluring strategies overwhelm our common sense. The dazzling plan our colleagues from Melbourne had sketched out, bearing the imprimatur of a renowned consulting firm, had blinded us to all the problems that might arise after the merger.

Third, in hindsight we came to understand how impossible it is to plant and nurture a smaller professional business organization in the infertile grounds of a megacorporation. We thought again about the gap between numbers-oriented management at the corporate level and market-focused management at the business-unit level. We reconfirmed that the two have great difficulty communicating with each other in an enormous, diversified corporation. We understood the devastation a megacorporation's incapacity to assess, deploy, and motivate its professional employees can cause.

Although we had discharged our legal obligations to our shareholders, we still wondered whether we could have arranged a different kind of merger—one that would not only have

ensured an equitable price for stockholders and fair treatment for employees but that would also have sustained another decade or so of productive capacity in the U.S. economy for the operation we had built.

All of us, as directors serving on several boards, are aware that much has been written and said in recent years about the moral obligations of directors to their investors. We have concluded, however, that the most difficult ethical problems of takeover do not center on constantly asking what is best for the shareholders. To be sure, that issue is frustratingly complex, but its legal and moral framework is well developed. Guidance for it comes from many sources, ranging from new directors' primers to analyses in the business and legal press.

Nor do the hardest ethical problems lie in what happens to the company's managers and employees after a merger, although we certainly are concerned about this complicated issue. Admittedly, recent practice has entailed much abuse, but the precedent is ample for setting up protective measures of the type that are fair to both shareholders and managers.

The most vital, difficult ethical problems in takeover relate to the productive capacity of a corporate organization—to the board's role in developing and maintaining this capacity and then in preserving it in times of crisis. These are governance problems, compounded of managerial and economic factors along with the ethical dimension. They are problems relatively unaddressed today.

The current conception of a board's responsibility during a takeover is too narrow. Directors have a moral obligation to be mindful of all the repercussions a merger will have. Takeovers have destroyed countless finely tuned, productive organizations when they were absorbed into remote superstructures. That is a cost the entire economy will have to bear.

Paul O. Gaddis

Commentaries

When it comes to takeovers, there are as many perspectives as there are players, so HBR asked several sea-

soned executives to look at Mr. Gaddis's case and tell our readers what they saw. The comments that follow give us the viewpoints of a takeover artist, a former chairman of the New York Stock Exchange, and a director and retired CEO.

T. Boone Pickens, Jr.
General Partner
Mesa Limited Partnership
and
Chairman
United Shareholders
Association

Experienced players in the oil industry will know the situation Mr. Gaddis is describing and will sympathize with his concern about the breakup of this company's management team after its acquisition. The executives were first-rate, and it is a shame that the new owner did not keep them.

But there is more to this story than post-takeover turf battles. As a result of previous mistakes, the company was so mired in debt that its prospects for long-term growth were minimal. Given the subsequent collapse of oil and gas prices, it was fortunate that interested buyers with deep pockets appeared on the scene.

Unfortunately, these directors found it difficult to discharge their fiduciary duties to the shareholders who had elected them. When other companies began offering more value than the company was capable of achieving by remaining independent, the board's responsibility was to negotiate the best deal possible for the owners. Instead, Mr. Gaddis and his colleagues categorized potential acquisitions on the basis of how they would affect the company's executives. The board even resorted to the discriminatory practice of greenmail in a futile effort to preserve executive employment at the shareholders' expense.

Perhaps the misplaced loyalty of the directors reflects their meager stock ownership. One of Mr. Gaddis's fellow directors, for example, owned only 350 shares, worth less than $1,500. For a company with $150 million in annual revenues, the price of boardroom admission was cheap. Little wonder that the company's "independent" directors seemed to feel more rapport with the managers than with the owners.

James J. Needham
International Business Consultant,
Former Chairman
New York Stock Exchange, and
Former Commissioner
Securities and Exchange Commission

Mr. Gaddis's article is a revealing and candid expression of the self-appraisal he and his colleagues underwent before and after their difficult decision to support the sale of the company they served as directors. I appreciate his willingness to share his experience, and I empathize with him.

Being a director sometimes requires the combined skills of a juggler and a high-wire performer. Boards under the pressures Mr. Gaddis describes must deal with several critical issues simultaneously while maintaining the coolness of mind we associate with those who walk the high wire. Generally, boards do well with the first objective. It is the second that they often have trouble with. Emotional detachment is not completely possible for human beings—nor should we want it to be. Boards must be particularly mindful of that fact when they are making decisions that affect the groups to whom they are accountable.

The reactions of Mr. Gaddis and his colleagues reflect their lack of total detachment, not a failure to discharge their responsibility in selling the company. That commentary will bring small comfort to Mr. Gaddis, but I hope it will give him another perspective on his state of mind.

The current environment as well as my long-standing personal convictions call my attention to other, less philosophical matters. It is impossible for me to visualize any circumstance in which greenmail payments could be justified. Those who have authorized such payments should come forward and submit their views to analysis by critics of the practice. Needless to say, I think such persons lack the detachment I have mentioned. To be more blunt, the approval of greenmail is a

vain attempt to maintain the status quo by a management group and a board who naively believe they are so entrenched and so endowed with all the answers that they have nothing to learn—or to regret. Mr. Gaddis vividly presents the consequences of this belief.

As for Mr. Gaddis's proposal that boards assume some responsibility for the macroeconomic affairs of this nation, a reminder is required. Boards are elected bodies whose constituencies are small and whose authority and objectives are delineated in the constitutions of their companies. If boards continue to direct all their efforts to the business of their companies, they can rest assured that the economic well-being of our nation will be served.

Peter Scotese
Retired CEO
Springs Industries, Inc. and Member of the Board
National Distillers & Chemical Corporation,
Bell & Howell Company, and ARMTEK

The case Paul Gaddis presents leaves me somewhat ambivalent about how due diligence and the business judgment rule apply to the actions of his board. On the one hand, these directors showed a considerable amount of ethical responsibility, logic, and forethought in their consideration of the many consequences and scenarios that could evolve. On the other hand, they gave unusual emphasis to preserving the management team, which I find somewhat unrealistic. A management team is a product of good leadership, recruiting, selection, training, and opportunity for upward mobility. This especially talented management team might have been very difficult to retain in any event, given a rapidly declining industrial environment, a falling stock price, and the vulnerability of such talent to outside recruiting.

Certainly the directors showed a deep understanding of the legal pitfalls in takeovers and were meticulous about seeking counsel to protect the company from "vulture capitalists" and unwanted suitors. But they appear to have neglected other options that might have maintained and pos-

sibly improved the company's market valuation by rationalizing its assets. Breakup moves such as asset spin-offs, going public with part of the company, repurchasing stock, a leveraged buyout through management—any one of these might have been a realistic alternative. Certainly the management LBO route was worth the same kind of thought and attention given to choosing a proper suitor in light of the board's desire to preserve the 40-person management team and its potential capacity for achievement.

The Type A, Type B suitor classifications were imaginative. The greenmail paid to one shareholder was an act I deplore, regardless of the rationale. Other antitakeover steps taken long in advance might have prevented the need for this.

What happened after the takeover shows how hard it is to read the past or predict what will happen after the honeymoon is over. The company's demise as a stand-alone operating unit with a worldwide petroleum focus may have been due to the difficulty of merging foreign and domestic business cultures. But the turf war, the unraveling, and the mistreatment of the board must have been at least partially triggered by the deteriorating conditions in the industries being served and the need for drastic cost cutting.

I share the author's conclusion that the current concept of boardroom obligations is too narrow. Our laws support only the shareholders' interests without regard to moral and ethical responsibilities. And except in privately held or family-owned and -controlled businesses, no consideration seems to be given to preserving jobs and the economic base of enterprise in communities. Yet time and events are moving us toward these broader concepts. The recent Wall Street scandals and the rising tide of public opinion in favor of legislation to address these shortcomings assure that changes will occur.

Reprint 87404

Acquisitions and
Corporate Diversification

Diversification via acquisition: creating value

A successful diversification move yields a return higher than the risk-adjusted cost of capital necessary to make the acquisition

Malcolm S. Salter and
Wolf A. Weinhold

When debating whether to try to acquire a business that will take their company into either a related or an unrelated field, top corporate officers must answer this vital question: Will it create value for our shareholders? The interest of top management is in improving operating results, which, it hopes, will eventually be reflected in a higher value for the company's stock. Unless management has good reason to believe that the transaction can produce a market value higher than the investor could obtain himself by diversifying his own portfolio, the company should not make the acquisition. The authors discuss the misconceptions that maintain the popularity of corporate diversification programs (many of them unsuccessful) and then outline ways in which a merger can create value for stockholders.

Mr. Salter is professor of business administration at the Harvard Business School, where he special-

izes in the strategic and organizational problems of diversified companies. This is his fourth HBR article. His previous articles have concentrated on the relationship between corporate strategy and top executive pay. Mr. Weinhold divides his time between being a research associate at the Harvard Business School and being an independent management consultant. He is a graduate of the Massachusetts Institute of Technology's Sloan School of Management and specializes in financial economics. Salter and Weinhold have collaborated in research and course development activities and on advising companies on diversification strategies. This article is taken from their forthcoming book *Diversifying Acquisitions: A Framework for Strategic and Economic Analysis.*

During the past 25 years an increasing proportion of U.S. companies have seen wisdom in pursuing a strategy of diversification. Between 1950 and 1970, for example, single-business companies comprising the *Fortune* "500" declined from 30% to 8% of the total. Acquisition has become a standard approach to diversification.

In recent years the productivity of capital of many multibusiness companies has lagged behind the economy. Nevertheless, diversification through acquisition remains popular; between 1970 and 1975, acquired assets of large manufacturing and mining companies averaged slightly more than 11% of total new investment in those companies, and most of that activity was diversifying acquisition.[1] In the past few years the pace of activity has been slower than in the hectic 1967–1969 period, but the combination of high corporate liquidity, depressed stock prices, and slow economic growth has meant that for many companies acquisitions are among the most attractive investment alternatives. Since mid-1977, hardly a week has gone by without at least one major acquisition being announced by a diversifying corporation.

In light of this continuing interest and the apparent economic risks in following such a strategy, we present a review of the theory of corporate diversification. We begin by discussing seven common misconceptions about diversification through acquisition. We then turn to the basic question facing companies wanting to adopt the strategy: How can

1. Bureau of Economics, Federal Trade Commission, *Statistical Report on Mergers and Acquisitions* (Washington, D.C., November 1976), p. 93.

2. Richard P. Rumelt first articulated this useful definition in his *Strategy, Structure, and Economic Performance* (Boston: Division of Research, Harvard Business School, 1974).

3. William F. Sharpe, *Portfolio Theory and Capital Markets* (New York:

a company create value for its shareholders through diversification?

Our consideration of value creation leads to an examination of the potential benefits of the alternatives available—related-business diversification and unrelated-business diversification. Businesses are related if they (a) serve similar markets and use similar distribution systems, (b) employ similar production technologies, or (c) exploit similar science-based research.[2]

Common misconceptions

There are seven common misconceptions about diversification through acquisition that we can usefully highlight in the context of recent history. They relate to the economic rationale of this strategy and to the management of a successful diversification program.

1. *Acquisitive diversifiers generate larger returns (through increased earnings and capital appreciation) for their shareholders than nondiversifiers do.*

This notion gained a certain currency during the 1960s, in part because of the enormous emphasis that securities analysts and corporate executives placed on growth in earnings per share (EPS). Acquisitive diversifiers that did not collapse at once from ingesting too many businesses often sustained high levels of EPS growth.

However, once it became apparent that a large proportion of this growth was an accounting mirage and that capital productivity was a better indicator of management's performance and a business's economic strength, the market value of many acquisitive companies plunged.

Many widely diversified companies have had low capital productivity in recent years. *Exhibit I* on page 172 shows the performance of a sample originally selected by the Federal Trade Commission in 1969 as representative of companies pursuing strategies of diversification and not classifiable in standard industrial categories. While the average return on equity of the sample was 20% higher than the average of the *Fortune* "500" in 1967, it was 18% below the *Fortune* average in 1975. Even the surge in profits in 1976 and 1977 and the impact of nonoperating, accounting profits in several corporations failed to bring the sample average up to the *Fortune* average. What is even more telling than the return on equity figures is that the sample's return on assets was 20% or more below the *Fortune* "500" average throughout the ten-year period.

So it is not surprising that acquisitive diversifiers have had low price-earnings ratios. On December 31, 1977, the average P/E of the sample, which includes many busy diversifiers, was 30% below that of the New York Stock Exchange stocks as a whole. This discount has changed little over several years. Even high return-on-equity performers like Northwest Industries, Teledyne, and Textron have P/Es well below the market's average.

Such low market values imply great uncertainty about the size and variability of future cash flows. And when they are uncertain about a company's cash flow, investors and stock analysts view them as less valuable than reliable and predictable earnings streams, so they are inclined to discount the company's future earnings heavily. The high discount rates of acquisitive diversifiers produce growth with less capital appreciation than that of nondiversifiers, whose earnings streams appear to be more predictable. What will create value is growing cash flows with little uncertainty about their size or variability.

2. *Unrelated diversification offers shareholders a superior means of reducing their investment risk.*

Unrelated diversification may be attractive from an investor's point of view—its use is frequently offered to justify or defend conglomerate mergers—but it is not a superior means of reducing investment risk. (By *investment risk* we mean the variability of returns over time, *returns* being defined as capital appreciation plus dividends paid to investors.)

According to contemporary financial theory, a security's risk and return can be decomposed into two elements: (1) what is specific to each company and called "unsystematic" because it can be diversified away and (2) what is "systematic" because it is common to all securities (the securities market) and hence nondiversifiable.[3] Since the unsystematic risk of any security can be eliminated through simple portfolio diversification, the investor does not need widely diversified companies like Litton Industries and Gulf & Western Industries to eliminate the risk for him.

Contemporary financial economists believe that prices of securities reflect the consensus of many knowledgeable buyers and sellers concerning a company's prospects. This consensus leads to an efficient capital market, where the investor finds it extremely difficult to consistently make risk-adjusted

Analysis of systematic risk

Since portfolio theory tells us that reducing systematic risk is impossible through portfolio diversification, let us analyze a portfolio of assets against a diversified company's assets similar in size and allocation. This risk analysis requires three kinds of information: (1) the investment composition, by industry, of the diversified company; (2) the size of the investment the company has made in each industry; and (3) the systematic risk of each of those industries.

Summing the industries' systematic risks, weighted by their relative size in the portfolio, results in a measure of the portfolio's systematic risk. The last step before comparing the portfolio's systematic risk with the diversified company's systematic risk is to adjust for differences in financial risk. Once he has done this, the analyst can determine, within statistical limits, whether the diversifying corporation has reduced its systematic risk.

The results of a risk analysis of Gulf & Western Industries, a high return-on-equity performer for over a decade, are presented in *Table A*. An analysis of a comparable portfolio for G&W is given in *Table B*. Both tables reflect a five-year period ending in July 1975. The businesses of G&W's eight divisions overlap very little. Grouping these divisions with Gulf & Western's investment portfolio produces a well-diversified comparable portfolio.

As *Table A* indicates, Gulf & Western's systematic risk, adjusted for financial leverage, differs insignificantly from that of a comparable portfolio. All three systematic risk measurements are within one standard deviation of each other. Whatever benefits Gulf & Western provides its shareholders, reduction of investment risk apparently is not one of them.*

Table A
Portfolio comparison

	Systematic risk (Beta)	Standard deviation
Gulf & Western's portfolio statistics		
Leverage = .37*		
Systematic risk (according to Merrill Lynch, Pierce, Fenner & Smith)	1.15	.20
Systematic risk (according to Value Line)	1.35	.20
Comparison portfolio's statistics		
Weighted average leverage = .30†		
Weighted average systematic risk†	1.15	
Systematic risk when leverage = .37	1.26	.15

*Market value of debt divided by the sum of the market values of debt and equity.
†Taken from *Table B*.

*A more thorough presentation of this method of making a comparative risk analysis is available from the authors at Harvard Business School, Soldiers Field, Boston, Massachusetts 02163.

profits in excess of those the market realizes as a whole. While it does not claim that the price of every security always accurately reflects its underlying (systematic) risk, the theory does suggest that when one views all securities over time, the "overvaluations" and "undervaluations" by the market balance out.[4]

Several researchers have extended this efficient capital market concept to the analysis of conglomerate mergers. Their studies suggest that unrelated corporate diversification has little to offer investors with respect to risk reduction over a diversified portfolio of comparable securities.

They also suggest that if diversified companies cannot increase returns or reduce risks more than comparable portfolios do, these companies can at best offer the investor only value comparable to that of a mutual fund. Indeed, widely diversified companies with systematic risks and returns equivalent to those of a mutual fund may actually be *less* attractive investment vehicles because of their higher management costs and their inability to move into or out of assets as quickly and as cheaply as mutual funds do.[5] For a specific case involving systematic risk, see the ruled insert above comparing Gulf & Western Industries with a portfolio having like assets.

4. For summaries of empirical evidence supporting the efficient market theory, see Eugene F. Fama, "Efficient Capital Markets: A Review of Theory and Empirical Work," *Journal of Finance*, May 1970, p. 383; and Michael C. Jensen, "Capital Markets: Theory and Evidence," *Bell Journal of Economics and Management Science*, Autumn 1972, p. 35.

5. See Keith V. Smith and John C. Shreiner, "A Portfolio Analysis of Conglomerate Diversification," *Journal of Finance*, June 1969, p. 413; J. Fred Weston and Surenda K. Mansinghka, "Tests of Efficiency Performance of Conglomerate Firms," *Journal of Finance*, September 1971, p. 919; and R. Hal Mason and Maurice B. Gondzwaard, "Performance of Conglomerate Firms: A Portfolio Approach," *Journal of Finance*, March 1976, p. 39.

Table B
Systematic risk analysis of a portfolio similar to that of Gulf & Western Industries (dollars in millions)

Group	Standard & Poor's industry category	Industry average: sales/assets	Industry average: debt/assets	G&W's 1974 sales	Assets of a company comparable to G&W group	Debt of a company comparable to G&W group	Comparable company's assets as percentage of portfolio's assets	Industry's systematic risk	Weighted systematic risk of comparable companies in portfolio
Food and agricultural products	Sugar	2.1	.45	$ 175	$ 85	$ 37	4.3%	.6	.026
Natural resources	Lead and zinc	1.2	.1	178	150	15	7.5	.72	.054
Paper and building products	Paper	2.1	.4	405	190	75	9.5	.9	.085
Financial services	Small loan finance	.6	.15	494	446	70	22.4	1.35	.302
Leisure time	Movies	1.8	.3	298	165	50	8.3	1.65	.137
Automotive replacement and parts	Automotive replacement and parts	3.0	.1	225	75	7	3.8	1.7	.063
Consumer products	Tobacco	2.1	.3	212	100	30	5.0	.85	.042
Manufacturing	Automotive OEM	2.3	.3	327	140	45	7.0	1.25	.104
	Capital goods: machinery	1.8	.25	285	160	40	8.0	1.3	.068
	Electrical	2.0	.2	195	100	20	5.0	1.3	.088
Operating group's total				$2,794	$1,611	$389	80.8%		.969
Intangibles					100		5.0	.969*	.048
Investments					284	211	14.2	.95	.135
Total					$1,995†	$600	100.0%		1.15

*Intangibles arise from an excess investment over the equity acquired. Its risk matches that of the underlying assets (operating portfolio).

†G&W's 1974 annual report listed this investment as $1,983 million (within 1% of the comparison portfolio).

3. *Adding countercyclical businesses to a company's portfolio leads to a stabilized earnings stream and a heightened valuation by the marketplace.*

This misconception is an extension of the previous one. For decades, proponents of unrelated or conglomerate diversification have argued that when a company diversifies into an industry with a business cycle or a set of economic risks different from its own, it enhances the "safety" of its income stream. In essence, this sense of safety is a very simple form of the "risk pooling" concept underlying insurance.

In light of the poor performance of many diversified companies, it should be obvious that safety is difficult to attain. Because of the complex interactions of the U.S. and other nations' economies, finding genuinely countercyclical businesses is very hard. At the most, there are industry cycles that

either lead or lag behind the general economy (e.g., housing and capital goods, respectively) or that are less cyclical than the general economy (e.g., consumer goods and tobacco products).

Even if diversifying companies can identify the countercyclical businesses, diversifiers find it difficult to construct balanced portfolios of businesses whose variable returns balance one another. Moreover, inasmuch as businesses grow at various rates, widely diversified companies face the continual challenge of rebalancing their business portfolios through very selective acquisitions.

Quite apart from this argument, the low stock market values of widely diversified companies during the past eight years indicate that the marketplace has heavily discounted the future cash returns to investors in companies consisting of purportedly countercyclical businesses. While there are undoubtedly many reasons for this situation, it suggests that the market may be more interested in growth and the productivity of invested capital than in earnings stability per se. In addition, investors have little incentive to bid up the prices of diversified companies since an investor can obtain the benefits of stabilizing an income stream through simple portfolio diversification.

4. *Related diversification is always safer than unrelated diversification.*

This misconception rests on the notion of corporate executives that they reduce their operating risks when they stick to buying businesses they think they understand. They want to limit their diversification to businesses with similar marketing and distribution characteristics, similar production technologies, or similar science-based R&D efforts.

While this presumption often has merit, making related acquisitions does not guarantee results superior to those stemming from unrelated diversification. For example, Xerox's entry into data processing via its acquisition of Scientific Data Systems, which Xerox justified on the ground of technological, marketing, and manufacturing compatibility, led to a great drain on earnings for years. The management of Singer decided to take advantage of the company's competence in electromechanical manufacturing as the basis for its diversification program. The result was dramatic failure, leading to a $500 million write-off of assets.

A close reading of the Xerox and Singer cases suggests that successful related diversification depends on both the quality of the acquired business and the organizational integration required to achieve the possible benefits of companies exchanging their skills and resources. Such exchange has been called *synergy*.

Even more important, the perceived relatedness must be real, and the merger must give the partners a competitive advantage. Unless these conditions are met, related diversification cannot be justified as superior or even comparable to unrelated diversification as a means of reducing operating risks or increasing earnings.

5. *A strong management team at the acquired company ensures realization of the potential benefits of diversification.*

Many companies try to limit their pool of acquisition candidates to well-managed companies. This policy is rarely the necessary condition for gaining the potential benefits of diversification.

As we shall stress later in this article, the potential benefits of related diversification stem from augmenting the effective use of the surviving company's core skills and resources. Usually such improvement requires an exchange of core skills and resources among the partners. The benefits of unrelated diversification are rooted in two conditions: (1) increased efficiency in cash management and in allocation of investment capital and (2) the capability to call on profitable, low-growth businesses to provide the cash flow for high-growth businesses that require significant infusions of cash.

Whether pursuing related or unrelated diversification, it is often the acquiring company's management skills and resources—not those of the acquired company—that are critical to achieving the potential benefits of diversification. Indeed, if the acquired company is well managed and priced accordingly by the capital market, the acquirer must exploit the potential synergies with the acquiree to make the transaction economically justifiable.

6. *The diversified company is uniquely qualified to improve the performance of acquired businesses.*

During the height of the merger and acquisition activity of the 1960s, executives of conglomerates often argued that they could improve the profitability of acquired companies by "modernizing" administrative practices and exerting more operating discipline than that demanded by the marketplace.

Consider the testimony of Harold S. Geneen, then chairman and president of International Telephone & Telegraph Corporation, at a government hearing concerning how ITT provided "constructive bases for merger."

"We can afford to price fairly," Geneen said, "and to exchange our own equity stocks with the shareholders of an incoming company. We can improve operating efficiencies and profits sufficiently to make this valuation worthwhile to both sets of shareholders." In a document outlining ITT's acquisition philosophy and submitted to the hearing, Geneen wrote that from 1960 to 1965 the company had "developed the ability through management skills, routines, and techniques to set and progressively meet higher competitive standards and achieve them in practically every line and product that we have undertaken."[6]

The claims that Geneen and many other successful diversifiers have invoked are not benefits of diversification per se but simply the benefits of that nebulous factor, "good management." Single-business companies pursuing vertical integration or horizontal expansion through acquisition can achieve identical results. To gain the benefits Geneen claimed, a company needs only to allow managers with the requisite skills to implement their desired improvements in the organization.

Rarely, it may be argued, does an organization willingly take steps that could alter its traditional administrative and managerial practices. Under these circumstances, change will occur only when forced from the outside, and diversifying companies often represent such a force. Nevertheless, the benefits achieved are not, strictly speaking, benefits of diversification.

7. *Great deals are made by professional "deal makers."*

The most potentially dangerous misconception on our list is the one that credits the imaginative work of investment bankers and other brokers with the success of a diversifying acquisition. The investment banker's role is to provide attractive ideas, but it is the company's role to select the ideas that have the greatest strategic and economic value.

This role involves developing diversification objectives and acquisition guidelines that fit a carefully prepared concept of the corporation. It also involves the company's ability to recognize and exploit the potential for creating value through diversifying acquisitions. Every experienced corporate diversifier has learned, often painfully, that he must live with an acquisition long after it has ceased being a "great deal."

Ways to create value

A company following a diversification strategy can create value for its shareholders only when the combination of the skills and resources of the two businesses satisfies at least one of the following conditions:

☐ An income stream greater than what could be realized from a portfolio investment in the two companies.

☐ A reduction in the variability of the income stream greater than what could be realized from a portfolio investment in the two businesses—that is, reduced systematic risk.

6. Hearings before the Antitrust Subcommittee of the Committee of the Judiciary, U.S. House of Representatives, November 20, 1969.

Included in both conditions is explicit comparison of corporate diversification on the shareholder's behalf with independent portfolio diversification on the investor's part. This comparison deserves comment.

Most benefits derived from reducing unsystematic corporate risk through diversification are, of course, equally available to the individual investor. Diversified companies can achieve trade-offs between total risk and return that are superior to the trade-offs available to single-business companies. Diversified companies cannot create value for their stockholders merely by diversifying away unsystematic risk.

Inasmuch as investors can diversify away unsystematic risk themselves, in efficient capital markets unsystematic risk is irrelevant in the equity valuation process. A diversifying company can create value for its shareholders only when its risk-return trade-offs include benefits unavailable through simple portfolio diversification.

There are seven principal ways in which acquisition-minded companies can obtain returns greater than those obtainable from simple portfolio diversification. The first four are particularly relevant to related diversification, while the last three are more relevant to unrelated diversification.

1. *A diversifying acquisition can raise the productivity of capital when the particular skills and one merger partner's knowledge of the industry are applied to the competitive problems and opportunities facing the other partner.*

When the reinforcement of skills and resources critical to the success of a business within the combined company leads to higher profitability, value is created for its shareholders. This reinforcement is the realization of synergy.

The acquisition by Heublein, Inc. of United Vintners in 1968 is a good case in point. Heublein's strategy during the 1960s was to obtain high margins in marketing liquor and specialty food products through intensive, innovative advertising. At the time, Heublein stood out in this respect because the industry was production- and distribution-oriented. The company's liquor products division accounted for more than 80% of 1965 sales. Its principal product was the premium-priced Smirnoff vodka, the fourth largest and fastest growing liquor brand in the United States.

The 1968 acquisition of United Vintners, the marketing arm of a large grape growers' cooperative that owned two of California's best-known wine brands, gave Heublein the opportunity to raise its investment in an industry where it had some experi-

Exhibit I
Performance data of 36 diversified manufacturers (1967, 1973, 1975, 1977)

Company	1967 Year-end total assets (in millions of dollars)	1967 Return on assets	1967 Return on equity	1973 Year-end total assets (in millions of dollars)	1973 Return on assets	1973 Return on equity
Avco	$1,618.5	3.4%	14.7%	$1,412.2	(1.3)%	(3.6)%
Bangor Punta	144.4	4.0	13.6	328.1	0.5	1.3
Bendix	833.4	5.5	11.3	1,427.0	4.1	11.1
Boise Cascade	865.2	3.3	11.3	1,585.4	9.0*	21.1*
City Investing	338.9	4.0	18.5	3,622.8	2.0	10.3
Colt Industries	197.1	6.1	16.7	266.0	4.0	10.0
FMC	931.8	6.6	13.6	680.5	5.7	11.6
GAF	473.5	4.1	6.9	627.0	4.6	8.7
General Tire	741.7	4.1	8.4	1,233.9	6.2	12.9
W.R. Grace	1,578.4	3.4	8.6	2,003.8	4.2	11.3
Gulf & Western	749.4	6.4	26.8	2,364.1	3.8	13.4
ICI	865.5	2.3	4.0	1,736.6	3.0	6.0
ITT	2,961.2	4.0	11.4	10,133.0	5.2	14.1
Walter Kidde	253.1	7.0	14.7	739.5	5.1	12.5
Koppers	326.5	4.3	7.7	520.3	5.7	11.2
LTV	845.1	4.8	18.3	1,829.1	2.7*	23.7*
Litton	945.0	7.4	19.0	2,116.2	2.0	5.2
Martin Marietta	527.2	7.0	11.9	1,074.0	5.3	11.4
3M	1,034.7	14.2	19.9	2,280.9	13.0	20.6
NL Industries	576.4	8.9	13.4	987.8	4.8	10.9
Northwest Industries	1,286.3	3.0	6.0	964.8	5.9*	13.4*
Norton Simon	463.8	3.3	6.7	1,120.0	7.0	15.5
Ogden	381.7	5.3	14.1	713.6	3.7	12.9
Rapid-American	337.8	4.8	14.9	1,755.5	1.7	13.7
SCM	451.4	5.6	19.7	552.7	3.3	7.8
Signal	1,090.3	4.5	9.1	1,378.1	4.2	8.7
Singer	1,049.2	4.8	11.1	1,897.0	5.0	11.9
Sperry Rand	1,095.2	5.9	11.9	1,840.6	4.9	10.6
Studebaker-Worthington	561.0	5.9	12.1	995.1	3.3	10.5
TRW	710.9	7.6	17.3	1,446.1	6.6	15.1
Teledyne	337.7	6.4	15.8	1,229.6	5.3	12.6
Tenneco	3,589.3	4.1	11.8	5,127.3	4.5	12.3
Textron	669.7	9.2	20.4	1,310.4	7.7	16.1
U.S. Industries	162.3	7.4	20.5	1,033.5	6.5	12.7
White Consolidated	277.3	3.8	14.7	597.4	5.9	15.1
Whittaker	118.0	7.4	29.3	589.4	(1.0)*	(3.3)*
Sample average		5.3	13.9		4.0	12.2
Fortune "500"		7.8	11.7		5.0	12.4

Criteria for the selection of companies in the Federal Trade Commission sample:
(a) Each company in 1969 had total assets of $250 million or more.
(b) Each company had 50% or more of its total sales derived from manufactured products.
(c) Each company had less than 50% of its total sales in any one industry and was engaged in three or more product lines.
*Extraordinary items included.

1975				1977			
Year-end total assets (in millions of dollars)	Return on assets	Return on equity		Year-end total assets (in millions of dollars)	Return on assets	Return on equity	EPS growth rate (1967-1977)
$1,250.4	4.9%*	12.1%*		$4,125.6	2.8%*	18.6%*	3.6%
234.9	3.6	8.7		395.4	4.6	13.9	2.1
1,567.6	5.1	11.1		1,810.6	6.5	14.1	7.7
1,569.5	4.1	7.5		1,799.0	6.4	12.1	7.8
3,938.0	0.8	5.0		4,721.0	1.8	10.2	14.7
866.3	6.0	14.8		1,112.2	6.3	13.8	9.3
1,843.9	5.9	13.7		2,141.5	5.6	12.7	6.8
705.4	4.4	8.4		762.4	(6.2)	(14.2)	—
1,427.3	4.4	9.1		1,587.3	7.3	13.3	12.9
2,523.8	6.6	18.8		2,941.0	4.8	11.4	3.0
3,305.7	4.2	17.5		4,159.1	3.6	12.2	8.0
2,241.7	2.2	5.3		2,613.2	3.0	7.1	6.5
10,408.0	3.8	9.6		12,285.5	4.5	10.7	4.8
854.9	5.1	12.3		1,107.2	5.1	11.0	3.2
679.7	8.9	17.6		851.9	7.8	14.1	14.2
1,962.8	0.7	3.9		2,067.0	(1.9)*	(10.1)*	—
2,185.7	1.6	4.4		2,063.8	2.7	6.5	(4.1)
1,139.0	4.9	9.4		1,376.8	7.4	14.1	8.5
3,016.8	8.7	15.0		3,529.6	11.7	18.2	10.0
1,059.5	4.3	9.1		1,325.8	5.0	9.4	(1.2)
1,184.1	8.6	18.6		1,764.6	7.3	18.2	13.4
1,355.7	6.1	11.9		1,487.2	6.9	12.4	12.9
926.0	5.1	14.8		1,021.7	4.9	15.4	6.1
1,481.0	(0.6)	(4.9)		1,485.3	3.2*	22.5*	7.8
704.1	4.0	10.1		767.9	4.9	10.9	0.0
1,866.8	2.2	5.3		2,152.8	4.7	11.6	6.0
1,797.1	(25.2)	(96.0)		1,461.9	6.5*	20.6*	0.8
2,533.1	5.2	12.9		2,841.5	5.5	12.1	10.1
883.6	3.4	9.1		915.2	7.6	15.5	12.1
1,686.5	6.2	14.1		2,056.7	7.5	16.7	8.0
1,141.9	8.9	20.5		1,420.1	13.7	28.4	32.3
6,584.2	5.2	15.0		8,278.3	5.2	13.9	8.4
1,433.3	6.7	13.1		1,738.3	7.9	14.8	5.5
941.7	1.1	2.1		837.4	5.1	8.4	(3.8)
858.2	5.5	16.0		934.2	5.9	15.5	13.1
508.9	0.6	1.6		481.2	3.3	9.7	1.6
	3.6	9.5			5.3	12.4	
	5.7	11.6			6.5	13.3	

Exhibit II
Relationship between cash used and cash generated by business areas of Genstar, 1971-1974

Area	Cash use ratio*
Building supplies	1.01
Cement	.31
Housing and land development	1.72
Construction	1.67
Chemicals and fertilizers	.38
Marine activities	1.87
Imports and exports	.46
Investments	.52
Total for the company	1.02

* The cash use ratio is cash used divided by cash generated. A business area's cash use ratio is determined by comparing its cash used with its cash generated. A cash use ratio higher than 1 indicates that the business area is a net cash user, while a ratio of less than 1 indicates a net cash generator. Cash generated is defined as net income after tax plus depreciation and deferred tax.

ence (it was the U.S. distributor for Lancers wine) and to extend the application of its proven skills in promoting specialty products. By identifying and then exploiting an emerging consumer preference for lighter-bodied, often slightly flavored products, Heublein helped United Vintners launch two new products—Cold Duck (a champagne-sparkling burgundy combination) and Bali Hai (a fruit-flavored wine).

By the end of 1969, one year after its acquisition of United Vintners, Heublein had increased sales by over 2.5 million cases and augmented the subsidiary's profitability. Heublein's marketing strategy was so successful that during the 1960s and early 1970s its return on equity averaged over 30% and the marketplace valued Heublein at over 35 times its earnings. Heublein discovered in its diversification efforts, however, that its strategy of aggressive advertising was not the key success factor in either brewing (Hamm's beer) or fast foods (Kentucky Fried Chicken), and its market valuation suffered accordingly. By 1977, Heublein had seen its P/E fall to 10 and its stock price to one-third of its previous high.

2. *Investments in markets closely related to current fields of operation can reduce long-run average costs.*

A reduction in average costs can accrue from scale effects, rationalization of production and other managerial efforts, and technological innovation. For example, a marketing department's budget as a percent of sales will decline if existing resources can be used to market new or related products.

Similarly, a large company like Procter & Gamble can expect its per-unit distribution costs to decline when it augments the use of its existing distribution system to move products to the marketplace. This notion has been the basis of many acquisitions made by consumer products companies.

3. *Business expansion in an area of competence can lead to the generation of a "critical mass" of resources necessary to outperform the competition.*

In many industries, companies have to achieve a certain size, or critical mass, before they can compete effectively with their competitors.

For example, the principal way many small laboratory instrumentation companies hope to offer sustained competition against such entrenched companies as Hewlett-Packard, Tektronix, Beckman Instruments, and Technicon is to attain a size giving them sufficient cash flow to underwrite competitive research and development programs. One way to reach this size is to make closely related diversifying acquisitions.

4. *Diversification into related product markets can enable a company to reduce systematic risks.*

Many of the possibilities for reducing risk through diversification are implicit in the previous three ways to increase returns because risk and return are closely related measurements. However, diversifying by acquiring a company in a related product market can enable a company to reduce its technological, production, or marketing risks. If these reduced business risks can be translated into a less variable income stream for the company, value is created.

Although there is no evidence that General Motors' strategy was developed with this notion in mind, an important result of GM's diversification within the motor vehicle industry has been its ability to easily absorb changes in demand for any one automotive product. GM's extensive related-product line reduces the company's marketing risk and enables GM's managers to concentrate on production efficiencies. As a result, GM's income stream tends to be less volatile than those of its competitors and of portfolios of discrete investments in unassociated, though automotive-related, companies.

5. *The diversified company can route cash from units operating with a surplus to units operating with a deficit and can thereby reduce the need of individual businesses to purchase working capital funds from outside sources.*

Through centralizing cash balances, corporate headquarters can act as the banker for its operating subsidiaries and can thus balance the cyclical working capital requirements of its divisions as the economy progresses through a business cycle or as its divisions experience seasonal fluctuations. This type of working capital management is, of course, an operating benefit completely separate from the recycling of cash on an investment basis.

6. *Managers of a diversified company can direct its currently high net cash flow businesses to transfer investment funds to the businesses in which net cash flow is zero or negative but in which management expects positive cash flow to develop. The aim is to improve the long-run profitability of the corporation.*

This potential benefit is a by-product of the U.S. tax code, which imposes double taxation of dividends—once via corporate profits taxes and once via personal income taxes. By reinvesting its surplus cash flow, the company defers taxes that stockholders otherwise would have to pay on the company's dividends.

In November 1975, Genstar, Ltd. of Canada justified this way of creating value in a submission to the Royal Commission on Corporate Concentration. There Genstar argued that the well-managed, widely diversified company can call on its low-growth businesses to maximize net cash flow and profits in order to enable it to reallocate funds to the high-growth businesses needing investment. By so doing, the company will eventually reap benefits via a higher ROI and the public will benefit via lower costs and, presumably, via lower prices.

As *Exhibit II* shows, two of Genstar's major business areas—cement as well as chemicals and fertilizers—used far less cash (for working capital and reinvestment) in 1971–1974 than they generated (*cash generated* being defined as net income after taxes plus depreciation and deferred taxes). Genstar recycled the excess cash flow into its housing and land development, construction, and marine activities. So Genstar was able not only to employ its assets more productively than before but also to reap economic benefits beyond those possible from a comparable securities portfolio.

Genstar's argument for cross-subsidization has an important extension. Diversified companies have access to information that is often unavailable to the investment community. This information is the internally generated market data about each industry in which it operates, data that include information about the competitive position and potential of each company in the industry.

With this inside information, diversified enterprises can enjoy a significantly better position in assessing the investment merits of particular projects and entire industries than individual investors can. Such access enables the companies to choose the most attractive projects and thereby to allocate capital among "their" industries more efficiently than the capital markets can.

7. *Through risk pooling, the diversified company can lower its cost of debt and leverage itself more than its nondiversified equivalent. The company's total cost of capital thereby goes down and provides stockholders with returns in excess of those available from a comparable portfolio of securities.*

As the number of businesses in the portfolio of an unrelated diversifier grows and the overall variability of its operating income or cash flow declines, its standing as a credit risk should rise. Because the company pools its own divisions' risks and supports any component threatened with bankruptcy, theoretically (at least) the company should have a some-

Exhibit III
Potential benefits of diversification

	Related-business diversification	Unrelated-business diversification
Product-market orientation	Diversification into business with similar marketing and distribution characteristics, similar production technologies, or similar science-based research activities.	Diversification into product markets with key success variables unrelated to the key success variables of the acquirer's principal business.
Transferable resources	Operating and/or functional skills; excess capacity in distribution systems, production facilities, or research operations.	General management skills; surplus financial resources.
Nature of potential benefits	Increased productivity of corporate resources through operating synergy, improved competitive position accruing from greater size of business and lower long-run average costs, all leading to reduction in the variability of the income stream and/or a larger income stream than that available from simple portfolio diversification.	Efficient cash management and allocation of investment capital, reduced cost of debt capital, and growth in profits through cross-subsidization, all leading to a larger income stream than that available from simple portfolio diversification; unlikely reduction of systematic (market-related) risk.
Relative ease of achieving potential benefits	Difficult because of organizational problems associated with integrating formerly self-sufficient companies into the acquiring company.	Easy-to-achieve capital efficiencies and benefits from cross-subsidization.

what lower cost of debt than that of companies unable to pool their risks. More important, the reduced variability of the diversified company's cash flow improves its ability to borrow.

This superior financial leverage enables the corporation's shareholders to shift some risk to government and thereby reduce the company's total cost of capital. (Since interest, in contrast to dividends, is tax deductible, the government shoulders part of the cost of debt capitalization in a business venture.) These benefits become significant, however, only when the enterprise aggressively manages its financial risks by employing a high debt-equity ratio or by operating several very risky, unrelated projects in its portfolio of businesses.

While this type of company can enjoy a lower cost of capital than a less diversified company of comparable size, it can also have a higher cost of *equity* capital than the other type. This possibility stems from the fact that part of the financial risk of debt capitalization is borne by the equity owners. In addition, investors' perceptions of risk are not solely conditioned by the degree of diversification in corporate assets. Indeed, the professional investor may be unwilling to lower the rate of return on equity capital just because a company has acquired a well-balanced or purportedly countercyclical collection of businesses.

The risks and opportunities the investor perceives for a company greatly depend on the amount and clarity of information that he or she can effectively process. As a company becomes more diversified, its business can become less clearly defined and its investors' uncertainty about its risks and opportunities can rise. The greater this uncertainty, of course, the higher the risk premium the equity investor demands and the higher the company's cost of equity capital becomes.

The most significant benefits to the stockholder occur in related diversification when the special skills and industry knowledge of one merger partner apply to the competitive problems and opportunities facing the other. Shareholders' benefits from unrelated or conglomerate diversification can occur where more efficient capital and asset management leads to a better return for investors than that available from a diversified portfolio of securities of comparable systematic risk. *Exhibit III* summarizes the benefits that are attainable from the two types of diversification.

Unfortunately, the benefits that offer the greatest potential are usually the ones least likely to be implemented. Of the synergies usually identified to justify an acquisition, financial synergies are often unnoted while operating synergies are widely trumpeted. Yet our experience has been that the benefits most commonly achieved are those in the financial area.

It is not hard to understand why. Most managers would agree that the greatest impediment to change is the inflexibility of the organization. The realization of operating benefits accompanying diversification usually requires significant changes in the company's format and administrative behavior. These changes are usually slow to come; and so are the accompanying benefits.

Nevertheless, diversification does offer potentially significant benefits to the corporation and its shareholders. When a company has the ability to export or import surplus skills or resources useful in its competitive environment, related diversification is an attractive strategic option. When a company possesses the skills and resources to analyze and manage the strategies of widely different businesses, unrelated diversification can be the best strategic option. Finally, when a diversifying company has both of these abilities, choosing a workable strategy will depend on the personal skills and inclinations of its top managers.

Reprint 78408

Diversification strategies

An unrelated-business diversifier is a company pursuing growth in product markets where the main success factors are unrelated to each other. Such a company, whether a conglomerate or simply a holding company, expects little or no transfer of functional skills among its various businesses. In contrast, a related-business diversifier uses its skills in a specific functional activity or product market as a basis for branching out.

Strategic analysis for more profitable acquisitions

A seller's market demands more careful evaluation than ever before

Alfred Rappaport

As more and more corporations see acquisitions and mergers as an important part of their growth strategy, the acquisitions market has become intensely competitive, and buyers are paying a substantial premium for target companies. This author describes a framework for acquisitions analysis that evaluates both the buying and the selling company and helps the buyer decide, among other things, the maximum price he should pay for a particular company as well as the best way to finance the acquisition.

Mr. Rappaport is the Leonard Spacek Professor of Accounting and Information Systems and director of the Accounting Research Center at the Graduate School of Management, Northwestern University. He is consulting editor for Prentice-Hall's Contemporary Topics in Accounting Series and is currently serving on the Financial Accounting Standards Board's Task Force on Funds Flow and Liquidity. He is a consultant to corporations on financial control systems and merger and acquisition analysis.

Less than a decade after the frantic merger activity of the late 1960s, we are again in the midst of a major wave of corporate acquisitions. In contrast to the 1960s, when acquirers were mainly freewheeling conglomerates, the merger movement in the 1970s includes such long-established giants of U.S. industry as General Electric, Gulf Oil, and Kennecott Copper. Because of the decline in the value of the dollar and the greater political stability of the United States, foreign companies also have become increasingly active buyers of U.S. companies during the past few years.

Most acquisitions are accomplished with cash today, rather than with packages of securities as was common in the 1960s. Finally, the current merger movement involves the frequent use of tender offers that often lead to contested bids and to the payment of substantial premiums above the premerger market value of the target company. In 1978, cash tender offer premiums averaged more than 70% above premerger market values.

The popular explanation for the recent merger rage is that the market is "undervaluing" many solid companies, thus making it substantially cheaper to buy rather than to build. Couple this belief with the fact that many corporations are enjoying relatively strong cash positions and the widely held view that government regulation and increased uncertainty about the economy make internal growth strategies relatively unattractive, and we see why mergers and acquisitions have become an increasingly important part of corporate growth strategy.

Despite all of the foregoing rationale, more than a few of the recent acquisitions will fail to create value for the acquirer's shareholders. After all, shareholder value depends not on premerger market valuation of the target company but on the actual acquisition price the acquiring company pays compared with the selling company's cash flow contribution to the combined company.

Only a limited supply of acquisition candidates is available at the price that enables the acquirer to earn an acceptable return on investment. A well-conceived financial evaluation program that minimizes the risk of buying an economically unattractive company or paying too much for an attractive one is particularly important in today's seller's market. The dramatic increase in premiums that must be paid by a company bidding successfully calls for more careful analysis by buyers than ever before.

Because of the competitive nature of the acquisition market, companies not only need to respond wisely but often must respond quickly as well. The growing independence of corporate boards and their demand for better information to support strategic decisions such as acquisitions have raised the general standard for acquisition analysis. Finally, sound analysis convincingly communicated can yield substantial benefits in negotiating with the target company's management or, in the case of tender offers, its stockholders.

Malcolm S. Salter and Wolf A. Weinhold outlined seven principal ways in which companies can create value for their shareholders via acquisition.[1] In this article, I will show how management can estimate how much value a prospective acquisition will in fact create. In brief, I will present a comprehensive framework for acquisition analysis based on contemporary financial theory—an approach that has been profitably employed in practice. The analysis provides management and the board of the acquiring company with information both to make a decision on the candidate and to formulate an effective negotiating strategy for the acquisition.

Steps in the analysis

The process of analyzing acquisitions falls broadly into three stages: planning, search and screen, and financial evaluation.

The acquisition planning process begins with a review of corporate objectives and product-market strategies for various strategic business units. The acquiring company should define its potential directions for corporate growth and diversification in terms of corporate strengths and weaknesses and an assessment of the company's social, economic, political, and technological environment. This analysis produces a set of acquisition objectives and criteria.

Specified criteria often include statements about industry parameters, such as projected market growth rate, degree of regulation, ease of entry, and capital versus labor intensity. Company criteria for quality of management, share of market, profitability, size, and capital structure also commonly appear in acquisition criteria lists.

The search and screen process is a systematic approach to compiling a list of good acquisition prospects. The search focuses on how and where to look for candidates, and the screening process selects a few of the best candidates from literally thousands of possibilities according to objectives and criteria developed in the planning phase.

Finally comes the financial evaluation process, which is the focus of this article. A good analysis should enable management to answer such questions as:

> What is the maximum price that should be paid for the target company?

> What are the principal areas of risk?

> What are the earnings, cash flow, and balance sheet implications of the acquisition?

> What is the best way of financing the acquisition?

Corporate self-evaluation

The financial evaluation process involves both a self-evaluation by the acquiring company and the evaluation of the candidate for acquisition. While it is possible to conduct an evaluation of the target company without an in-depth self-evaluation first, in general this is the most advantageous approach.[2] The scope and detail of corporate self-evaluation will necessarily vary according to the needs of each company.

Two fundamental questions posed by a self-evaluation are: (1) How much is my company worth? (2) How would its value be affected by each of several scenarios? The first question involves generating a "most likely" estimate of the company's value based on management's detailed assessment of its objectives, strategies, and plans. The second question calls for an assessment of value based on the range of plausible scenarios that enable management to test the joint effect of hypothesized combinations of product-market strategies and environmental forces.

Corporate self-evaluation viewed as an economic assessment of the value created for shareholders by various strategic planning options promises potential benefits for all companies. In the context of the acquisition market, self-evaluation takes on special significance.

First, while a company might view itself as an acquirer, few companies are totally exempt from a possible takeover. During 1978 alone, 80 acquisitions exceeding $100 million were announced. The recent roster of acquired companies includes such names as Anaconda, Utah International, Babcock & Wilcox, Seven Up, Pet, Carborundum, and Del Monte. Self-evaluation provides management and the board with a continuing basis for responding to tender offers or acquisition inquiries responsibly and quickly. Second, the self-evaluation process might well call attention to strategic divestment opportunities. Finally, self-evaluation provides acquisition-minded companies a basis for assessing the comparative advantages of a cash versus an exchange-of-shares offer.

Acquiring companies commonly value the purchase price for an acquisition at the market value of the shares exchanged. This practice is not economically sound and could be misleading and costly to the acquiring company. A well-conceived analysis for an exchange-of-shares acquisition requires sound valuations of *both* buying and selling companies. If the acquirer's management believes the market is undervaluing its shares, then valuing the purchase price at market might well induce the company to overpay for the acquisition or to earn less than the minimum acceptable rate of return.

Conversely, if management believes the market is overvaluing its shares, then valuing the purchase price at market obscures the opportunity of offering the seller's shareholders additional shares while still achieving the minimum acceptable return.

Valuation of acquisitions

Recently *Business Week* reported that as many as half of the major acquisition-minded companies are relying extensively on the discounted cash flow (DCF) technique to analyze acquisitions.[3] While mergers and acquisitions involve a considerably

more complex set of managerial problems than the purchase of an ordinary asset such as a machine or a plant, the economic substance of these transactions is the same. In each case, there is a current outlay made in anticipation of a stream of future cash flows.

Thus the DCF criterion applies not only to internal growth investments, such as additions to existing capacity, but equally to external growth investments, such as acquisitions. An essential feature of the DCF technique is that it explicitly takes into account that a dollar of cash received today is worth more than a dollar received a year from now, because today's dollar can be invested to earn a return during the intervening time.

To establish the maximum acceptable acquisition price under the DCF approach, estimates are needed for (1) the incremental cash flows expected to be generated because of the acquisition and (2) the cost of capital—that is, the minimum acceptable rate of return required by the market for new investments by the company.

In projecting the cash flow stream of a prospective acquisition, what should be taken into account is the cash flow contribution the candidate is expected to make to the acquiring company. The results of this projection may well differ from a projection of the candidate's cash flow as an independent company. This is so because the acquirer may be able to achieve operating economies not available to the selling company alone. Furthermore, acquisitions generally provide new postacquisition investment opportunities whose initial outlays and subsequent benefits also need to be incorporated in the cash flow schedule. Cash flow is defined as:

(earnings before interest and taxes [EBIT]) $\times$ (1-income tax rate) + depreciation and other noncash charges − capital expenditures − cash required for increase in net working capital

In developing the cash flow schedule, two additional issues need to be considered: (1) What is the basis for setting the horizon date—that is, the date beyond which the cash flows associated with the acquisition are not specifically projected? (2) How is the residual value of the acquisition established at the horizon date?

A common practice is to forecast cash flows period by period until the level of uncertainty makes management too "uncomfortable" to go any farther. While practice varies with industry setting, management policy, and the special circumstances of the acquisition, five or ten years appears to be an arbitrarily set forecasting duration used in many

1. Malcolm S. Salter and Wolf A. Weinhold, "Diversification via Acquisition: Creating Value," HBR July-August 1978, p. 166.

2. For a more detailed description on how to conduct a corporate self-evaluation, see my article, "Do You Know the Value of Your Company?" *Mergers and Acquisitions*, Spring 1979.

3. "The Cash-Flow Takeover Formula," *Business Week*, December 18, 1978, p. 86.

Exhibit I
One company's average cost of capital

	Weight	Cost	Weighted cost
Debt	.20	.05	.01
Equity	.80	.15	.12
Average cost of capital			.13

Exhibit II
Premerger financial statements for Alcar and Rano (in millions of dollars)

Statement of income (year ended December 31)

	Alcar	Rano
Sales	$600.00	$50.00
Operating expenses	522.00	42.50
EBIT	78.00	7.50
Interest on debt	4.50	.40
Earnings before taxes	73.50	7.10
Income taxes	36.00	3.55
Net income	$37.50	$3.55
Number of common shares outstanding (in millions)	10.00	1.11
Earnings per share	$3.75	$3.20
Dividends per share	1.30	.64

Statement of financial position (at year-end)

Net working capital	$180.00	$7.50
Temporary investments	25.00	1.00
Other assets	2.00	1.60
Fixed assets	216.00	20.00
Less accumulated depreciation	(95.00)	(8.00)
	$328.00	$22.10
Interest-bearing debt	$56.00	$5.10
Shareholders' equity	272.00	17.00
	$328.00	$22.10

situations. A better approach suggests that the forecast duration for cash flows should continue only as long as the expected rate of return on incremental investment required to support forecasted sales growth exceeds the cost-of-capital rate.

If for subsequent periods one assumes that the company's return on incremental investment equals the cost-of-capital rate, then the market would be indifferent whether management invests earnings in expansion projects or pays cash dividends that

shareholders can in turn invest in identically risky opportunities yielding an identical rate of return. In other words, the value of the company is unaffected by growth when the company is investing in projects earning at the cost of capital or at the minimum acceptable risk-adjusted rate of return required by the market.

Thus, for purposes of simplification, we can assume a 100% payout of earnings after the horizon date or, equivalently, a zero growth rate without affecting the valuation of the company. (An implied assumption of this model is that the depreciation tax shield can be invested to maintain the company's productive capacity.) The residual value is then the present value of the resulting cash flow perpetuity beginning one year after the horizon date. Of course, if after the horizon date the return on investment is expected to decline below the cost-of-capital rate, this factor can be incorporated in the calculation.

When the acquisition candidate's risk is judged to be the same as the acquirer's overall risk, the appropriate rate for discounting the candidate's cash flow stream is the acquirer's cost of capital. The cost of capital or the minimum acceptable rate of return on new investments is based on the rate investors can expect to earn by investing in alternative, identically risky securities.

The cost of capital is calculated as the weighted average of the costs of debt and equity capital. For example, suppose a company's aftertax cost of debt is 5% and it estimates its cost of equity to be 15%. Further, it plans to raise future capital in the following proportions—20% by way of debt and 80% by equity. *Exhibit I* shows how to compute the company's average cost.

It is important to emphasize that the acquiring company's use of its own cost of capital to discount the target's projected cash flows is appropriate only when it can be safely assumed that the acquisition will not affect the riskiness of the acquirer. The specific riskiness of each prospective candidate should be taken into account in setting the discount rate, with higher rates used for more risky investments.

If a single discount rate is used for all acquisitions, then those with the highest risk will seem most attractive. Because the weighted average risk of its component segments determines the company's cost of capital, these high-risk acquisitions will increase a company's cost of capital and thereby decrease the value of its stock.

Case of Alcar Corporation

As an illustration of the recommended approach to acquisition analysis, consider the case of Alcar Corporation's interest in acquiring Rano Products. Alcar is a leading manufacturer and distributor in the industrial packaging and materials handling market. Sales in 1978 totaled $600 million. Alcar's acquisition strategy is geared toward buying companies with either similar marketing and distribution characteristics, similar production technologies, or a similar research and development orientation. Rano Products, a $50 million sales organization with an impressive new-product development record in industrial packaging, fits Alcar's general acquisition criteria particularly well. Premerger financial statements for Alcar and Rano are shown in *Exhibit II.*

Acquisition for cash

The interactive computer model for corporate planning and acquisition analysis used in the Alcar evaluation to follow generates a comprehensive analysis for acquisitions financed by cash, stock, or any combination of cash, debt, preferred stock, and common stock. In this article, the analysis will concern only the cash and exchange-of-shares cases. In the cash acquisition case, the analysis follows six essential steps:

> Develop estimates needed to project Rano's cash flow contribution for various growth and profitability scenarios.

> Estimate the minimum acceptable rate of return for acquisition of Rano.

> Compute the maximum acceptable cash price to be paid for Rano under various scenarios and minimum acceptable rates of return.

> Compute the rate of return that Alcar will earn for a range of price offers and for various growth and profitability scenarios.

> Analyze the feasibility of a cash purchase in light of Alcar's current liquidity and target debt-to-equity ratio.

> Evaluate the impact of the acquisition on the earnings per share and capital structure of Alcar.

Step 1—cash flow projections: The cash flow formula presented earlier may be restated in equivalent form as—

Exhibit III
Most likely estimates for Rano's operations under Alcar control

	Years		
	1-5	6-7	8-10
Sales growth rate (g)	.15	.12	.12
EBIT as a percentage of sales (p)	.18	.15	.12
Income tax rate (T)	.46	.46	.46
Capital investment per dollar of sales increase (f)	.20	.20	.20
Working capital per dollar of sales increase (w)	.15	.15	.15

Employing the cash flow formula for year 1:

$$CF_1 = 50(1+.15)(.18)(1-.46) - (57.5-50)(.20+.15) = 2.96$$

$$CF_t = S_{t-1} (1+g_t) (p_t) (1-T_t) - (S_t - S_{t-1}) (f_t + w_t)$$

where
CF = cash flow,
S = sales,
g = annual growth rate in sales,
p = EBIT as a percentage of sales,
T = income tax rate,
f = capital investment required (i.e., total capital investment net of replacement of existing capacity estimated by depreciation) per dollar of sales increase,
w = cash required for net working capital per dollar of sales increase.

Once estimates are provided for five variables, g, p, T, f, and w, it is possible to project cash flow.

Exhibit III shows Alcar management's "most likely" estimates for Rano's operations, assuming Alcar control; *Exhibit IV* shows a complete projected ten-year cash flow statement for Rano.

Before developing additional scenarios for Rano, I should make some brief comments on how to estimate some of the cash flow variables. The income tax rate is the effective cash rate rather than a rate based on the accountant's income tax expense, which often includes a portion that is deferred. For some companies, a direct projection of capital investment requirements per dollar of sales increase will prove a difficult task.

To gain an estimate of the recent value of this coefficient, simply take the sum of all capital investments less depreciation over the past five or ten years and divide this total by the sales increase from the beginning to the end of the period. With this approach, the resulting coefficient not only represents the capital investment historically required per dollar of sales increase but also impounds any cost increases for replacement of existing capacity.

One should estimate changes in net working capital requirements with care. Actual year-to-year balance sheet changes in net working capital may not provide a good measure of the rise or decline in funds required. There are two main reasons for this:

Exhibit IV
Projected ten-year cash flow statement for Rano (in millions of dollars)

| | Years | | | | | | | | | |
	1	2	3	4	5	6	7	8	9	10
Sales	$57.50	$66.12	$76.04	$87.45	$100.57	$112.64	$126.15	$141.29	$158.25	$177.23
Operating expenses	47.15	54.22	62.36	71.71	82.47	95.74	107.23	124.34	139.26	155.97
EBIT	$10.35	$11.90	$13.69	$15.74	$18.10	$16.90	$18.92	$16.95	$18.99	$21.27
Income taxes on EBIT	4.76	5.48	6.30	7.24	8.33	7.77	8.70	7.80	8.74	9.78
Operating earnings after taxes	$5.59	$6.43	$7.39	$8.50	$9.78	$9.12	$10.22	$9.16	$10.25	$11.48
Depreciation	1.60	1.85	2.13	2.46	2.84	3.28	3.74	4.25	4.83	5.49
Less capital expenditures	(3.10)	(3.57)	(4.12)	(4.74)	(5.47)	(5.69)	(6.44)	(7.28)	(8.22)	(9.29)
Less increase in working capital	(1.13)	(1.29)	(1.49)	(1.71)	(1.97)	(1.81)	(2.03)	(2.27)	(2.54)	(2.85)
Cash flow	$2.96	$3.41	$3.92	$4.51	$5.18	$4.90	$5.49	$3.86	$4.32	$4.84

(1) the year-end balance sheet figures may not reflect the average or normal needs of the business during the year, and (2) both the accounts receivable and inventory accounts may overstate the magnitude of the funds committed by the company.

To estimate the additional cash requirements, the increased inventory investment should be measured by the variable costs for any additional units of inventory required and by the receivable investment in terms of the variable costs of the product delivered to generate the receivable rather than the absolute dollar amount of the receivable.[4]

In addition to its most likely estimate for Rano, Alcar's management developed two additional (conservative and optimistic) scenarios for sales growth and EBIT-sales ratio. *Exhibit V* gives a summary of all three scenarios. Alcar's management may also wish to examine additional cases to test the effect of alternative assumptions about the income tax rate and capital investment and working capital requirements per dollar of sales increase.

Recall that cash flows should be forecast only for the period when the expected rate of return on incremental investment exceeds the minimum acceptable rate of return for the acquisition. It is possible to determine this in a simple yet analytical, nonarbitrary, fashion. To do so, we compute the minimum pretax return on sales (P min) needed to

earn the minimum acceptable rate of return on the acquisition (k) given the investment requirements for working capital (w) and fixed assets (f) for each additional dollar of sales and given a projected tax rate (T). The formula for P min is:

$$P_{min} = \frac{(f+w)\ k}{(1-T)\ (1+k)}.$$

Alcar's management believes that when Rano's growth begins to slow down, its working capital requirements per dollar of additional sales will increase from .15 to about .20 and its effective tax rate will increase from .46 to .50. As will be shown in the next section, the minimum acceptable rate of return on the Rano acquisition is 13%. Thus:

$$P_{min} = \frac{(.20+.20)\ (.13)}{(1-.50)\ (1+.13)}$$
$$= .092.$$

Alcar's management has enough confidence to forecast pretax sales returns above 9.2% for only the next ten years, and thus the forecast duration for the Rano acquisition is limited to that period.

Step 2—estimate minimum acceptable rate of return for acquisition: In developing a company's average cost of capital, measuring the aftertax cost of debt is relatively straightforward. The cost of equity capital, however, is more difficult to estimate.

Rational, risk-averse investors expect to earn a rate of return that will compensate them for accepting greater investment risk. Thus, in assessing the company's cost of equity capital or the minimum expected return that will induce investors to buy the company's shares, it is reasonable to assume that they will demand the risk-free rate as reflected in the current yields available in government bonds, plus a premium for accepting equity risk.

4. For an illustration of this calculation, see my article, "Measuring Company Growth Capacity During Inflation," HBR January-February 1979, p. 91.

5. For example, see Roger G. Ibbotson and Rex A. Sinquefield, *Stock, Bonds, Bills, and Inflation: The Past (1926-1976) and the Future (1977-2000)* (New York: Financial Analysts Research Foundation, 1977), p. 57. They forecast that returns on common stocks will exceed those on long-term government bonds by 5.4%.

6. For a discussion of some of the problems in estimating beta as a measure of risk, see Eugene F. Brigham, *Financial Management: Theory and Practice* (Hinsdale, Ill.: The Dryden Press, 1977), p. 666.

Recently, the risk-free rate on government bonds has been in the neighborhood of 8.8%. By investing in a portfolio broadly representative of the overall equity market, it is possible to diversify away substantially all of the unsystematic risk—that is, risk specific to individual companies. Therefore, securities are likely to be priced at levels that reward investors only for the nondiversifiable market risk—that is, the systematic risk in movements in the overall market.

The risk premium for the overall market is the excess of the expected return on a representative market index such as the Standard & Poor's 500 stock index over the risk-free return. Empirical studies have estimated this market risk premium (representative market index minus risk-free rate) to average historically about 5% to 5.5%.[5] I will use a 5.2% premium in subsequent calculations.

Investing in an individual security generally involves more or less risk than investing in a broad market portfolio, thus one must adjust the market risk premium appropriately in estimating the cost of equity for an individual security. The risk premium for a security is the product of the market risk premium times the individual security's systematic risk, as measured by its beta coefficient.

The rate of return from dividends and capital appreciation on a market portfolio will, by definition, fluctuate identically with the market, and therefore its beta is equal to 1.0. A beta for an individual security is an index of its risk expressed as its volatility of return in relation to that of a market portfolio.[6] Securities with betas greater than 1.0 are more volatile than the market and thus would be expected to have a risk premium greater than the overall market risk premium or the average-risk stock with a beta of 1.0.

For example, if a stock moves 1.5% when the market moves 1%, the stock would have a beta of 1.5. Securities with betas less than 1.0 are less volatile than the market and would thus command risk premiums less than the market risk premium. In summary, the cost of equity capital may be calculated by the following equation:

$k_E = R_F + B_j (R_M - R_F)$
where
k_E = cost of equity capital,
R_F = risk-free rate,
B_j = the beta coefficient,
R_M = representative market index.

The acquiring company, Alcar, with a beta of 1.0, estimated its cost of equity as 14% with the foregoing equation:
$k_E = .088 + 1.0(.052)$
    $= .140$

Exhibit V
Additional scenarios for sales growth and EBIT/sales

Scenario	Sales growth Years 1-5	6-7	8-10	EBIT/sales Years 1-5	6-7	8-10
1. Conservative	.14	.12	.10	.17	.14	.11
2. Most likely	.15	.12	.12	.18	.15	.12
3. Optimistic	.18	.15	.12	.20	.16	.12

Exhibit VI
Alcar's weighted average cost of capital

	Weight	Cost	Weighted Cost
Debt	.23	.051	.012
Equity	.77	.140	.108
Average cost of capital			.120

Exhibit VII
Risk-adjusted cost of capital for Rano acquisition

	Weight	Cost	Weighted cost
Debt	.23	.054*	.012
Equity	.77	.156	.118
Average risk-adjusted cost of capital			.130

*Before-tax debt rate of 10% times 1 minus the estimated tax rate of 46%.

Since interest on debt is tax deductible, the rate of return that must be earned on the debt portion of the company's capital structure to maintain the earnings available to common shareholders is the aftertax cost of debt. The aftertax cost of borrowed capital is Alcar's current beforetax interest rate (9.5%) times 1 minus its effective tax rate of 46%, which is equal to 5.1%. Alcar's target debt-to-equity ratio is .30, or, equivalently, debt is targeted at 23% and equity at 77% of its overall capitalization as *Exhibit VI* shows Alcar's weighted average cost of capital. The appropriate rate for discounting Alcar cash flows to establish its estimated value is then 12%.

For new capital projects, including acquisitions, that are deemed to have about the same risk as the overall company, Alcar can use its 12% cost-of-capital rate as the appropriate discount rate. Because the company's cost of capital is determined by the weighted average risk of its component segments, the specific risk of each prospective acquisition should be estimated in order to arrive at the discount rate to apply to the candidate's cash flows.

Exhibit VIII
Maximum acceptable cash price for Rano – most likely scenario, with a discount rate of .130 (in millions of dollars)

Year	Cash flow	Present value	Cumulative present value
1	$ 2.96	$ 2.62	$ 2.62
2	3.41	2.67	5.29
3	3.92	2.72	8.01
4	4.51	2.76	10.77
5	5.13	2.81	13.59
6	4.90	2.35	15.94
7	5.49	2.33	18.27
8	3.86	1.45	19.72
9	4.32	1.44	21.16
10	4.84	1.43	22.59
Residual value	11.48	26.02*	48.61
Plus temporary investments not required for current operations			1.00
Less debt assumed			5.10
Maximum acceptable cash price			$44.51
Maximum acceptable cash price per share			$40.10

$$*\frac{\text{Year 10 operating earnings after taxes}}{\text{Discount rate}} \times \text{Year 10 discount factor} =$$

$$\frac{11.48}{.13} \times .2946 = 26.02$$

Rano, with a beta coefficient of 1.25, is more risky than Alcar, with a beta of 1.0. Employing the formula for cost of equity capital for Rano:

$$k_E = .088 = 1.25(.052)$$
$$= \underline{.156}$$

On this basis, the risk-adjusted cost of capital for the Rano acquisition is as shown in *Exhibit VII*.

Step 3—compute maximum acceptable cash price: This step involves taking the cash flow projections developed in Step 1 and discounting them at the rate developed in Step 2. *Exhibit VIII* shows the computation of the maximum acceptable cash price for the most likely scenario. The maximum price of $44.51 million, or $40.10 per share, for Rano compares with a $25 current market price for Rano shares. Thus, for the most likely case, Alcar can pay up to $15 per share, or a 60% premium over current market, and still achieve its minimum acceptable 13% return on the acquisition.

Exhibit IX shows the maximum acceptable cash price for each of the three scenarios for a range of discount rates. To earn a 13% rate of return, Alcar can pay at maximum $38 million ($34.25 per share), assuming the conservative scenario, and up to $53

million ($47.80 per share), assuming the optimistic scenario. Note that as Alcar demands a greater return on its investment, the maximum price it can pay decreases. The reverse is, of course, true as well. For example, for the most likely scenario, the maximum price decreases from $44.51 million to $39.67 million as the return requirement goes from 13% to 14%.

Step 4—compute rate of return for various offering prices and scenarios: Alcar management believes that the absolute minimum successful bid for Rano would be $35 million, or $31.50 per share. Alcar's investment bankers estimated that it may take a bid of as high as $45 million, or $40.50 per share, to gain control of Rano shares. *Exhibit X* presents the rates of return that will be earned for four different offering prices, ranging from $35 million to $45 million for each of the three scenarios.

Under the optimistic scenario, Alcar could expect a return of 14.4% if it were to pay $45 million. For the most likely case, an offer of $45 million would yield a 12.9% return, or just under the minimum acceptable rate of 13%. This is as expected, since the maximum acceptable cash price as calculated in *Exhibit VIII* is $44.51 million, or just under the $45 million offer. If Alcar attaches a relatively high probability to the conservative scenario, the risk associated with offers exceeding $38 million becomes apparent.

Step 5—analyze feasibility of cash purchase: While Alcar management views the relevant purchase price range for Rano as somewhere between $35 and $45 million, it must also establish whether an all-cash deal is feasible in light of Alcar's current liquidity and target debt-to-equity ratio. The maximum funds available for the purchase of Rano equal the postmerger debt capacity of the combined company less the combined premerger debt of the two companies plus the combined premerger temporary investments of the two companies. (Net working capital not required for everyday operations of the business is classified as "temporary investment.")

In an all-cash transaction governed by purchase accounting, the acquirer's shareholders' equity is unchanged. The postmerger debt capacity is then Alcar's shareholders' equity of $272 million times the targeted debt-to-equity ratio of .30, or $81.6 million. Alcar and Rano have premerger debt balances of $56 million and $5.1 million, respectively, for a total of $61.1 million.

The unused debt capacity is thus $81.6 million minus $61.1 million, or $20.5 million. Add to this the combined temporary investments of Alcar and Rano of $26 million, and the maximum funds avail-

Exhibit IX
Maximum acceptable cash price for three scenarios and a range of discount rates

| Scenarios | Discount rates | | | | |
	.11	.12	.13	.14	.15
1. Conservative					
Total price ($ millions)	$48.84	$42.91	$38.02	$33.93	$30.47
Per share price	44.00	38.66	34.25	30.57	27.45
2. Most likely					
Total price ($ millions)	57.35	50.31	44.51	39.67	35.58
Per share price	51.67	45.33	40.10	35.74	32.05
3. Optimistic					
Total price ($ millions)	68.37	59.97	53.05	47.28	42.41
Per share price	61.59	54.03	47.80	42.59	38.21

able for the cash purchase of Rano will be $46.5 million. A cash purchase is therefore feasible within the tentative price range of $35 to $45 million.

Step 6—evaluate impact of acquisition on Alcar's EPS and capital structure: Because reported earnings per share (EPS) continue to be of great interest to the financial community, a complete acquisition analysis should include a comparison of projected EPS both with and without the acquisition. *Exhibit XI* contains this comparative projection. The EPS stream with the acquisition of Rano is systematically greater than the stream without acquisition. The EPS standard, and particularly a short-term EPS standard, is not, however, a reliable basis for assessing whether the acquisition will in fact create value for shareholders.[7]

Several problems arise when EPS is used as a standard for evaluating acquisitions. First, because of accounting measurement problems, the EPS figure can be determined by alternative, equally acceptable methods—for example, LIFO versus FIFO. Second, the EPS standard ignores the time value of money. Third, it does not take into account the risk of the EPS stream. Risk is conditioned not only by the nature of the investment projects a company undertakes but also by the relative proportions of debt and equity used to finance those investments.

A company can increase EPS by increasing leverage as long as the marginal return on investment is greater than the interest rate on the new debt. However, if the marginal return on investment is less than the risk-adjusted cost of capital or if the increased leverage leads to an increased cost of capital, then the value of the company could decline despite rising EPS.

Primarily because the acquisition of Rano requires that Alcar partially finance the purchase

Exhibit X
Rate of return for various offering prices and scenarios

| Scenarios | Offering price | | | | |
| | Total ($ millions) | $35.00 | $38.00 | $40.00 | $45.00 |
	Per share	$31.53	$34.23	$36.04	$40.54
1. Conservative		.137	.130	.126	.116
2. Most likely		.152	.144	.139	.129
3. Optimistic		.169	.161	.156	.144

Exhibit XI
Alcar's projected EPS, debt-to-equity ratio, and unused debt capacity—without and with Rano acquisition

| Year | EPS | | Debt/equity | | Unused debt capacity (in millions of dollars) | |
	Without	With	Without	With	Without	With
0	$ 3.75	$ 4.10	.21	.26	$25.60	$20.50
1	4.53	4.89	.19	.27	34.44	9.42
2	5.09	5.51	.17	.28	44.22	7.00
3	5.71	6.20	.19	.29	40.26	4.20
4	6.38	6.99	.21	.30	35.45	.98
5	7.14	7.87	.24	.31	29.67	−2.71
6	7.62	8.29	.26	.31	22.69	−7.77
7	8.49	9.27	.27	.32	14.49	−13.64
8	9.46	10.14	.29	.33	4.91	−22.34
9	10.55	11.33	.31	.34	−6.23	−32.36
10	11.76	12.66	.32	.35	−19.16	−43.88

Note: Assumed cash purchase price for Rano is $35 million.

7. See William W. Alberts and James M. McTaggart, "The Short-Term Earnings Per Share Standard for Evaluating Prospective Acquisitions," *Mergers and Acquisitions*, Winter 1978, p. 4; and Joel M. Stern, "Earnings Per Share Don't Count," *Financial Analysts Journal*, July-August 1974, p. 39.

Exhibit XII
Most likely estimates for Alcar operations without acquisition

| | Years | | |
	1-5	6-7	8-10
Sales growth rate	.125	.120	.120
EBIT as a percentage of sales	.130	.125	.125
Income tax rate	.460	.460	.460
Capital investment per dollar of sales increase	.250	.250	.250
Working capital per dollar of sales increase	.300	.300	.300

Exhibit XIII
Estimated present value of Alcar equity – most likely scenario, with a discount rate of .120 (in millions of dollars)

Year	Cash flow	Present value	Cumulative present value
1	$ 6.13	$ 5.48	$ 5.48
2	6.90	5.50	10.98
3	7.76	5.53	16.51
4	8.74	5.55	22.06
5	9.83	5.58	27.63
6	10.38	5.26	32.89
7	11.63	5.26	38.15
8	13.02	5.26	43.41
9	14.58	5.26	48.67
10	16.33	5.26	53.93
Residual value	128.62	345.10*	399.03
Plus temporary investments not required for current operations			25.00
Less debt outstanding			56.00
Present value of Alcar equity			$368.03
Present value per share of Alcar equity			$ 36.80

$$*\frac{\text{Year 10 operating earnings after taxes}}{\text{Discount rate}} \times \text{Year 10 discount factor} =$$

$$\frac{128.62}{.12} \times .32197 = 345.10$$

price with bank borrowing, the debt-to-equity ratios with the acquisition are greater than those without the acquisition (see *Exhibit XI*). Note that even without the Rano acquisition, Alcar is in danger of violating its target debt-to-equity ratio of .30 by the ninth year. The acquisition of Rano accelerates the problem to the fifth year. Whether Alcar purchases Rano or not, management must now be alert to the financing problem, which may force it to issue additional shares or reevaluate its present capital structure policy.

Acquisition for stock

The first two steps in the acquisition-for-stock analysis, projecting Rano cash flows and setting the discount rate, have already been completed in connection with the acquisition-for-cash analysis developed in the previous section. The remaining steps of the acquisition-for-stock analysis are:

> Estimate the value of Alcar shares.

> Compute the maximum number of shares that Alcar can exchange to acquire Rano under various scenarios and minimum acceptable rates of return.

> Evaluate the impact of the acquisition on the earnings per share and capital structure of Alcar.

Step 1—estimate value of Alcar shares: Alcar conducted a comprehensive corporate self-evaluation that included an assessment of its estimated present value based on a range of scenarios. In the interest of brevity, I will consider here only its most likely scenario.

Management made most likely projections for its operations, as shown in *Exhibit XII.* Again using the equation for the cost of equity capital, the minimum EBIT as a percentage of sales needed to earn at Alcar's 12% cost of capital is 10.9%. Since management can confidently forecast pretax return on sales returns above 10.9% for only the next ten years, the cash flow projections will be limited to that period.

Exhibit XIII presents the computation of the value of Alcar's equity. Its estimated value of $36.80 per share contrasts with its currently depressed market value of $22 per share. Because Alcar management believes its shares to be substantially undervalued by the market, in the absence of other compelling factors it will be reluctant to acquire Rano by means of an exchange of shares.

To illustrate, suppose that Alcar were to offer $35 million in cash for Rano. Assume the most likely case, that the maximum acceptable cash price is $44.51 million (see *Exhibit VIII*); thus the acquisition would create about $9.5 million in value for Alcar shareholders. Now assume that instead Alcar agrees to exchange $35 million in market value of its shares in order to acquire Rano. In contrast with the cash case, in the exchange-of-shares case Alcar shareholders can expect to be worse off by $12.1 million.

With Alcar shares selling at $22, the company must exchange 1.59 million shares to meet the $35 million offer for Rano. There are currently 10 million Alcar shares outstanding. After the merger, the combined company will be owned 86.27%—i.e., (10.00)/(10.00 + 1.59)—by current Alcar shareholders and 13.73% by Rano shareholders. The $12.1 million loss by Alcar shareholders can then be calculated as shown in *Exhibit XIV*.

Step 2—compute maximum number of shares Alcar can exchange: The maximum acceptable number of shares to exchange for each of the three scenarios and for a range of discount rates appears in *Exhibit XV*. To earn a 13% rate of return, Alcar can exchange no more than 1.033, 1.210, and 1.442 million shares, assuming the conservative, most likely, and optimistic scenarios, respectively. Consider, for a moment, the most likely case. At a market value per share of $22, the 1.21 million Alcar shares exchanged would have a total value of $26.62 million, which is less than Rano's current market value of $27.75 million—that is, 1.11 million shares at $25 per share. Because of the market's apparent undervaluation of Alcar's shares, an exchange ratio likely to be acceptable to Rano will clearly be unattractive to Alcar.

Step 3—evaluate impact of acquisition on Alcar's EPS and capital structure: The $35 million purchase price is just under ten times Rano's most recent year's earnings of $3.55 million. At its current market price per share of $22, Alcar is selling at about six times its most recent earnings. The acquiring company will always suffer immediate EPS dilution whenever the price-earnings ratio paid for the selling company is greater than its own. Alcar would suffer immediate dilution from $3.75 to $3.54 in the current year. A comparison of EPS for cash versus an exchange-of-shares transaction appears as part of *Exhibit XVI*. As expected, the EPS projections for a cash deal are consistently higher than those for an exchange of shares.

However, the acquisition of Rano for shares rather than cash would remove, at least for now, Alcar's projected financing problem. In contrast with a cash acquisition, an exchange of shares enables Alcar to have unused debt capacity at its disposal throughout the ten-year forecast period. Despite the relative attractiveness of this financing flexibility, Alcar management recognized that it could not expect a reasonable rate of return by offering an exchange of shares to Rano.

Exhibit XIV
Calculation of loss by Alcar shareholders (in millions of dollars)

Alcar receives 86.27% of Rano's present value of $44.51 million (see *Exhibit VIII*)	$38.4
Alcar gives up 13.73% of its present value of $368.03 million (see *Exhibit XIII*)	(50.5)
Dilution of Alcar shareholders' value	$12.1

Exhibit XV
Maximum acceptable shares to exchange for three scenarios and a range of discount rates (in millions)

Scenarios	Discount rates				
	.11	.12	.13	.14	.15
1. Conservative	1.327	1.166	1.033	0.922	0.828
2. Most likely	1.558	1.367	1.210	1.078	0.967
3. Optimistic	1.858	1.630	1.442	1.285	1.152

Exhibit XVI
Alcar's projected EPS, debt-to-equity ratio, and unused debt capacity—cash vs. exchange of shares

Year	EPS		Debt/equity		Unused debt capacity (in millions of dollars)	
	Cash	Stock	Cash	Stock	Cash	Stock
0	$ 4.10	$ 3.54	.26	.21	$20.50	$25.60
1	4.89	4.37	.27	.19	9.42	35.46
2	5.51	4.93	.28	.17	7.00	46.62
3	6.20	5.55	.29	.18	4.20	48.04
4	6.99	6.23	.30	.20	0.98	46.37
5	7.87	7.00	.31	.21	−2.71	44.29
6	8.29	7.37	.31	.23	−7.77	40.90
7	9.27	8.22	.32	.24	−13.64	36.78
8	10.14	8.98	.33	.26	−22.34	29.90
9	11.33	10.01	.34	.27	−32.36	21.79
10	12.66	11.17	.35	.29	−43.88	12.29

Note: Assumed purchase price for Rano is $35 million.

Concluding note

The experience of companies that have implemented the approach to acquisition analysis described in this article indicates that it is not only an effective way of evaluating a prospective acquisition candidate but also serves as a catalyst for reevaluating a company's overall strategic plans. The results also enable management to justify acquisition recommendations to the board of directors in an economically sound, convincing fashion.

Various companies have used this approach for evaluation of serious candidates as well as for initial screening of potential candidates. In the latter case, initial input estimates are quickly generated to establish whether the range of maximum acceptable prices is greater than the current market price of the target companies. With the aid of a computer model, this can be accomplished quickly and at relatively low cost.

Whether companies are seeking acquisitions or are acquisition targets, it is increasingly clear that they must provide better information to enable top management and boards to make well-conceived, timely decisions. Use of the approach outlined here should improve the prospects of creating value for shareholders by acquisitions.▽

Reprint 79409

Competitive edge

The competitive significance of leading-edge strategic planning is underscored by something that the chief executive of one of America's most successful companies said recently. In responding to a question asking him to identify the reasons for his company's outstanding and long-sustained leadership position in its industry, he said: "In the main, our competitors are acquainted with the same fundamental concepts and techniques and approaches that we follow, and they are as free to pursue them as we are. More often than not, the difference between their level of success and ours lies in the relative thoroughness and self-discipline with which we and they develop and execute our strategies for the future."

From
Dick Neuschel, "The Chief Executive's Strategic Role and Responsibilities," a Special Study prepared for The Presidents Association, the Chief Executive Officers' division of American Management Associations. Copyright © 1977 by The Presidents Association. All rights reserved.

Choosing compatible acquisitions

Through a tailor-made screening system, companies can find a profitable match

Malcolm S. Salter and Wolf A. Weinhold

In today's low-growth yet volatile environment, many companies choose to diversify through acquisition. An acquisition candidate with high potential will be one that can create economic value by leading to a free cash flow for the combined company that is either larger or less risky than that of a comparable investment portfolio. Candidates with the greatest promise for value creation will be those offering a good fit with the acquirer's unique set of skills and resources. The authors examine how an assessment of these skills and resources can help companies decide (1) whether related or unrelated acquisitions make sense, (2) which economic, strategic, and managerial variables should be stressed in evaluating an acquisition candidate's risk-return profile, and (3) what potential exists for successful integration with the acquiring company.

Mr. Salter is professor of business administration at the Harvard Business School, where he specializes in the strategic and organizational problems of diversified companies. This is his fifth article for HBR.

Mr. Weinhold is both a research collaborator with Mr. Salter at the Harvard Business School and an independent management consultant. Salter and Weinhold are coauthors of *Diversification Through Acquisition: Strategies for Creating Economic Value* (Free Press, 1979).

Illustrations by Richard A. Goldberg.

Though some view large-scale acquisitions primarily as the province of adventurous conglomerates, in fact many old-line conservative giants are actively involved in such activities. General Electric, for instance, paid $2 billion in stock for Utah International, Exxon paid $1.2 billion in cash for Reliance Electric, and Allied Chemical and Kennecott Copper each paid more than $500 million for their respective acquisitions of Eltra and Carborundum.

When such corporate acquisitions succeed, it is often because the acquirers have a mechanism for identifying candidates that offer the greatest potential for creating value for the company's shareholders. In a previous article, we pointed out that value is created when diversifying acquisitions lead to a free cash flow for the combined company (1) that is greater than could be realized from a portfolio investment in the two companies or (2) whose variability is smaller than it would be with a portfolio investment in the two companies.[1]

Effective systems for identifying and screening acquisitions have four important properties. First, they must provide means of evaluating a candidate's potential for creating value for the acquirer's shareholders. Second, they must be able to reflect the special needs of each company using the system. Relying on checklists or priorities with supposed universal applicability is the surest possible way of placing an entire acquisition program in jeopardy. Third, they must be easy to use—but not overly rigid. Since most structured frameworks of analysis run the risk of promoting mechanical solutions to complicated policy issues, formal screening and evaluation procedures must not be allowed to crowd out more

1. See our article, "Diversification via Acquisition: Creating Value," HBR July-August 1978, p. 166.

informal, spontaneous contributions to the decision-making process.

Fourth, and perhaps most important, an effective acquisition screening system must serve as a mechanism for communicating corporate goals and personal knowledge among the parties involved. The analytic concepts and language inherent in such a system can significantly aid managers in implementing an acquisition program that is conceptually sound, internally consistent, and economically justifiable.

This article will focus on guidelines for screening acquisitions that diversify the acquirer's operations. Our interest in such acquisitions is prompted by two considerations:

First, in today's low-growth yet volatile environment, most companies with high-growth goals or an imbalanced portfolio of businesses find diversification necessary. Only a few companies have both the organizational and the technological traits for successful diversification through internal development, so acquisition becomes the only alternative.

Second, large companies seeking expansion opportunities often find significant antitrust barriers in their pursuit of those acquisition candidates that make the greatest strategic and business sense. These high-potential acquisitions are companies closely related to existing businesses. However, the company that reaches for the benefits of scale economies, production efficiencies, or market rationalizations will, in many cases, run afoul of antitrust legislation.

Acquisitions for diversification can be related or unrelated to the original business. Each type has important variants:

Related acquisitions that might be called "supplementary" involve entry into new product markets where a company can use its existing functional skills or resources. Such acquisitions are typically most valuable to companies with a strong competitive position and a desire to extend their corporate competence to new areas of opportunity. The base on which this form of diversifying acquisition is built can either be a proprietary functional skill, as is the case for many of the major pharmaceutical and chemical companies, or a more general corporate capability, such as Gillette showed in disposable consumer products or United Technologies in capital goods.

Related acquisitions that are "complementary" rather than supplementary involve adding functional skills or resources to the company's existing distinctive competence while leaving its product-market commitment relatively unchanged. This type of acquisition is most valuable to companies in attractive industries whose competitive or strategic position could be strengthened by changing (or adding to) their value-added position in the commercial chain.

A classic example would be an original-equipment automotive parts manufacturer expanding into the distribution of replacement parts to secure a more stable, controllable market. Such a strategy often leads to a form of vertical integration as these new functional skills and/or resources are more closely linked to the diversifying company's core businesses. The acquisitions of American Television and Communications by Time, Inc. or Cardiac Pacemakers by Eli Lilly represent this complementary type of strategy.

Unrelated acquisitions involve entry into businesses with product markets or key success factors unrelated to existing corporate activities. These unrelated businesses can be managed either actively or passively. In active management, the corporate office becomes heavily involved in evaluating the new division's objectives and in establishing a highly competitive internal market for capital funds. Conglomerates such as Teledyne, Gulf & Western, and International Telephone and Telegraph typify companies pursuing this approach. In passive management, corporate headquarters usually limits its involvement to investment reviews, but there may be a centralized financing or banking function. The recent U.S. acquisitions by Thomas Tilling, Thyssen, and the Flick Group are all examples of this strategy. Diversified U.S. companies like U.S. Industries, IU International, and Alco Standard have historically followed this strategy, though recent economic events have forced the corporate office in each of these instances to take a more active management role.

The choice of a particular acquisition strategy largely depends on identifying the route that best uses the company's existing asset base and special resources. When a company can export (or import) surplus functional skills and resources relevant to its industrial or commercial setting, it should consider related acquisitions as an attractive strategic option. On the other hand, a company that has a special capacity to (1) analyze the strategies and financial requirements of a wide range of businesses, (2) tolerate—and even encourage—a lack of uniformity in the organization's structure, and (3) transfer surplus financial resources and general management skills among subsidiaries when necessary can exploit the potential benefits of unrelated acquisitions.

Acquisition guidelines

The decision to pursue a specific type of diversifying acquisition provides the context for drawing up precise guidelines. While every acquisition-minded company should undertake an audit of corporate strengths and weaknesses as well as an analysis of its risk-return profile and cash flow characteristics, the process of developing acquisition guidelines for related diversification should differ in focus and in content from what is used for unrelated diversification.

Related diversification

The most significant shareholder benefits from related acquisitions accrue when the special skills and industry knowledge of one merger partner can help improve the competitive position of the other. It is worth stressing again that not only must these special skills and resources exist in one of the two partners but they must also be transferable to the other. Thus, acquisition guidelines would describe those companies with functional skills and resources that would either add to or benefit from the company's resource package.

Lest such identification appear too obvious or elementary, consider the dilemma that Ciba-Geigy Corporation faced in its 1974 acquisition of Airwick Industries. Ciba-Geigy's products were almost entirely specialty chemicals and pharmaceuticals. Its corporate objectives were to continue to improve its long-term profits through new products derived from its extensive research program and from acquisitions in related fields. An attractive acquisition, according to Ciba-Geigy's acquisition task force, should:

> Participate in growing markets.
> Have a proprietary position in its markets.
> Have operations likely to be favorably affected by Ciba-Geigy's know-how in both research and development and the manufacture and marketing of complex synthetic organic chemicals.
> Be product rather than service oriented.
> Have sales of $50 million or more.
> Earn a good gross profit margin on sales.
> Have the potential for a return on investment of 10% or more.
> Be involved in such activities as specialty chemicals; proprietary pharmaceuticals; cosmetic and toiletry products; animal health products; proprietary household and garden products; medical supplies; products and services related to air, liquid, and solid waste treatment; or photochemicals and related products.

The search—a model of intelligent acquisition behavior—involved reviewing more than 18,000 companies in-house, along with an outside computer review. In addition, the company circulated the acquisition criteria among commercial and investment banking firms for their suggestions, and the task force worked with the company's divisions to identify attractive candidates. All told, about 100 companies came through this screen and were scrutinized more closely. Among these was Airwick Industries.

Airwick had 1973 sales of $33.5 million, net earnings of $2.7 million, and a return on shareholders' investment of 22.5%. The company's principal products were air fresheners and a full line of sanitary maintenance items (such as disinfectants, cleansers, insecticides with odor-counteracting features, and some swimming pool products). Over the previous five years, the rapidly growing air freshener market had become extremely competitive. Bristol-Myers, American Home Products, and S.C. Johnson had all entered the market. While Airwick's financial performance had been good, it was clearly facing financial pressures in meeting the marketing onslaught of these major consumer products companies.

After several weeks of extensive interviews and analysis, Ciba-Geigy's task force concluded that Airwick was a sound company that had numerous potential synergies with Ciba-Geigy. The task force reported that acquisition of Airwick would be an attractive way of entering the household products business, *if* Ciba-Geigy had a strategic interest in this area. The tentativeness of this conclusion suggests that the acquisition guidelines failed to provide sufficient criteria for a final choice of the acquisition candidate.

Related diversification requires that new businesses or activities have a coherence or "fit" with the existing businesses of the acquirer. Achieving this fit involves exploring a range of possible choices. A quick review of Ciba-Geigy's eight acquisition guidelines finds only two that express any notion of strategic fit (third and fourth). The company's distinctive skills lay in its sophisticated research in organic chemicals and its technologically advanced production skills. Relative to many other companies, Ciba-Geigy did not require nor perhaps encourage an advanced marketing program.

If Ciba-Geigy's objectives were to build on these skills and talents a strategy of related-supplementary diversification, attractive acquisition candidates

would have similar critical success variables. Specifically, such businesses would:

1. Require high levels of chemically based research and development skills.

2. Manufacture products by chemical processes requiring a high degree of engineering or technical know-how.

3. Sell principal products on technically based performance specifications.

4. Not require heavy advertising or expensive distribution systems that would take resources away from the maintenance of distinctive R&D and manufacturing capabilities.

Ciba-Geigy would have steered away from businesses that were either marketing intensive or involved in the production of commodity chemicals, including many of those businesses it had targeted.

Alternatively, if Ciba-Geigy had wished to add important skills and resources in new functional activities—a related-complementary diversification strategy—attractive acquisition candidates would have experience in large-scale manufacturing, marketing, and distribution of chemically based products. They would be businesses:

1. Whose resource inputs could include Ciba-Geigy's specialty chemicals.

2. Whose success depends highly on chemical usage or application.

3. Whose production and/or distribution involve chemically based products.

4. Whose key success factor is marketing oriented. This may include, but is not limited to, companies with extensive distribution systems, well-known brand names, and/or a tradition of customer acceptance.

These quite different sets of acquisition guidelines, though both seeking related diversification, help explain the task force's dilemma with Airwick. Lacking precise diversification objectives and acquisition guidelines, the task force analyzed Airwick according to related-supplementary criteria, which required skills similar to those of Ciba-Geigy. However, Airwick's key success factors were quite different from Ciba-Geigy's, and Ciba-Geigy's functional strengths were largely irrelevant to Airwick's future. Naturally, the task force felt the need to hedge its recommendations until it had more meaningful acquisition guidelines for marketing-oriented companies.

The lesson of this case is simple but fundamental. Companies pursuing a strategy of growth into related fields must decide whether to expand existing skills and resources into new product markets or whether to add new functional skills and resources.

Unrelated diversification

The principal benefits for companies pursuing unrelated acquisitions stem from improved corporate management of working capital, resource allocation, or capital financing and lead to a cash flow for the combined company that is either larger or less risky than its component parts. A company pursuing unrelated acquisitions can therefore usefully focus its acquisition criteria on the size and riskiness of a business's cash flow and the compatibility of this cash flow pattern with its own cash flow profile. Once again, lest this appear too obvious, consider the uncertainty faced by General Cinema Corporation.

General Cinema, the nation's largest operator of multiple-auditorium theater complexes and largest soft drink bottler, has compiled an enviable financial record. Both return on equity and earnings growth have exceeded 20% for the last decade. By the mid-1970s, the company had reduced the large amount of debt it had incurred while actively acquiring soft drink bottlers. It then began an acquisition search for a "third leg of the stool."

General Cinema's acquisition guidelines indicated a preference for well-run small to medium-sized companies ($5 million to $20 million in pretax earnings) whose consumer- or leisure-oriented products had unique characteristics that protected them against competition. Senior managers spoke of using the company's competence in any new acquisition. All this suggests some very general related-diversification strategy.

General Cinema's actions suggest, however, that this strategy was not followed. Its soft drink bottling business is not closely related to the multiple-auditorium theater business in either a product-market or a functional skill sense, nor were several of its previous diversification attempts, which involved bowling alleys, FM radio stations, and furniture retailing.

Thus, in General Cinema's case, the difference between the company's espoused theory of diversification and its actual behavior is clear. Assuming, therefore, it had a realistic interest in unrelated diversification, what additional acquisition guidelines could usefully structure General Cinema's search for an attractive unrelated acquisition candidate?

Turning first to General Cinema's risk profile, one finds a high level of risk at the corporate level (its

stock had a beta in excess of 1.8) but relatively low levels of risk at the operating subsidiary level. This divergence in risk levels was due to management's policy of aggressive financial leverage with a debt-to-equity ratio (including capitalized leases) exceeding 3 to 1. By incurring high levels of financial leverage to increase its risk level, rather than assuming either operating or competitive risk, General Cinema was creating value for its shareholders.

A cash flow analysis of General Cinema's product-market portfolio reinforces these conclusions. All of General Cinema's divisions were classic cash cows—the largest competitors in mature, low-growth industries. In addition, the competitive positions of both the theater and bottling divisions were especially strong due to the franchise nature of both markets. Since both movie theaters and bottling operations are capital-intensive businesses, their cash flows, relative to many industries, were high. General Cinema's cash flow strength was likely to increase as continued growth in revenues and financial leverage interacted to generate an increasing surplus of cash funds.

In short, General Cinema showed many of the characteristics of a well-managed, unrelated diversifier. In fact, the distinctive competence General Cinema's senior managers often referred to consisted of well-developed planning and control skills in the corporate office, a key success variable for many such companies. Thus, additional acquisition guidelines for General Cinema, reflecting an unrelated-active strategy, could be as follows:

1. The acquisition candidate should be asset intensive. The assets could either be fixed, such as buildings and equipment, or intangible, such as trademarks, franchises, or goodwill. In either case, they should be well established with significant ongoing value in order to be "bankable."

2. Since high levels of debt would be used, the acquisition's assets should create high barriers to entry. This implies products relatively immune to technological obsolescence or markets not exposed to significant levels of internal competition or external pressure.

3. Since General Cinema's surplus cash flow is increasing, an attractive acquisition should have significant growth potential over an extended period of time.

4. The acquisition candidate may have a low pre-tax return on invested capital (say 16%). However, total invested capital (debt, leases, and equity) should be at least three times the equity investment. Reflecting this (potential) leverage, the pretax return on equity should be high (at least 30%).

5. The requirements for relative immunity to market change and a high growth rate imply that the acquisition would be service oriented rather than technology based.

6. For senior managers to feel comfortable with the acquisition, they should market or distribute products or services to the consuming public.

7. Since General Cinema lacks surplus general managers, the acquisition should have good operating managers. Successful integration into General Cinema requires that the acquisition be adaptable to intensive planning and financial controls.

Most of the guidelines are as applicable to companies managing unrelated acquisitions passively as to companies operating actively. However, the criteria requiring integration into an intensive planning and financial control system and a corporate-managed resource allocation process embody those elements found in most actively managed portfolios of unrelated businesses.

The Ciba-Geigy and General Cinema cases clearly show how closely tied acquisition guidelines should be to overall corporate strategy. Effective acquisition guidelines must reflect carefully thought-out corporate objectives. In situations where the objectives (and especially diversification objectives) lack specificity or relevance, acquisition guidelines will be vague and have limited use in structuring a process for productive acquisition search and screening.

Screening the candidates

Once an acquisition-minded company has established detailed and comprehensive guidelines, it can develop its own system for identifying promising candidates. This screening system should identify candidates with the greatest potential of creating value for the acquiring company's shareholders.

As we said earlier, economic value is created only when diversifying acquisitions lead to a free cash flow for the combined company (1) that is greater than could be realized from a portfolio investment in the two companies or (2) whose variability is smaller than would occur from a portfolio investment in the two companies.

We have identified eight principal ways in which one or both of these conditions can be met through diversifying acquisitions as well as several additional ways that are not, strictly speaking, due to diversification.[2] Each involves the way in which the two companies' resource structures can be successfully integrated to form a more efficient business unit.

The following list briefly outlines those economic, strategic, and managerial variables that have the greatest potential impact on value creation. These variables can be divided into two broad categories—those dealing with the candidate's risk-return profile and those dealing with the candidate's integration potential.

Risk-return variables

Return characteristics principally concern the size and timing of an acquisition's prospective cash flows. While such characteristics are often thought of as company specific, many industries show readily identifiable cash flow patterns over their business cycles and/or their life cycles:

Size and period of cash flow. These variables focus on the pattern of free cash flows into and out of the acquisition over time. Generally, a period of investment (negative cash flow) during industry growth is followed by a period of return (positive cash flow) during maturity. A specific acquisition's cash flow pattern will reflect its capital intensity, profitability, growth rate, and stage of maturity.

Noncapitalized strategic investments. These are investments in assets that are not reflected on the company's balance sheet but are nevertheless important to its competitive success. Such assets as R&D skills, production technology, and market power (through advertising or distribution presence) are typically highly illiquid but are often the most effective competitive weapons and market entry barriers a company has.

Returns due to unique characteristics. Returns from the intangible assets developed through "strategic expenses" are often high, since along with specialized management skills they usually represent a company's distinctive competence. Alternatively, high returns may reflect entrepreneurial talents or access to one-of-a-kind sources of supply. Care should be given to distinguishing between company characteristics that can be developed and unique characteristics such as entrepreneurial talent, government franchises, or access to low-cost natural resources.

Investment liquidity. Liquidity primarily depends on the marketability of the investment's underlying assets. Generally, the less risky an asset and the higher its collateral value, the easier it is to convert into cash. Highly liquid assets seldom provide distinct competitive advantages, however, or yield high rates of return.

Every return (or cash flow) has some level of risk; normally, the greater the potential returns, the greater the risks. A critical part of management's job is to control these risks so that the risk-return trade-off becomes more attractive than otherwise.

Vulnerability to exogenous changes in supply or demand. These risks arise from exposure to changes outside the company's control or, alternatively, the inability of managers to influence their business environment. The risks faced by a company depend on how critical a specific environmental factor is to the company, how readily available substitutes are, and how specialized the company's internal resources are. The greater the company's ability to lay off or pass on these environmental risks in the marketplace, the more stable its cash flow and the lower its risk.

Ease of market entry and exit. Generally, the easier market entry or exit is, the more likely it is that industry rates of return will be driven toward normal or risk-adjusted levels. Entry-exit barriers can include capital requirements, specialized skills and resources, market presence, and government licenses or permits. Michael E. Porter described how knowledge about and use of entry and exit barriers can be critical in corporate strategy and competitive rivalry.[3]

Excess productive capacity. The risk of excess capacity is directly linked to market growth and the nature of capital investment to meet that growth. If it is most efficient to add new productive capacity in large increments of fixed investment (with corresponding sunk costs) and if these assets are long-lived (or with similar technological efficiencies), significant incentives to maintain volume through price cutting will exist whenever one competitor's relative demand falls off. Where market demand is relatively price inelastic, everyone in the industry will suffer revenue losses and reduced profitability.

Gross margin stability. This is closely related to production capacity risks and the ease of market entry and exit. Gross margins are good indicators of profitability and the availability of cash flow to support the development of more competitive technological, marketing, or administrative systems. The stability of gross margins also indicates the relative attractiveness of increasing operating leverage by substituting capital investment (with its fixed costs) for variable costs in the production process.

2. See our book, *Diversification Through Acquisition: Strategies for Creating Economic Value* (New York: Free Press, 1979).

3. Michael E. Porter, "How Competitive Forces Shape Strategy," HBR March-April 1979, p. 137.

Competitive strength. This depends on market share position, vulnerability to external forces in the marketplace, and position vis-à-vis suppliers and purchasers. Substantial evidence shows that in many industries companies with high market share have higher cash flows and higher returns on investment than those with low market share. If, however, a high market share position requires large investments in relatively specialized assets (fixed or intangible), these companies may also be highly vulnerable to major changes in the marketplace. Such external market risks include technological obsolescence, swift changes in consumption patterns, and new distribution or marketing systems accompanying changing demographics or technology. Finally, shifts in the bargaining strengths, or competitive positions, of suppliers or purchasers may substantially alter the costs or benefits of internal market share positions.

Societal liabilities. The increasing legislation concerning social issues and the public welfare has altered the costs and rates of returns of many companies. Driving forces behind this legislation include environmental concerns, consumer protectionism, and employee safety and benefits.

Political risk. Many companies have discovered that political and environmental risks may be significantly greater than the strategic, competitive, or technological risks faced in day-to-day business. The Mideast crisis and the continued turbulence in much of the Third World are only the most obvious instances. Unstable economic and monetary policy in the United States and trade policy in Japan are other, equally important, facets. Failure to assess and manage these risks correctly may render an otherwise successful corporate strategy irrelevant.

Each of these risk measures reflects one particular aspect of an asset's or a company's risk profile. How managers handle these risks as well as the inherent economic characteristics of the asset can be summarized through the following two capital market risk measures:

☐ Financial risk. This refers to the burden of fixed contractual payments incurred to own an asset. The greater this fixed burden (usually through debt or lease payments), the greater the financial risk. Skilled managers often use financial risk as an integral part of corporate strategy.

☐ Systematic and unsystematic risk. These measure the volatility (or the riskiness) of the returns of an asset or a business relative to the returns of all other assets in the marketplace. Systematic or market-related risk, which is most relevant to equity investors because it directly influences market value, reflects a company's inherent cash flow volatility and financial risk relative to the volatility of the economy in general. Unsystematic risk measures the risk specific to a particular company or asset. It can be reduced or eliminated by investors through portfolio diversification.

Integration potential

The second set of criteria a diversifying company should consider in developing its screening program concerns the acquisition's potential for successful integration. Such criteria are often much more important for a related diversifier than for an unrelated diversifier. In fact, a related diversifier may well focus most of its efforts in this area, since its corporate strategy and business commitments will render many risk-return criteria meaningless. Nevertheless, issues of organizational compatibility and the availability of general management skills are critical to the success of all diversifying companies:

Supplementary skills and resources. These criteria principally reflect a related-supplementary diversification strategy. Consequently, they focus on a company's ability to transfer and effectively use the skills and resources of one partner to the competitive advantage of the other. Generally, the potential benefits of this type of merger increase as the shared skills and resources constitute an increasingly larger element in the cost of doing business.

Complementary skills and resources. These criteria reflect a related-complementary diversification strategy. They focus on improving the competitive position of the business by adding new functional skills and resources to the existing resource base.

Financial fit-risk pooling benefits. These criteria are more important in unrelated than in related diversification. They focus on developing an internal capital market that is more efficient than the external capital marketplace. These benefits can arise out of improved working capital (cash) management, improved investment management (cross-subsidization), improved resource allocation, or more aggressive financial leverage.

Availability of general management skills. Talented general managers are essential whenever value creation depends on the revitalization of underused assets. A surplus of general management resources in either partner must always be considered an extremely positive feature.

Organizational compatibility. As any experienced diversifier will know, this is a critical issue. All of the previous criteria identify the potential for value creation, which can be realized only by an organization that can effectively exploit this potential and thereby create a more competitive enterprise.

Meeting individual corporate needs

An acquisition screening system should reflect a company's specific objectives. For example, a currently cash-rich company expecting to face substantial capital investment demands in five years might articulate its size and period of investment criteria as: "The most favorable investment pattern (purchase price plus subsequent infusion of funds into the acquisition) is a maximum of $100 million over the next three-year period. The acquired company should become financially self-sufficient by the end of the third year and generate surplus cash flow by the fifth year."

By composing such statements, a company can tailor generic guidelines often found in acquisition screening grids to its own unique needs. Where guidelines or screening criteria are complex or especially important to the acquiring company, any particular measure may require more than one statement. Similarly, the desired characteristics of industries and companies may be expressed in either positive or negative terms depending on the acquiring company's resources and objectives.

Developing these criteria should involve all members of the group or task force responsible for formulating and implementing the acquisition program. Each should generate descriptive statements based on his or her understanding of the company's objectives and needs. Subsequent discussions among these persons can then lead to a single set of generally accepted and explicit screening criteria.

Once formal statements or criteria have been developed, it is sometimes useful to establish weightings or scoring ranges for each measure. These scoring ranges will reflect the importance of each item to the acquiring company.[4] Specific designation of the value of each measure forces managers to discuss the entire acquisition in terms of corporate objectives, resources, and skills.

Such a discussion also ensures internal consistency of the program. Wide discrepancies may signal that managers differ in their perceptions of the

company's objectives, strategy, or distinctive competence or, alternatively, that they have either overlooked or understood only implicitly key elements in the diversification strategy.

As the acquisition task force screens industries, industry subgroups, and individual companies, the process will typically be iterative, reducing the potential acquisition universe to a smaller and smaller size. Industry subgroups (companies sharing the same key success factor or similar products and/or markets) will replace industries, and companies will replace industry subgroups until a limited set of candidates exists.

At each step in the screening process, the managers involved should individually evaluate the potential candidates and then meet to analyze their evaluations and discuss any major differences. Managers should ask: Do the results make intuitive sense? Why is there such a wide (or narrow) spread in the point scores? Has some critical element been overlooked?

As the screening process develops, company strategists should modify both the explicit screening criteria and their scoring ranges as new information about the potential acquisition and/or the environment emerge. Some diversifiers may also be useful to make the statements more detailed as the screening process narrows attention to fewer candidates or to eliminate certain criteria altogether. Generally, the need to revise statements will be less for related diversifiers than for unrelated diversifiers, since the former typically have a smaller universe of candidates to choose from. Clear communication of objectives and differences of opinion is particularly important since, once an acquisition decision has been made, a company can reverse itself only with very high financial and organizational costs.

This procedure should stimulate the flow of information and judgments among those responsible for the acquisition program and lead to a questioning of assumptions, provide a critical analysis of differences of opinion, and improve the consistency between corporate objectives and resources. Just as the capital budget or the operating budget can be used as a communications tool, so too can the acquisition screening grid serve an important communications function.

Potential for value creation

The last step in the screening process is determination of the candidate's potential for value creation

4. See our book, *Diversification Through Acquisition*, p. 194, for a detailed explanation of how to develop a weighting system.

for the shareholders of the acquiring company. This potential should then be compared to the cost of the acquisition as well as to the company's other investment opportunities (including the repurchase of its own stock).

In many ways, this procedure is similar to capital budgeting exercises that use the notion of net present value or discounted cash flow, but the analysis of a potential acquisition is significantly more complex than most capital budgeting decisions. Whereas the typical investment project involves assets with risks reasonably similar to those already in the company's portfolio and under the control of familiar managers, this is not the case with many acquisition candidates. Not only may the acquired asset's risks be different but the managers of an acquired company are often of unknown quality. Even where some familiarity exists, the managers' attitudes and motivation can change radically after the acquisition is consummated.

Another significant difference between an acquisition and the typical investment project is that the capital marketplace acts as a pricing mechanism to equate the value of a company with its risk-return characteristics. A lucky acquirer may well find a bargain or, more precisely, a company whose intrinsic value is greater than its market value plus the transaction costs necessary to acquire it.

Much more likely, however, is the case where an acquisition candidate is not undervalued relative to its existing level of cash flow and risk but rather is underusing its asset base. In this case, the acquirer will have to make extensive changes in the acquired company's management and/or use of assets for the acquisition to be economically justifiable. These changes will result typically in a company whose risk and expected cash flow are vastly different from what they previously were. Historic measures of this asset's performance may well be useless in the evaluation of future prospects.

The specific mechanics of net present value (or the discounted cash flow valuation process) appear in almost any financial handbook and are in the repertoire of most investment bankers or management consultants.[5] For discounted cash flow to be useful in acquisition analysis, it should be readily adaptable in the following three areas:

1. Developing detailed cash flow projections (including additional capital investments) over the acquired company's period of ownership.

2. Establishing relevant rates of return for the acquired company (and its constituent parts) based on its prospective risk characteristics and its capital structure.

3. Performing sensitivity analyses under the various economic, operating, and financial scenarios likely to be faced.

While this approach seems straightforward and objective, it is in practice much more complex and intuitive. Wherever operating, financial, or strategic changes are to be made in the acquired company's businesses, simple extrapolation or projection of current performance is, at best, risky. Similarly, if integration with the acquirer is to occur, as in related diversification, managers must evaluate changes in the cash flows and risk levels of both acquirer and acquired. Virtually every attempt to achieve one of the several potential benefits of diversification will lead to subtle yet important changes in the combined company's cash flow and risk characteristics. Careful use and a thorough understanding of the valuation process are of paramount importance, for slight errors in estimating these cash flows or risk levels can lead to valuation prices that differ by 30% or 40%.

Nevertheless, a careful application of the method we have outlined will force a company to be as concrete as possible in its assessment of future risks and returns. No one formula or method, least of all a simplified discounted cash flow analysis, should be expected to reveal by itself the best option or decision. The worth of any screening and evaluation system will vary according to both the quality of information used and the ability of managers to use this tool without crowding out important intuitive judgments about the compatibility of corporate cultures, the quality of an acquisition candidate's management, and the long-term strength of a candidate's competitive position.

The room for error in making these judgments is considerable. The anticipated benefits of an acquisition are often greater than those finally realized. Reaping benefits that stem from operating synergies requires considerable time and management effort. The knowledge of which benefits are achievable and at what costs comes from both prior experience and a strong sense of administrative feasibility. These personal characteristics of decision makers, along with the ability to value future returns accurately, lie at the base of a successful acquisition screening system.

---

5. For a good summary of this valuation process, see Alfred Rappaport, "Strategic Analysis for More Profitable Acquisitions," HBR July-August 1979, p. 99.

Preparing the ground

Executives often ask why they should have elaborate acquisition guidelines when such decisions must often be made without sufficient time for detailed, comprehensive analysis or when candidates best suited to their company's needs are not available. To summarize, formal acquisition guidelines can help companies prepare themselves for swift action in three ways:

First, working through a formal process in periods of relative calm tends to reinforce a broad understanding among executives of the company's objectives. Given the complexities of organizational life in the modern corporation, this benefit is not trivial.

Second, experience with a structured process, such as articulating acquisition guidelines or writing specific screening criteria, leads to widely shared assumptions about the company's strengths and weaknesses and its special needs and to a general agreement on what is most important for future profitability and corporate development.

Third, working within a formal system develops a common language or set of concepts relevant to the acquisition decision. This language system and the analytic framework it represents serve to ensure that key decision makers follow similar logic when acquisition opportunities suddenly appear and quick decisions are necessary.

The issue concerning the availability of acquisition candidates is often overemphasized. Most companies, especially those that are publicly owned, are available at a price. In the capital markets, where there is a continual auction of corporate securities, companies change hands every day. The real question is not whether attractive candidates are available but whether the company's potential to create value for the acquirer's shareholders is sufficient to justify the purchase price.▽

Reprint 81109

Willard F. Rockwell, Jr.

How to acquire a company

*From one business leader's experience,
his many successes as well as some failures,
10 "commandments" for merger planning*

Foreword

For the executive who wants to "go to school" to learn the art of successful mergers and acquisitions, there is no better source of knowledge than the practical experience which has been accumulated during the past two decades. Here a leader of many merger negotiations looks searchingly into that body of experience—at successes and failures, problems and opportunities, shortcuts and pitfalls—and draws useful lessons for future use. These lessons are grouped under 10 major rules or commandments.

Mr. Rockwell is Chairman of the Board of North American Rockwell Corporation, formed by the merger of North American Aviation and Rockwell-Standard Corporation in September 1967. After serving as a director of Rockwell-Standard Corporation, he became that company's president in 1963 and served as such until the merger in 1967. A registered professional engineer, he has also been a director of Rockwell Manufacturing Company (unrelated to Rockwell-Standard) since 1940, was its president from 1947 to 1964, and has been its vice chairman of the board since 1964. Mr. Rockwell has long been active in the Chamber of Commerce of Greater Pittsburgh; from 1959 to 1962 he was president of the organization. He is a director of Mellon National Bank & Trust Co., Hickok Manufacturing Company, The Coleman Company, Inc., Merex (Buenos Aires, Argentina), and other corporations.

"If current trends continue," says Richard Gilbert, Jr., managing editor of *Mergers and Acquisitions*, "one out of every three American companies will merge in the next ten years."[1]

But a study by Booz, Allen & Hamilton points out that only 64 out of 120 companies making acquisitions would acquire the companies they did if they had it to do over again. And in the experience of Jerome S. Hollender, vice president, mergers and acquisitions, for Shearson, Hammil & Co., out of 100 acquisitions consummated over a 10-year period, only 41 "equalled or exceeded expectations"; while 34 were "some-

1. Quoted in *Newsweek*, April 25, 1966, p. 72.

what disappointing," and 25 were "extremely disappointing."

Although the growth potential of a well-considered merger program is virtually unlimited, there is clearly a more sobering side to the picture that is well worth consideration by those with a roving eye for other companies. As one president I know puts it, "The glittering aspects of the merger route have been so greatly stressed, it is all too easy to overlook the ruts in the road."

Ruts there are in abundance, and I have tripped over my share during the 30-odd acquisitions I have been involved in during the past 10 years. Still, experience pays off in this field as in any other. The merger route *can* be all that its most enthusiastic proponents claim it to be—*if* the reasons for merging are right, the planning is sound, major pitfalls are anticipated, and the chief executive is a stark realist and pragmatist. Admittedly, the *if* is a big one.

What steps can management take to analyze a prospective acquisition with perceptiveness and sound judgment, probing behind the seemingly attractive facade which is so often created by a deft corporate makeup artist? How can management keep from merging for the wrong reasons? How can it foresee whether this company or that will mesh naturally and harmoniously with its own growth pattern?

There is no simple answer. Each merger possibility is unique and should be considered on its own merits. But there are certain key considerations that apply to virtually every merger. They may not guarantee success. But taking full cognizance of them will help immeasurably. The 10 factors which comprise the main body of this article (see the ruled insert on page 73) have been structured out of my own experience. They take into consideration both the hits and the misses. (Some of my own merger ventures did not work out; others exceeded expectations. I am fortunate in being able to say that in recent years the successes have greatly outnumbered the failures.)

As experience has repeatedly borne out both to me and to Dupuy Bateman, our vice president of mergers and acquisitions at North American Rockwell, these 10 factors are of special importance for any company deciding to buy or sell. But I regard the first 4 factors as critical and have thus labeled them the "must" factors. These 4 apply to any and all mergers. In my view, if any one of them is violated, the chances of a successful wedding are virtually nil.

1. Pinpoint the objectives

Overanxiety has resulted in more than one rash corporate marriage. Some presidents are so eager to pull off a brilliant merger deal that they don't take the time to specify what "brilliant" means. To quote Mr. Hollender again, "You would be surprised at the number of companies that initiate programs of search, evaluation and negotiation before they have even defined their goals."[2] Without good goal definition, he believes, most merger negotiations are doomed either to abandonment or to failure after consummation.

Another pitfall is the bigness lure; executives want to buy size for their companies. Bigness by itself has little intrinsic value, however, if the size fails to produce increased earnings or a more favorable price/earnings ratio. Also, unplanned expansion can generate all kinds of headaches and complications.

Focus on earnings

A study of successful mergers shows there is only one valid all-encompassing objective for making an acquisition: to produce increased earnings for the stockholders of both companies. All lesser goals, my experience indicates, should be set with this one master objective in mind. Let me illustrate:

□ At North American Rockwell we are shooting for an annual growth rate of 10% or better in per-share earnings and an average return of 15% or better on shareowners' equity. This goal was agreed on during the planning stages of the merger of North American Aviation and Rockwell-Standard. Other objectives are to improve further the market diversification of net income; to upgrade, while increasing total sales, the balance between government and commercial business; and to develop and maintain a working environment which would enable the company to attract and retain high-talent employees at all levels. Also, we are seeking profitable markets for the company's technological resources in government contracts, programs to meet the growing problems of the human community, and commercial areas where new technologies are needed.

Another carefully spelled out objective helped to guide Rockwell-Standard's acquisition activities prior to its merger with North American Aviation. This was to diversify into expanding fields with countervailing cycles in order to smooth the peaks and valleys of company business into a more constant incline of sales and earnings. We found that when a company is involved in a variety of cycles, it avoids the danger of burrowing too deeply into any one.

The acquisition history of virtually every successful merger-minded company that I know of proves that earnings growth is inevitable when the hunt for likely candidates is predicated on a merger policy based on objectives. It didn't

2. See Paul J. Keil, "Expert Stresses Need for Planning," *California Business*, July 5, 1966, p. 8.

take long after I approached North American Aviation's president, Lee Atwood, for both of us to see that the merger goals of the two companies dovetailed neatly:

☐ Rockwell-Standard's annual sales of about $636 million were largely commercial. North American Aviation's sales of $2 billion were 95% government funded.

☐ One Rockwell-Standard objective was to graduate into areas where North American Aviation had already excelled, its activities spanning the entire spectrum of defense and space technology and of systems management techniques. In building capabilities in these areas, North American Aviation had assembled 17,000 professional employees, including 2,900 with master's degrees and more than 600 with doctorates.

☐ North American Aviation sought the kind of marketing, commercial, and international know-how that Rockwell-Standard already possessed. Rockwell-Standard, at the time of the merger, was the nation's leading independent manufacturer of automotive components and industrial gears. It ranked fourth in private and business aircraft.

Once the goals of the two companies were compared and assessed, the mutual advantages of the merger became as clear as the goals themselves. What has emerged from the wedding is, as has been described by the financial community, a "concept" or "thesis" company focused on sophisticated technological development.

Drawing the line

Another thing experience teaches in setting goals is that it is just as important to clarify what management does not want as it is to spell out the things it is after. Our company has no interest, for example, in becoming a so-called conglomerate. We are highly diversified in 19 different industries, but this diversification is in specific fields of growth that are well integrated and closely related to existing services, resources, and talents. In considering possible acquisitions, we must be assured that our technological or marketing resources can make a significant contribution to the other company, and it to us. This keeps us from extending our lines to areas outside our competence.

Assuming goals are continually reassessed and kept up to date, they should be observed strictly, even when the temptation to stray is great.

The 10 "commandments"

'Must' factors

1. Pinpoint and spell out the merger objectives.

2. Specify substantial gains for the stockholders of both companies.

3. Be able to convince yourself that the acquired company's management is—or else can be made—competent.

4. Certify the existence of important dovetailing resources—but do not expect perfection.

Other key considerations

5. Spark the merger program with the chief executive's involvement.

6. Clearly define the business you are in (e.g., bicycles or transportation).

7. Take a depth sounding of strengths, weaknesses, and other key performance factors—the target acquisition company's and your own.

8. Create a climate of mutual trust by anticipating problems and discussing them early with the other company.

9. Don't let caveman advances jeopardize the courtship.

10. Most important of these latter six rules, make people your No. 1 consideration in structuring your assimilation plan.

I have been guilty of succumbing to that temptation at least once in my recollection, and the incident taught me a valuable lesson:

☐ A seemingly attractive company was up on the block, and we bought it for one dollar. This may sound like a great bargain, but it turned out to be anything but! It was a sick company, and we bought its debts and obligations as well as its assets. The result was not inspiring. We wound up liquidating or selling off 80% of the business and keeping the 20% that was profitable. The lesson we learned was that while some managements make a specialty of nursing sick companies back to health, that job is not our cup of tea. We are not business doctors!

2. Specify gains for owners

The perfect merger does not exist and probably never will. But the *ideal* merger does. In almost every case this is the merger which results in positive and apparent gains for both companies. But what kinds of gains?

T.R. Gamble, Pet Milk Company's chief executive officer, believes that a company contemplating a merger should first develop a plan of benefits and then ask itself two key questions: (1) Can the acquired company benefit from our assets? (2) Does it have the ability to use them? This philosophy makes good sense. I don't hold with the view that a company's profit performance is the sole criterion of whether or not it is worth acquiring. Even where both companies are well in the black, the merger will stand small chance of coming off successfully unless definite values are exchanged to produce the desired synergistic effect.

Every experienced and successful merger team that I know of shares this belief. And the top pros take special pains to analyze the two-way benefits in depth and to describe them in detail and in writing very early in the negotiations. If the benefits are substantial, one president told me, that fact alone "can iron out a lot of minor wrinkles and help pave the way to a swift and satisfactory deal."

There are many ways for mutual benefits to be attained. It is a good idea to develop a list of as many values as come to mind and to keep adding to the list as experience suggests new entries. You will then be able to test each potential acquisition as it comes along by dividing a sheet of paper into two sections, one for each company, and balancing the pluses that appear on each side of the sheet. To get you started, here is a brief sampling of some of the more important benefits. The merger may:

○ Provide a much needed diversification opportunity.
○ Fill a gap in technical or scientific expertise.
○ Produce financial capabilities for capital expansion.
○ Strengthen an internal management or operating weakness.
○ Buy valuable time for management (e.g., so sufficient development time can be allowed for a product-line change).
○ Provide a system of reporting that will produce faster and more comprehensive management decisions.
○ Open new market capabilities.
○ Reduce the company's dependence on a limited field of growth.
○ Produce important savings through the ability to make volume purchases.
○ Shore up a vulnerable patent position.
○ Increase the stock's price/earnings ratio.
○ Provide better and more reliable quality control.

○ Give a needed boost to the company's image and reputation in the marketplace.
○ Provide important research facilities and expertise.
○ Allow management to reap the benefits of a tax-loss carryover.
○ Flesh out a product line for either or both companies.
○ Put excess management or physical facilities to use.
○ Provide needed management expertise in marketing, finance, acquisitions, international operations, or other fields.

The more such values apply to both partners, the greater the chances that the merger will succeed.

3. Check management ability

The corporate asset in shortest supply these days is good, skilled, experienced, loyal management. When you acquire a new company, the top leadership that comes along with the package is at least as important as the rest of the assets you buy.[3]

What to look for

How can you identify management competence? It is not easy, for executive styles vary enormously. One successful president will keep communications pipelines open to dozens of his subordinates; another will deal almost exclusively with two or three top aides. One good man will hammer his points home by gentle persuasion; another will use brute force. One man will strut an impressive array of advanced degrees; another may never have gone to college. As one president told me, "The only common denominator of competence is success."

Still, there are certain basic characteristics to look for, and certain basic questions to ask. Says John R. Shad, vice president of E.F. Hutton & Co.:

"Three common characteristics of able executives are unusually high degree of motivation, energy, and intelligence. Not all successful executives have all three, but few have less than two."[4]

3. See John Kitching, "Why Do Mergers Miscarry?" HBR November-December 1967, p. 84.

4. "How Investment Bankers Appraise Corporations," *The Commercial and Financial Chronicle*, August 2, 1962, p. 15.

Motivation is particularly important, I think. When evaluating a potential acquisition where the continued participation of the president is a key factor in the operation's success, the first thing I want to know is what, specifically, he wants for himself and his company. If I am satisfied by this answer, other questions pose themselves. What kind of judgment does the chief executive have? Does he possess an open mind? How well does he work with his people?

Sometimes paying close attention to the way a man works and deals with his associates can be particularly instructive. What kind of rapport exists between them? Do they have a genuine respect for his ability and judgment? Is the air between them clear of rancor and bitterness? Does a brand of enthusiasm and spontaneity prevail that is indicative of a harmonious and rewarding relationship?

Equally important, how well will the other company's chief executive work *with your own management team*? I know of one president who sold out to a larger company because he felt it was in the best interests of his stockholders to do so. But this man had been accustomed to being a dominant force in business most of his life. He soon found that he was unable to subordinate himself to the will of others. He balked at taking what was tantamount to orders, however tactfully and diplomatically they were voiced. This man was unquestionably the company's single most powerful asset, but after six months he pulled out of the operation and went into another line of business.

The point is this: even clearly indicated competence will not suffice if it differs too sharply from the kind you expect and are accustomed to in your own operation.

Judging the future

Even in cases where competence is coupled with compatibility, another vital aspect must be considered. Presumably, you have taken certain steps to gauge the competence of the prospective company's top management. Whatever you have learned, whatever judgment you have reached, it will be based wholly on past experience, past activities, and past reputation. But what of the future?

Where a company's top management is a key ingredient in the success formula, as it is in most cases, you must assure yourself to the best of your ability that the management team will be "on deck" when the company goes out under

its new flag. Age may be a key factor. Does the chief executive of the acquired company wish to convert his ownership into marketable securities in order to separate himself from the business? Is he well fixed financially, but bored with his present activities? Is he seeking new challenges—a venture into politics, perhaps, or exploration into new fields of endeavor? Has he grown weary of the pressures of the competitive race? Has he decided to take life easy, devote more time to hobbies? Does he plan to put in the hours and effort you expect of him?

Soul-searching questions indeed, and difficult to cope with at times! But sidestepping them can lead to all kinds of problems later on. Getting the answers will clear the air and pave the way to better understanding and a more certain chance of success.

4. Seek a good fit

How long should it take for a merger-minded company to find a likely candidate and get serious negotiations under way? I know of some cases where this took three years; others where it took four weeks. It is impossible to generalize. Looking for a merger prospect, I find, is a game of "fits." It is a matter of meshing your resources into the resources of the other company and coming up with a whole that is greater than the sum of the parts—the well-known synergistic formula. The only trouble is that some presidents search so hard for a nonexistent perfect match that they miss out on prime opportunities along the way.

My personal experience leads me to conclude that you have to look hard, but you can't look too hard or too long. You have to know when you should compromise in what you are after, and when you should pack up your gear and explore other fields of endeavor. The suitors who most often wind up as bachelors are the ones who carry on the most elaborate studies. By the time they identify the ideal mate, someone else has grabbed her first!

In mergers the trick is to come up with the maximum number of fits you can, measure the potential gains against the risk involved, and move decisively when the time is right. A chief executive puts his neck on the block every time he sanctions a merger action. There is never any guarantee that the deal won't go sour. If you don't risk making mistakes, you won't seize many opportunities either; and often the failure

Exhibit I. Typical "good fits"

Company A	Company B
Excellent technical, financial, and management resources. Good marketing teams, fine R&D facilities. But the company anticipates long-range obsolescence of its principal product line.	Smaller company producing a high-grade line of quality products in a dynamic growth field. Excellent research team disgruntled by lack of facilities. Short on capital resources, lacking in marketing know-how.
Good, solid, well-established company with excellent reputation, top standing in the financial community, first-rate plant and research facilities. Top management team with two thirds of members past age 60 and no successors available.	Young growth-oriented company with a top-rated management team averaging 49 years of age. Company seeking to upgrade the value of its stock and to broaden its toehold in the market.
Pharmaceutical company with sales from $5 million to $10 million. Buckling under high R&D costs and quality control expenses in a heavily government-regulated industry.	Pharmaceutical company in virtually the same situation.*
Medium-sized, technically oriented company. Heavy, unused plant resources. Engaged in cyclical business with low price/earnings ratio of stock. Company seeking to boost its price/earnings ratio and to put its equipment into production.	Smaller, technically oriented company, with dovetailing talents and product mix. Also valuable patents which compensate for larger company's patent vulnerability. Desirous of expanding into foreign markets but needing the larger company's resources and expertise to make this move.
Engineering company with strong technological expertise in limited areas. Seeking to beef up its technical and marketing capabilities in the information systems field.	Engineering company with neatly dovetailing resources and capabilities, expert where the other company is weak. Unsophisticated in areas where the other company is strong.

*The two companies pooled their resources to achieve operating economies and strengthen their marketing organizations.

to make a move turns out to be the biggest mistake of all.

Exhibit I contains a sampling of five typical "good fit" situations. The descriptions are based on a number of mergers I either was involved in or evaluated during the past decade. The examples are limited to a few major characteristics only. Supplemented by a variety of "subfits," each of these prospective matches is well worth exploring further.

5. Involve the head man

In my experience, the difference between running a company and conducting an acquisition program is like the difference between playing checkers and playing chess. You don't just plan your next move in chess; you plot out the whole game. A special kind of vision is required to achieve this goal, and in many companies only the chief executive officer is in a position to possess this perspective. I believe that the chart-

5. Quoted in *Newsweek*, April 25, 1966, p. 73.

ing of corporate growth is the president's No. 1 responsibility. In my case it is a daytime, a nighttime, an all-the-time occupation. I don't get involved in mergers every once in awhile; I am always involved in them. Quite frankly, I cannot afford not to be.

An investment broker said recently, "I cannot call to mind a single successful acquisition where the head man was not deeply and personally involved."

Conrad Jones, who runs Booz, Allen & Hamilton's Growth Services Division, echoes this sentiment. "The biggest reason for flops," he says, "is the failure of a company's chief executive to take an intense, direct and continuing interest in the company being acquired." [5]

The chief executive can delegate portions of the investigation program and the mountainous detail of work involved in bringing a merger from the early courtship stages through the marriage ceremony. But the setting of the basic merger policy is his "baby." And so is the facing of risk. To illustrate:

☐ The president of a small company was considering a merger with another organization of equal size. He told his controller to review the facts and come up with a decision. The controller hemmed and hawed until it was too late. Off the record, he admitted quite frankly, "It was the boss's decision. If he was unwilling to stick his neck out, I certainly had no intention of doing it for him." He was absolutely right.

The president's participation does not cease when the right company is located and the merger deal consummated. Often it is at this point that the most critical period begins. Once the agreement has been signed, it is the president's job to get the wheels moving and keep them moving, to start the cross-pollination of ideas, and to convert hopeful thinking to profitable action. In making a merger work, you have to do a great deal more than simply push a button. There is a lot of hand cranking involved; the machinery will not run by itself.

6. Define your business

"What business are you in?" This question was asked recently of a merger-minded president. His answer ran through a string of enterprises in a variety of industries. It made me wonder what guidelines, if any, his company had drawn for itself in the kind of acquisitions it sought.

A growing trend among progressive companies today is what I sometimes refer to as "totalization." For example:

☐ One company was formerly engaged in the fields of finance, banking, and insurance. Today it thinks of itself as a "total credit" company, and it is diversifying into credit cards, factoring and other related fields.

☐ Mohasco Industries, Inc. makes carpets, furniture, cushions, and the like. It regards itself as a "total supplier of home furnishings."

☐ Kinney National Services, Inc., with a variety of enterprises ranging from parking lots to funeral parlors, is in the "total services" business.

☐ Genesco is well on its way toward becoming a "total apparel" organization.

☐ Our own orientation at North American-Rockwell is in the direction of "total technology." All of our products, from aircraft to machine tools and from textile machinery to truck and auto parts, are highly engineered items. Our business calls for highly sophisticated technical capability, plus extensive research and development resources. Technology, in short, is the unifying thread that helps to pull our diverse operations together.

Our top management team is outspoken in its resolution not to become a team of "octopologists." We believe that the banker who attempts to produce tractors on the side is asking for trouble. And so is the pretzel manufacturer who decides to sell insurance as a sideline. Exaggerated though these examples may be, I think that the point is a valid one. It is useful for a company to know what business it is in and how deeply it wants to be involved.

7. Analyze performance factors

In many acquisitions I have witnessed, the seller does not know as much as he should about the acquiring company. This is easily explained. The buyer is usually the bigger company with the experienced acquisition team and with better facilities for search and analysis. A chemical company's president offers sound advice: when the president believes his organization is ill equipped to evaluate the potential values—and pitfalls—of a prospective merger, an industry specialist should be hired to take over the chore. The stakes are too high to slight this critical aspect of the merger procedure.

Points to investigate

How extensive should the investigation be? Obviously, the usual standard criteria should be considered. These include such items as gross and net profit margins, the ratio of sales and advertising expense to sales, the ratio of labor costs to sales, return on book value, working capital ratio, and so forth. But the probe should go beyond such conventional considerations. How far beyond is difficult to determine and impossible to generalize, but let me draw on my research and experience during the past ten years or so to offer a checklist of factors to consider and pitfalls to avoid:

General:
☐ Evaluate the buyer's experience in bringing off successful merger deals. Most unsuccessful corporate marriages are consummated by inexperienced suitors.

☐ In the investigative phase, deal with vital factors only. Don't become deeply involved in "housekeeping" details that can be resolved later and will only serve to stall your merger plans. The idea is to predict what conditions could hurt you later if bypassed during the earlier phases and to defer nonessentials until a later date.

☐ Investigate the possibility of existing or pending lawsuits that are unknown to you.

☐ Review any possible antitrust implications of the merger with your attorney.

☐ In weighing the pros and cons of the deal, estimate what it would cost you to achieve on your own the same goals you are hoping to achieve by means of the acquisition route.

Gathering Data:

☐ Open pipelines if you can to the chief competitors of the company you are seeking to acquire. They may prove to be your best source of information. Find out, for example, if they recently hired any good research or management people from the company being wooed. If the company is unable to hold onto its top producers, determine why.

☐ Take advantage of free or low-cost sources of information about the company and the industry under scrutiny; organizations like the Department of Commerce and the New York Stock Exchange often provide better material than some consultants do.

☐ If the prospective merger partner is large and complex, hire a top-rated consulting firm to do a general financial and management audit. (North American Aviation used one such firm to look over Rockwell-Standard before the merger; Rockwell-Standard used another firm to check North American Aviation.)

☐ If the company under consideration is in a foreign country, be wary of long and expensive surveys designed to report on the political and economic climate of the area involved. As I have learned the hard way, such reports can be costly; and they are often hedged with intangible political, economic, and technical factors that render them worthless. It is usually preferable to hire a knowledgeable manager with proven experience in the country who is willing to stake his future on your enterprise. If I were unable to find at least one such individual, this failure alone would give me considerable pause.

Strategy & planning:

☐ If you are the seller, and your plans include participation in the merged enterprise, take steps to identify the long-range goals of the acquiring company. Find out how you and your organization will be expected to contribute toward the fulfillment of the goals and whether *continuing* two-way benefits will be generated by the marriage.

☐ Check the status of important long-term selling and buying agreements. Also, check for contracts and commitments that do not show up on the records. Ask the right questions to determine that the company's vital profit factors are not in jeopardy.

☐ Check the demand for the target company's main products or services to make sure they are not declining or on the verge of being outdated by competitive innovations.

Finance:

☐ Determine the price/earnings range in the particular industry, and then use that to gauge the stock of the company in question.

☐ Consider testing the strength of the proposed merger by leaking the word that negotiations are under way. Then observe the movement of your stock. If it goes down, some serious second thoughts about the deal might be warranted.

☐ Evaluate the benefits of a tax-loss carryover if there would be one, but don't attach too much importance to it. This can be a deceptively alluring pitfall. I have seen too many companies get into trouble because of it. Can the condition which caused the loss be corrected? That is the No. 1 consideration.

☐ Do not overlook the value and importance of the tender offer if you are genuinely convinced that the merger or acquisition would be of real benefit to the shareowners of both companies. At times this strategy can be used as a legitimate, honest, and expeditious method of achieving the desired result. As former SEC member William L. Cary points out, "an honest tender offer is a force for challenging management . . . and if tender offers were discouraged [by law] it would help keep present management entrenched." [6] Needless to say, the tender offer should not be employed as a whip to force a company into submission.

Physical assets:

☐ Investigate the target company's main production facilities. Satisfy yourself that equipment is in good condition and adequately maintained. It is a simple matter for a company to dress itself up for acquisition by deferring

6. Quoted in *Business Week*, May 6, 1967, p. 138.

maintenance, machine replacement, and other significant costs.

□ Get a statement of research and development costs over the past five years or so. Then evaluate new products, innovations, and changes on the drawing boards as a result of this investment in order to determine dollar return on the company's R&D program.

□ Make a realistic evaluation of the other company's inventory. Look for obsolete items that could substantially reduce its value. Also, determine that the company's method of inventory depreciation jibes with your own computations.

□ Assess the current status of patents, trademarks, leases, and so forth.

□ Take a hard look at backlogged projects and normal processing that is months behind. Creating such conditions is a popular form of window dressing to impress company shoppers.

Management & personnel:

□ Get your labor and legal experts to take a long hard look at the labor situation. Find out if any serious problems are anticipated.

□ Try to find out if there are any significant changes in the wind and, if so, what their implications are. A key executive may be departing, for example, and taking important business with him. A shortage of vital supplies may be anticipated. Pinpoint the factors that are causing the company's main profit flow, and satisfy yourself that nobody is tampering with the shutoff valve.

□ Keep an ear open for significant dissension and internal conflict among the target company's executives.

□ Check the prospective company's employment rolls. Has it tried to brighten its earnings picture and inflate the value of its stock by cutting the payroll?

□ Evaluate the other company's compensation and benefits program to assure that it is compatible, or can be made compatible, with the program of your own company.

□ Finally, and particularly important, merger history shows that many deals fall flat, not because the wrong company is acquired, but because the acquiring company is not strong enough to take on the burden involved. The vast problems of assimilating another company and integrating two separately operating entities into a single, smoothly coordinated unit demand a structurally sound organization which is subject to a minimum of internal difficulties.

As one president I know puts it, "The act of compounding chaos has never served to dissipate it."

8. *Face problems early*

In the case of one merger, a company acquired a smaller firm in the same industry. For years the acquired firm had sold its consumer products on a selective franchise basis. It was a matter of great pride to the president and his top marketing people that theirs was a prestigious, carriage-trade type of operation. But this was not the operation the larger company had in mind when it purchased the business. Its policy was one of rapid growth through volume sales and mass distribution.

The merger went off smoothly enough at first, but some months later the acquired organization was ordered to convert to mass distribution. The president of the organization and his top officers balked. They refused to be swayed, and the effect was traumatic. The windup was a rash of resignations followed by bitter and costly reorganization.

Had this turn of events been anticipated, the president of the parent company confided in me, he would never have gone through with the deal. My reply was that it should have been anticipated.

This is not the only time I have run into such a situation. It comes from holding back information and sidestepping vital, delicate issues. In my view, the most important single strategy in paving the way to a successful integration is the establishment of a climate of mutual trust and good will.

Involvement in more than a score of mergers has taught my management team to anticipate as many major problems as possible, to set them on the table for both parties to digest, and jointly to hammer out a practical and mutually acceptable plan for coping with each issue. The more thorns we extract at the outset, the less chance of infection later on. The earlier we make our intentions known, the smaller the possibility of subsequent misunderstanding.

Particularly where personnel problems are involved, early consideration takes on special significance. The best time to tackle such delicate and knotty issues is while the impact of the merger move still has people in a slightly heady condition. Later on the grapevine hum simmers down, things revert to normal, and a different atmosphere prevails. A new period of watchfulness sets in; people become wary.

I have seen this change of mood happen time and again. Very often the post-closing period, when the merger is on trial, so to speak, is the most difficult of all. With sensitivities honed to a superfine edge, this is no time to meet a critical issue head-on with sledgehammer force.

9. Make the right advances

Corporate and boy-girl courtships are repeatedly compared—with good reason, I think. Both are easily thwarted by a clumsy overture, a thoughtless action, a carelessly voiced sentiment.

In mergers nothing is more valuable than a keen sense of timing. Knowing when to move and when to hold depends partly on instinct, partly on prevailing conditions. A president who travels the acquisition route should have a fine nose for opportunity. At times it is necessary to wait with infinite patience until an expected opportunity appears. When it does appear, often you must make your move with unwavering speed and decisiveness.

Opportunity itself can be elusive. It is influenced strongly by general economic conditions and market fluctuations as well as by the moods

---

In "How to Sell Your Company," Richard M. Hexter fills in a noticeable void in the growing literature on acquisitions and mergers. "What is frequently overlooked," Hexter states, "is the realization that selling a company is an investment decision—the most important one in the company's history." He goes on to show how to sell so that the value of the company's equity will grow faster than it could without a sale. (see page 15. —The Editors

---

of the wooers and the wooed. Stockholders take a dim view of merger prospects, for example, when new lows are posted by the suitor's shares. A case in point is a proposed deal some months ago for Consolidated Laundry to finance a Dunhill International takeover with a public offering of $50 million in convertible debentures. When the market suddenly faded, so did Consolidated's offer.

When is it wise to talk prices? Some argue that getting the price on the table early saves time and effort for all involved. There is a point to be made for this philosophy, but I do not

abide by it. In my view, the selling job comes first. The first priority, in my opinion, is to convince both yourselves and the other management that joining forces will be a good move for both sets of stockholders. My personal strategy is to parade the benefits of the merger before getting down to serious discussion about price. With the gains in sight, I have found, men become more amenable to compromise and reasonable discussion.

I was recently asked, "What's the first move you make when you are interested in a company that's for sale?" My answer was that no company is ever for sale, at least not admittedly. It is important to respect this reality. A company on the block is like a girl in search of a husband. If she asks the fellow to marry her, she frightens him off. If she's too cold and aloof, he looks for a warmer climate. There is a delicate balance to be maintained.

Executing the approach

When approaching a company, the first essential is to pinpoint the right person to contact. This is usually the president or chairman, but it could also be a major shareowner or a key member of the family. Most often your banker, attorney, supplier, or some other acquaintance can steer you to the right person. As for myself, in this area, as in many others, I lean heavily on our vice president of mergers and acquisitions, Mr. Bateman.

A mistake some presidents make in their initial approach is to go through their banker. The last thing the prospect wants bandied about is the news that his company is for sale. If the banking community knows this, he may reason, so does everyone else.

In our case, the direct approach has always worked best. Quite often Mr. Bateman or I will get an introduction to the person we want to meet through a director or a mutual acquaintance. If this cannot be arranged, we contact the man ourselves. The first step is to write him a letter communicating our desire to meet him without revealing why. At the end of the letter we mention that we will telephone him in a few days to set up an appointment. The time lapse is important. It gives him a chance to look us up, call some people, and ask some questions about us.

When we call him, we explain that we would like to see him on a matter of mutual interest. I have been using this introduction for years. I have not as yet come across one president who has refused to have lunch with me or a top assistant like Mr. Bateman. When we do meet, after exchanging pleasantries I do not wait too long to explain that my interest is to explore the possibilities of a merger. If he is reluctant to probe the subject, I may hint that looking into the situation could be part of his fiduciary responsibility. Approached this way, I have seen more than one chief officer lower his defenses.

The negotiations themselves are usually more sensitive than the door-opening procedure. A common mistake we used to make is getting too many managers into the act. It is difficult to negotiate with a crowd of people at the table. Too much conversation and too many "contributions" can cause a meeting to bog down. Still, as merger expert Myles L. Mace points out, it is often helpful to keep a good third-person intermediary on hand—a banker, consultant, or legal counsel—to clear the logjam should an impasse be reached. Another helpful tip is to avoid winding up a negotiations session on a take-it-or-leave-it note. Before ending one meeting, Mace suggests, it is a good idea for the next session to be arranged.[7]

Last-minute snarls

John Shad estimates that, even after the handshake, one out of two mergers fizzles. The reason: legal snarls, accounting complications, and the like. A lawyer, in particular, can block a merger, especially if he happens to be temperamentally or psychologically opposed to it. And then, of course, there is the possibility of trouble from Washington. Looking back at the merger of Rockwell-Standard and North American Aviation, for instance, I shudder to think how easily the Department of Justice almost thwarted our efforts:

☐ After several negotiating sessions, agreement was finally reached. We shook hands. At a final shareowner meeting, the icing was put on the cake. We were all set to go. All that remained were the final closing papers. That is when we were hit by the Justice Department requirement that Rockwell-Standard sell off its Jet Aircraft Division before the merger.

This little thunderbolt came at a sensitive time. Normally it could take months, even years, to dispose of a major division. In this case months or years could destroy countless hours of work and planning. We had to move

fast and we did. In three weeks a contract was signed with the Israeli group that took over the division. A $1 million check changed hands. The deal was finalized.

Had we not moved with swift decision, another meeting would have had to be held to approve the merger because of legal requirements. We would have had to clear with the SEC all over again. Anything could have happened.

10. Absorb people with care

Making a merger work, in my view, is the art of taking over a company without overtaking it. At North American Rockwell, during the stage when we are assimilating a newly acquired company, we make every effort to exercise a minimum of control over the new member of the family. We do our level best to keep its management at the helm; we encourage its executives to set their own goals and their own schedules. If we lacked confidence in their ability to do this successfully, we would not have considered the company for acquisition in the first place.

Especially important during the assimilation stage is effective dissemination of information. (The job is never more crucial than when the acquired company is smaller and less sophisticated than the parent.) Even a well-coordinated acquisition leaves suppliers, customers, and especially employees deeply concerned about where they stand, for virtually any merger will rock the boat a bit. Until the waves subside, the more people are told about how the new setup will affect them personally, the less they will imagine. To illustrate again with the management philosophy at North American Rockwell, we go out of our way to anticipate questions from all quarters. We prepare carefully worded statements to employees, suppliers, customers, the press—doing this well in advance of the merger announcement. We offer public relations assistance to the acquired company, but only if it is wanted. We do not believe in ramming our cooperation and support down the throats of the people we are trying to help.

I am a strong believer in the personal and informal approach during the assimilation period. I like to visit people in their offices. I like to sit on the edge of a desk with a dozen people clus-

7. Myles L. Mace and George G. Montgomery, Jr., *Management Problems of Corporate Acquisitions* (Boston, Division of Research, Harvard Business School, 1962).

tered about and informally answer their questions about our ideas, plans, programs, and goals. Of course, the head of a large corporation can stretch himself just so far. With the help of taped speeches, closed-circuit TV, and the like, however, he can multiply his coverage. The aim is to get the message through to every manager and every worker, whatever his job, wherever he may be.

Experience proves that delicate personnel situations are the kind most susceptible to misunderstanding—for example, an executive's particular pension arrangement, or defining the place where one manager's authority and responsibility end and another's begin. One thing I have found useful, when delicate matters of this type are discussed and resolved at the conference table, is to get the agreement down in writing as quickly as possible, before time is given the chance to magnify expectations and distort decisions.

Maintaining prestige

A broker told me recently that the best way to strew the acquisition path with rocks and ruts is to diminish the prestige of the acquired company's top management. I could not agree more. At North American Rockwell we bend over backwards and then a bit to maintain and, where possible, improve the status of the individual manager. Our merger with Draper Corporation is a case in point:

☐ In assimilating this vital company, we made every effort to protect the high level of trust and prestige enjoyed by the president and his top officers in both the company and the community. We had ample opportunity to prove our sincerity. In this particular merger, our early advances were strongly opposed by some of Draper's advisers. But after the merger was signed, we urged the president to maintain the same relations as before. "They're important to you," we reasoned, "so it automatically follows they are important to us." This attitude did much, I am told, to convince the Draper people that we meant what we said when we promised to keep the reins of the business in existing hands.

When one company is absorbed by another, I do not think that the importance of maintain-

ing individual status and prestige can be overplayed. In my experience it is easier to knock $20,000 off the purchase price of a company than it is to get a man to give up his car.

Questions of accountability

To whom will Manager X account? What form will the accounting take? These are delicate questions. They are likely to tread on a manager's sensitivities. This is all the more reason, I think, to deal with the problem openly, honestly, and in advance of the assimilation phase —and, equally important, to set down the resolution in writing to minimize the chance of subsequent misinterpretation and bitterness.

A related problem arises when the president of the acquired company has been long accustomed to running the show from the No. 1 seat. How will he feel as No. 2, 5, or 8 of a large organization? "You never know," says one man, "until it happens." In one case the president adjusted fairly well to the assimilation of his group into a large organization. He was still No. 1 in his own corporation. But what nagged at his craw was his having to deal with the acquiring company's financial vice president instead of with the chief executive. Small point? Perhaps. But in this man's view it was important enough to make him resign. The possibility of such a reaction is worth pondering when planning a merger and preparing for assimilation of the acquired company.

Conclusion

In this article I have attempted to outline the 10 vital factors capable of spelling the difference between success and failure in mergers and acquisitions. One factor in particular transcends, encompasses, and overrides all others.

In buying a company, you acquire its plant, its equipment, its methods and systems, its patents and know-how, its distribution and research facilities.

But these are secondary, I believe. What you acquire first of all when you buy a company is its people. They are the precious asset that can keep it imaginative, aggressive, inspired, and dynamic. In my view, if you keep this thought well in mind, you will not go wrong.

Reprint 68511

READ THE FINE PRINT

REPRINTS
Telephone: 617-495-6192
Fax: 617-495-6985

Current and past articles
are available, as is an
annually updated index.
Discounts apply to
large-quantity purchases.

Please send orders to
HBR Reprints
Harvard Business School
Publishing Division
Boston, MA 02163.

HOW CAN *HARVARD BUSINESS REVIEW* ARTICLES WORK FOR YOU?

For years, we've printed a microscopically small notice on the editorial credits page of the *Harvard Business Review* alerting our readers to the availability of *HBR* articles.

Now we invite you to take a closer look at some of the many ways you can put this hard-working business tool to work for you.

IN THE CORPORATE CLASSROOM.

There's no more effective, or cost-effective, way to supplement your corporate training programs than in-depth, incisive *HBR* articles.

Affordable and accessible, it's no wonder hundreds of companies and consulting organizations use *HBR* articles as a centerpiece for management training.

IN-BOX INNOVATION.

Where do your company's movers and shakers get their big ideas? Many find the inspiration for innovation in the pages of *HBR*. They then share the wealth and spread the word by distributing *HBR* articles to company colleagues.

IN MARKETING AND SALES SUPPORT.

HBR articles are a substantive leave-behind to your sales calls. And they can add credibility to your direct mail

campaigns. They demonstrate that your company is on the leading edge of business thinking.

CREATE CUSTOM ARTICLES.

If you want to pack even greater power in your punch, personalize *HBR* articles with your company's name or logo. And get the added benefit of putting your organization's name before your customers.

AND THERE ARE 500 MORE REASONS IN THE *HBR CATALOG*.

In all, the *Harvard Business Review Catalog* lists articles on over 500 different subjects. Plus, you'll find books and videos on subjects you need to know.

The catalog is yours for just $8.00. To order *HBR* articles or the *HBR Catalog* (No. 21019), call 617-495-6192. Please mention telephone order code 025A when placing your order. Or FAX us at 617-495-6985.

And start putting *HBR* articles to work for you.

**Harvard Business School
Publications**

Call 617-495-6192 to order the *HBR Catalog*.

(Prices and terms subject to change.)

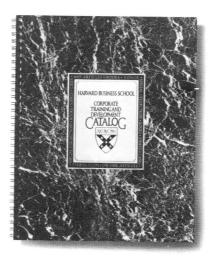

2768

2768